Presented To:

_____

From:

_____

Date:

_____

SECRETS OF A

SUPERNATURAL WORLD

SECRETS OF A
SUPERNATURAL WORLD

NEAR-DEATH REVELATIONS OF THE
ANCIENT WORLD AND THE FUTURE

Buck Stephens

DESTINY IMAGE® PUBLISHERS, INC.

P.O. Box 310, Shippensburg, PA 17257-0310

"Speaking to the Purposes of God for This Generation and for the Generations to Come."

This book and all other Destiny Image, Revival Press, MercyPlace, Fresh Bread, Destiny Image Fiction, and Treasure House books are available at Christian bookstores and distributors worldwide.

For a U.S. bookstore nearest you, call 1-800-722-6774.

For more information on foreign distributors, call 717-532-3040.

Reach us on the Internet: www.destinyimage.com.

ISBN 13 TP: 978-0-7684-3701-0
ISBN 13 HC: 978-0-7684-3702-7
ISBN 13 LP: 978-0-7684-3703-4
ISBN 13 Ebook: 978-0-7684-9020-6

For Worldwide Distribution, Printed in the U.S.A.
1 2 3 4 5 6 7 8 9 10 11 / 13 12 11

Dedication

This book is dedicated to all those who

ever looked at the world and wondered, to those who have dug in the dirt or gazed into space and wondered, why?

It is dedicated to all those who

have wondered why they are themselves and not someone else, those who want to know their future, their purpose, and their hope.

It is dedicated to all those who

seek to be part of the coming new world order.

But most of all it is dedicated to

the Mighty King!

In Memory of Our Friend and Partner in Ministry

Reverend Joseph Kingal

November 21, 1969 – October 18, 2010

Acknowledgments

This book has been a work in progress, not only for the last couple of years but for my whole life. Looking back, I realize that it has been in process since the day I was born. There have been a lot of people who have had input into this book because of what they have imparted into my life. My family, teachers, pastors, friends, and co-workers all have imparted something to me; all that has been imparted to me has become a part of everything that I do.

I wish to thank my family first and foremost for their love and support for what I am called to do. You are most precious to me, and I love you.

I wish to thank my wife and partner in ministry, Andi. Your support, input, and encouragement are part of this book, and you have contributed much from your wisdom, discernment, and insights that are recorded on the pages of this book. Thank you for your sacrifices in allowing this book to become a reality. Thank you for our precious children, Mindy and Ben, who are such a blessing. Mindy, thank you for being the gentle, precious woman of God you have become; thank you for bringing Chris into our lives and for our precious granddaughter, Briahna Rose. I pray she grows to be the woman of God you and your mother are. Briahna, you are such a joy, and I thank God for how you have blessed us. Ben, the calling on your life will bless many, and I look forward to what God will accomplish through you. I thank you for your wisdom and input and for being an inspiration to so many, including your dad.

I wish to acknowledge my teachers and professors at the Delaware County Christian School in Newtown Square, Pennsylvania, and at Houghton College in Houghton, New York. Thanks for enduring the difficult questions I asked and giving me your best. I especially want to thank two great scientists who were geologists and astronomers and who, most importantly of all, possessed the knowledge of the holy. To Dr. Frank Roberts, who went home to be with the Lord the week I completed work on this book; you will enjoy time with my professor Dr. S. Hugh Paine, who went on before you. You both spent much time patiently answering my questions and imparting your knowledge and understanding to me, and I am grateful for you. I only wish I could have shared this book with both of you, but of course, now you both do not need it.

Just before this work went to press, Andi and I spent a powerful week preaching in crusade meetings in Madang, Papua New Guinea, with one of my closest friends, Rev. Joseph Kingal, "the Billy Graham of the South Pacific," and his precious wife Susan. No person ever introduced us to each other, but our hearts were knitted together when independently the Lord led us to meet, introduced us, and we began a partnership in ministry. I am thankful that Pastor Kingal had the chance to read this manuscript and write his endorsement included in the book because, within hours of our parting in Madang, an automobile accident claimed his life and he was ushered into the presence of the Lord we served together and whom Joseph loved so much. I love and miss you, my brother, and I look forward to being with you again in the Kingdom! Our last words to each other were "to be continued," and I promise it will be!

Most of all, I wish to thank the Holy Spirit for coming to me when I was ill and for imparting to me knowledge from the unseen world and allowing me to share it with those who also seek the knowledge of the Kingdom.

Endorsements

This book will answer the questions you have always wondered about concerning the Bible and God. It will even fill in the gaps of many you have never contemplated.

Sid Roth, Host
It's Supernatural! Television
www.SidRoth.org

For over 12 years I have had the privilege of pastoring Buck Stephens and observing the development of his ministry. While most people first encounter Buck in his role as teacher and advisor in the area of financial stewardship, it is his gifting in prophetic ministry that often causes the greatest impact. With a rare and refreshing blend of consistent accuracy and gentle humility, Buck ministers the prophetic words and images he receives to the Body of Christ. Time and again the Lord has used him to deliver words of wisdom concerning future events that come to pass. His love for the integrity of Scripture and his commitment to Jesus Christ powerfully undergird the spiritual insights God has given him and are the foundation of everything he writes.

Pastor John Carter, Senior Pastor and Co-Founder
Abundant Life Christian Center
East Syracuse, New York
www.alcclife.org

Buck Stephens is a unique individual with a fascinating testimony. I sat mesmerized as I listened to him relate his near-death experience and visit to Heaven. He has a keen sensitivity to the spirit realm. This book promises to be a fascinating read.

Jonathan Bernis, President and CEO
Jewish Voice Ministries International
www.jewishvoice.org

I have enjoyed the ministry of Buck Stephens since I first met him through an act of God at the Oral Roberts University Campus in Tulsa, Oklahoma. Since then, I have invited Buck Stephens to speak in three of my major Gospel campaigns in Papua New Guinea. Despite the tough terrains, impassable road conditions, slippery mountain slopes, volcano dust, and blazing, unfriendly heat of the tropics, Buck ministered to God's people in my nation with love, sincerity of heart, and compassion. One of the things he taught my people is the subject of this book, *Secrets of a Supernatural World*. Papua New Guinea is one of the last frontiers on earth to be evangelized. Therefore, I thank God for the ministry of Buck Stephens to our nation. I am privileged and honored to call him my friend in the Gospel of Christ's Kingdom.

With a clear prophetic voice, my friend Buck Stephens captures an intriguing sense of purpose and destiny in *Secrets of a Supernatural World*. Truly, this masterpiece work will literally impact, affect, and infect this generation for Kingdom advancement. This thought-provoking and intellectually stimulating work clearly demonstrates God's infinite love for His "mudcake" creation. Buck's conversational style of writing will keep the reader intrigued and captivated from page to page. This is the Gospel expounded in its purest form. It is the spirit of an evangelist's appeal to the "mudcakes" to rebel and to return to their loving and eternal Father God. I highly recommend this Holy Spirit-inspired and anointed book to anyone willing and desiring to know his or her "origins and endings." I know in my spirit this book will ignite, inspire, and produce a Kingdom-oriented mindset in people for the coming new world order.

Moreover, the original mission statement for humanity was "to have dominion, be fruitful, fill, and subdue the earth." We were made to rule and reign on the earth. Just like Buck says, "this mudcake was so special because this is the only part of creation where God takes the unseen and mixes it with the 'seen'"! This mudcake is both physical and spiritual at the same time. We are indeed unique! May the pages of this book inspire and influence this generation and add more souls to His Kingdom on earth. May Heaven invade the earth through a God-appointed "redeemed mudcake rebellion." Thank you, Buck, for obeying God and releasing these wonderful truths to our generation.

Evangelist Joseph Kingal, Director and CEO
Joseph Kingal Ministries
Lae, Morobe Province
Papua New Guinea
www.josephkingalministries.org.pg

Truly my God is your God, Buck, and my people are your people. Shalom, my brother.

Rabbi Mark Greenberg
Tree of Life Bible
Messianic Jewish Family Bible Project Chairman
www.treeoflifebible.org

Contents

Foreword

A Unique Perspective on This Book

———•———

It is very, very early, and I look over to see that my husband has awakened and gone downstairs to his spot—that special place where I find him every morning, laptop open, earphones on, focusing on the many words seemingly flying out of his fingers. This has gone on for many months now.

What is he writing?

Is it not about finances and stewardship? That has been his focus for 15 years now and also the topic of his first book, *The Coming Financial Revolution*.

He has told me that I cannot see it until it is complete.

"Well," I say, "what is it about?"

He answers me with, "I can't tell you."

So every morning I come down and quietly make coffee, feeling so content that my man of God is immersed in writing for His King. I love it when Buck spends time with the Lord, for whatever reason! I will have to be patient.

Patient I was…not by nature, but by knowing that under a heavy anointing of the Holy Spirit and a great deal of love and commitment to God's great purpose, he carries on.

I am amazed at how quickly he types, hardly pausing, on and on, day after day.

Six months after his 1995 visit to the heavenly realms, he began to search out what this heavenly visit was all about. He remembered vividly the details of spending time in the presence of the Lord and the words Jesus spoke to him as He gave him instruction of what he was to teach His people.

Buck was so different after that.

He was so determined to follow to a "T" all that the Lord had shown him during that brief moment when he stopped breathing on the operating table. (Time did not seem brief in the presence of the Lord since Buck was with Him in eternity and there is no time there.)

Doors and opportunities began to open supernaturally for Buck to teach God's Word in a new and more powerful way. Churches and people were so affected by the message and, oh, how the Holy Spirit would move! The Lord had taught Buck so many things, and he was determined to share everything with the people of God. There was a fire and a passion in his soul, and I loved seeing him that way.

One day Buck finally finished the new book and handed it to me in the form of two large notebooks. I opened them and felt such an excitement to finally know what was the meaning and purpose of all those many words typed with such focus and diligence. I would finally find out what took so much focus, yet also seemed to flow from him.

I began to read about a time so very long ago before even people were formed from the dust of the ground. It was a time of great shaking and war in Heaven, and I also read about the times yet to come. The book told of eternity past, present, and future—where and how it all began and where it is all going. I read as it told of angels and demons, wars and peace, planets formed and angels warring. The book talked about secrets and mysteries humankind has struggled with, and then it amazingly answered those questions with understanding straight from the heavenly realms. It answers the big question, "If God is a loving God, how can He allow evil in this world?" It answers questions about dinosaurs, UFOs, and aliens, and then it ties them all together with a loving God's signature literally in the dirt as He carefully works out a plan to create a heavenly Kingdom on earth.

This book will make you cry, laugh, and get chills as you read it!

Is it not said that of all people, a wife will be the most honest?

My words to Buck when I finished reading this beautifully told story of time and eternity were, "It should be a Christian classic!"

I meant what I said!

Buck delves into the story of God's eternal plan in a beautiful and captivating way. I can honestly say that it is one of the best books I've ever read!

In case you wonder what the main point is of such a book, let me explain. Any Christian who reads the Word of God and studies it at all knows that we are living in the very end of the age. God has chosen to reveal many things and open up our understanding in these times. Amos 3: 7 says, *"The Lord God does nothing unless He reveals His secret counsel to His servants, the prophets"* (NASB).

To all those who have an ear to hear, the Spirit of the Lord is speaking loud and clear. It is more important now than ever to open our hearts and lives to the call of the Holy Spirit. This is a time of preparation for the Church to be sure that our lamps have oil (see Matt. 25:1-13), and it is a time for those outside of the Church to buy that oil without money (see Isa. 52:3). It is a time for their lamps to be trimmed and ready for the return of the bridegroom (see Matt. 25:1-13).

Buck stops along the way and presents the Gospel, giving opportunity for those who do not know the Lord Jesus personally to meet Him. There is no question what we need to do to be ready for the return of the King of kings, nor is there a question regarding who is that King of kings! Whether you know the Lord already or do not know Jesus as your Lord, through this book you will fall more in love with Him and have a pretty good understanding of what this thing called salvation is all about.

It is *fascinating, moving, and really, really interesting stuff!* The author's wife gives this book two thumbs up!

You will be blessed!

> *And there will be signs in the sun in the moon, and in the stars; and on the earth distress of nations, with perplexity, the sea and the waves roaring, men's hearts failing them from fear and the expectation of those things which are coming on the earth, for the powers of the heavens will be shaken.*
>
> *Then they will see the Son of Man coming in a cloud with power and great glory.*
>
> *Now when these things begin to happen, look up and lift up your heads, because your redemption draws near* (Luke 21:25-28 NKJV).

—Andrea P. Stephens

Preface

— ◆ —

Secrets of a Supernatural World is the result of an inner quest for knowledge and understanding that has spanned more than 50 years since I first looked in the mirror and wondered how I got in my body and why I was me and not someone else. My thirst to understand my origins and the origins of the difficult world around me raised more questions for every answer I was able to find and pushed me to keep on searching.

When my personal quest for understanding collided with a personal crisis, one that almost took my life just before my 42nd birthday, this book that is now in your hands was ordained to be written by the One who holds the answer to every question. Now at the 15th anniversary of that near-death experience, I have been released to share the answers I received to these questions. These very same questions are in the hearts and minds of so many people, who are just like me and you. We seek answers that come from the very heart of God for such a time as this, when a *new world order* is at hand, an order greater than what the world could possibly imagine. This book will help you understand why things are the way they are, why you are you, and what your eternal purpose is.

If you are a person who asks:

How did this world come to be, and why am I here? Am I here by accident, or was I created for a purpose?

Did this world evolve, or was it created? Why do we have fossilized life forms in the rock that do not exist today, and when did the dinosaurs live? How did all this happen?

If God created the world and He is an all-knowing God, why did He create lucifer, an angel who would rebel against Him and become "the devil"? Why did He create Adam and Eve if He knew that they would fail? Did God make a mistake? Did God know all this "in the beginning"?

If God is a loving God, how can He allow evil in this world? What is He going to do about it anyway? What is His plan, and why do Christianity and its plan of salvation seem so confusing? Who is Jesus anyway, and why would His death "save me"? Don't all religions lead to God?

Would a loving God condemn a person to hell for all eternity?

Is there any truth to the Bible, or is it just an old book full of confusing stories and contradictions? What about prophecies in the Bible? Are they real? Will the world end? Will it end in 2012 like Nostradamus, the Mayans, and others have predicted? What about global warming? Will it happen?

What about the aliens and the UFOs that supposedly have visited us—are they involved? Who are they anyway? What about angels and demons—can we see them? What is their purpose, and how did they get here? Is there such a thing as the supernatural?

What happens to me when I die? When my body is lifeless, where does that person inside of me go?

If you see yourself in these questions, then this book is for you. These questions, as well as many others, can and will be answered. Whether you are a scholar, theologian, or someone who does not know much about these subjects, you will find this book valuable.

Follow me through the pages of this book, and I will take you from before the beginning of time through all the ages until the times of this world's future become eternity. In this journey, you will discover why things are the way they are and why you are uniquely…you!

Follow me as we explore the creation of a new world order and the series of "Mudcake Rebellions" through which it will be accomplished. (You will learn what a mudcake is later on in this book.)

I am not any more special than you are, nor do I deserve anything more than you deserve. I am simply being used to help prepare us for this coming new world order, nothing more, nothing less. But I will tell you this emphatically:

The world is not prepared for what is coming!

Introduction

My family never looked quite as good as they did on Sunday morning. Everyone hustled about getting ready to go to church, dressing up, and gathering together the necessary things needed for the one hour of Sunday school. Then the traditional one hour of church would follow. We would sing a few hymns, the pastor or song leader waving his arm about like a band instructor, followed by a special musical performance by someone from the church—which was sometimes special and sometimes not so special. This would be followed by a few announcements, then our tithes and offerings...whatever they were. It never changed; it always happened in that order!

All I knew about tithes and offerings was that it was the time when I would drop in the plate the quarter my mom gave me. Usually I would be surprised when the plate got to me. I would promptly stand up in front of everyone and start digging in my pockets, first one and then the other, finally tossing that quarter into the plate missing the velvet pad and making it clang really loud on the metal rim. Everyone would smile though, everyone but my mom, that is; she would give me a look. My dad was usually taking up the offering, so he would see the whole thing too.

It was good to be cute sometimes; it took the edge off things!

"Bucko, are you dressed?" a shout would come up the stairs.

"Yeah!" I would yell back as I quickly looked for my pants. I knew Mom wouldn't come up and check; she was getting the beef roast ready to put in the oven and setting the timer for Sunday afternoon dinner. I quickly started putting on my clothes and checked myself out in the mirror, stopping to stare at myself, my mind wandering off again.

How come I am me? Why am I inside looking out of my eyes and not someone else's? How did I get in there? Where did I come from anyway? I just one day seemed to be here! If God created me, then why did He? What am I for? After all, everything is made for a reason!

I would do that often—get distracted with myself and wonder why I was me. I have found out over the years that many, if not all of you, have done the same thing. The truth is, I still do that once in awhile, but now I know the answers. I used to wish I was someone or something else, especially a bit taller during basketball season. I would always see improvements, usually influenced by my current circumstances, that God could have made when He created me.

As a young boy, I liked contemplating my existence in the mirror, but I never really came up with the answer. My wondering would abruptly stop when another shout came up the stairs, this time with great urgency and concern: "Bucko, are you ready? We have to go!"

I realized later when I had kids of my own that she would make her voice sound that way on purpose because she knew it would get my little buns moving for fear of being swatted! I confronted her about it when I had children of my own, and she confessed that she did do that, and then I confessed to her that I did the same thing to get my kids moving. It worked! You see, little buns become conditioned to the sound of a parent's voice and seem to know when they are in harm's way.

I would, with two swipes of my fingers through my hair, run down the steps where Mom, a comb in her hand, would catch me to check me over, combing my hair, which I had already combed with my fingers (looked good to me!).

"Did you brush your teeth?" she would ask.

"Uh huh," I would respond.

"Let me smell your breath. No, you didn't. Go brush your teeth! Hurry up!"

Mothers do weird things like smelling your breath. Stomping back up the stairs I would think to myself, *Huh, smells OK to me!* She would always get her way though, and soon we would all be in the car on our way to church.

Once we arrived, I would get one last check over outside the car, and then off I would go to my Sunday school class with my "Official Perfect Attendance Sunday School Award Bible" in hand, stuffed full of old Sunday school papers. That's how you can tell a committed Christian—they have a lot of papers, usually church bulletins, stuffed in their Bibles! Actually, I found out later that it was usually because the Bible had not been touched throughout the week, and then, of course, the next Sunday morning there wouldn't be any time to clean it out, so the pile of stuff grew!

I loved Sunday school; I would get to sit and goof around with my other buddies, and we would have our lesson, all of us sitting there with our hair nicely combed and our teeth brushed. Usually by then our shirts were all starting to get untucked from the little wrestling match we had just had in the boy's room before class. By the time we would leave for home after running around outside after church, we would be a mess again. It was a weekly process and ritual, and we guys, well, we got really good at it!

We would learn about God—that He created us and that He also created the world. We would learn about Jesus and that we needed to be "saved" in order to go to Heaven. We learned that we could be saved because Jesus died on the Cross to save us from our sins and that it was His blood that cleansed us from our sins. I very quickly learned the answers to the questions, and I believed I was saved. After all, I had a perfect attendance pin!

Actually, I really didn't understand how I could be cleansed from all sin because, as my buns would attest, I still was naughty sometimes. I did not understand how blood could fix anything; after all, it was messy. And I didn't understand how Jesus could be God and die and all that stuff. It all seemed a bit strange to me, but the grownups seemed to think it was a good idea.

When Sunday school was over, I would get a new paper to stuff in my Bible, and then it would be off to the main church service where I would have to sit with my mom, dad, and sister. For some strange reason, our parents would never allow me and my Sunday school buddies to sit together! They let us once, but after that...never again!

After tithes and offerings, Dad would come and sit with us as we sang another hymn. I would watch the song leader wave his arm around again, and then I would settle in for the sermon. That was usually when I read my Sunday school paper and did the puzzles. I never really understood much of what the pastor was saying, but I do remember that I would hear how we all needed to be "saved" and that we needed to do it before it was too late. I was not certain exactly what it was I needed to be "saved" from. After all, we could leave church and get hit by a truck or a bus or something, and then it would be too late.

I would not pay much attention; I figured I was already saved. I went to church, had an award Bible stuffed full of qualifying papers, *and* I had perfect attendance. Yeah, I was naughty and bit my sister once, but I hadn't murdered anyone! Surely I would be OK if that proverbial truck or bus that was supposedly always lurking outside the church door ran over me.

I would leave church, always stopping at the door just in case there was a truck or bus coming, but it wasn't long before I was back into things that little boys do.

As the years passed, I had questions. I wanted to know more, but frankly, some of the answers I really wanted answered no one seemed to know the explanation for. They accepted their salvation through Jesus, but they did not know why God had to do it that way.

If God created the world in seven days, when did the dinosaurs, mammoths, and saber-toothed tigers live? They were really neat, and I really wanted to know the answers. It seemed that what I was taught in science class and in Sunday school class were so different. Who was right?

How did God create the world, but better yet, *why* did He create the world? If God knows everything, then how come He did not know that lucifer, who became "the devil," would rebel against Him and cause Adam and Eve to do the same and create all this mess we live in?

I had lots of questions, and as I grew older, they became more and more sophisticated. But frankly, it seemed as if no person knew or could give me a completely satisfactory answer to my questions. Attempts to answer were always finalized by some ethereal statement like, "Well, we don't know; we have to just trust God and take it by faith and find out when we get to Heaven." That was a true statement, but that was not good enough for me.

My dad was very intrigued by subjects like creation, evolution, archaeology, and the Flood. He bought all kinds of books written on the subject; books like that were always good Christmas gift ideas. (And let me say this, he would have loved this book! Why? Keep reading.)

I recall sitting on Mom and Dad's bed looking at his books and the pictures in some of them. I have some of those books of his today. I remember one picture of a fully intact mammoth that had been encased in ice for "millions of years." I was truly intrigued, but could not understand the words. As I got older, I realized the books only raised more questions in my mind. I had questions, but I believed that the truth could be known without waiting "until I got to Heaven" for the answer. So I kept searching.

In high school, I tried to learn what I could about astronomy and geology and even assisted one of my teachers, a geologist, on his geological field trips to learn more. My high school biology teacher had been an evolutionist, yet he had tossed it all aside and accepted instead as truth that *"in the beginning God created the heavens and the earth"* (Gen. 1:1). I wanted to know why. I believed that too, but I wanted the answers to the questions in my head.

I especially wanted to have this question answered: *"Why am I me? What am I for? And if God created me, as I believe, what does He want me for?"* There just had to be an answer!

I searched and read all through high school and college, and then I continued to study, reading anything I could get my hands on, seeking but never finding the answers to all these questions. *Then one day something happened!*

Yes, *something happened* to give me the answers to my questions, and in this book, I want to share those answers with you in a way you can understand.

My wife, Andi, asked me if I would change anything about that time, which I describe as "a time when I was tortured by *nice* people." She asked if I would still go through it if I had the choice. I replied that I would not have changed a thing because it has so impacted and changed me. I believe I am to share with others the information I received in what the world calls a "near-death experience," and that this information will impact and change you as well for the good!

I know you want to know what happened, and I will tell you…in Chapter 3!

Don't you go jumping ahead now; this book is designed to give you information and then build on it chapter by chapter. Don't be tempted to read a chapter ahead of time because you find the chapter title interesting. The answers I give you are direct from the heart of God and from my heart.

Ready? Set? Go!

Chapter 1

In the Beginning...

———•———

"In the beginning God..." Ah yes, those famous words that start the Bible in Genesis 1:1. *"In the beginning God..."* Hmm.

The *beginning?*

The beginning of what? The beginning of time? The beginning of the Earth? I thought God did not have a beginning. (Now, as a kid, thinking about that was enough to make my hair go curly, and curly hair is exactly what I had—so that tells you how much I thought about it!) Well, that was what I was taught in church—that God always was, and I always wasn't! I was also taught that God made me and that He loved me.

But I had lots of questions!

I also learned as a child in Sunday school, if I did not know the answer to the teacher's question, to try "God!" If that wasn't right, then I tried, "Jesus!" One of those answers was always bound to get a smile and an approving nod from the teacher, even if I was wrong.

Now, on the other hand, the answer "satan" or "the devil" always got a frown and a disapproving and cautious look from the teacher. I never gave that answer unless I was sure I was right. I never wanted to yell out "satan" or "the devil" when the right answer was "God." That just wasn't good, and it made me wiggle in my seat when I was wrong, especially *that* wrong!

We did not talk much about satan; we did not want to pay any attention to him. After all, he was bad, and we should not talk very much about him, especially in church. He just always was the one we blamed the bad things on, especially the bad things we did. That was convenient, especially for a little boy like me. He was always lurking around the corner trying to trip us up. I learned to be cautious of and to fear him. He was my enemy. *And do you know who else's enemy he is? God's!* (Yes, class, that's the right answer here; I am smiling and nodding!)

What about these right answers? Who is "God"? Who is "Jesus"? What about "satan" or "the devil"? Who is he, and what does he want? Why does he not go away and let our lives be full of smiles and nods? Did not God create everything? Did God create satan? Why did He create such a monster who would make me bite my sister?

How did this whole mess happen anyway? Did God make a mistake? Did God not know that lucifer (satan) would rebel against Him? What is God going to do about it?

In order to understand this, we need to go back to the beginning. I know, I know—we don't really know when that was, but one thing I do know, it was before us!

"In the beginning, God..." implies that God was always there and was there at the beginning of the accounting of time as we know it. He did not start there, but already was and apparently always has been.

We have trouble understanding that because it is our human nature to package everything in a nice, neat box so that we can understand it. We often try to put God in a box so that we can understand Him.

When God starts to stick His hand out of that box and does something that stretches us a bit and challenges our faith, well then we think, *That's not of God.* Why? It's because it doesn't fit in the box we created for Him. God created a box (our bodies) for our spirits to live in while on Earth, and we have a tendency to do the same for Him. The box is called our "human understanding."

I am amazed at how many people try to match their wits with the One who created them; simply because they cannot understand God, they deny His existence and blame their intricate and sophisticated makeup on some cosmic accident that made them slither out of a puddle, swing in the trees, and grow to become a sophisticated biological machine with virtually untapped intellect who gives and receives love. I guess many of our ancestors did not get it, and that is why they are still swinging in the trees. How absurd!

You see, people who want to deny the existence of God rely on themselves and their intellects; they do not want to be held accountable to a higher authority. Unfortunately, many of them teach in our secular universities. They make up a theory, go out to find evidence to support that theory, and make a name for themselves.

Are you aware that this is how the theory of evolution developed?

This is how it happened.

Scientific thought takes evidence, researches it, and comes up with a hypothesis based on the evidence to explain what we are observing. Charles Darwin was one of these "my mind cannot understand a powerful God like this, so I will make up my own theory" people. He first came up with a theory and has had God-denying people hunting for evidence over the years to back it up! People have even admitted to fabricating evidence to support the theory to make a name for themselves. The facts supporting the theory are always changing, yet the Word of God has never changed.

The theory of evolution is much like believing that cars and airplanes evolved—that raw materials formed into a round wheel, which over the years added more and more parts while refining older ones. Some of them eventually grew wings and began to fly until we ended up with the amazing transportation technology of today. We know the truth: there was intelligent design building on the intelligence of the past and creating the automobile and other forms of transportation.

So it was and is with life. There *is* intelligent design, one with a mind more intelligent than ours. Even the smartest individuals in this world cannot take some dirt and water and make an intelligent and loving human being out of it, but God did, and some of us think we can understand that. Still today, the only way the smartest of us can create life is by using a biological process that was developed and put in motion by a more intelligent Creator. We don't fully understand how it works, but it is part of our nature to do it, and we, quite frankly, like doing so.

I remember hearing Dr. Gary Parker (who just happened to be my tenth grade biology teacher at Delaware County Christian School in the Philadelphia area years ago) at Dr. D. James Kennedy's creation conference talking about this very issue. Dr. Parker, a speaker with *Answers in Genesis*, is a card-carrying evolutionist-turned-child-of-God and creationist. He continued, however, to attend the evolutionists' conferences even after giving up his atheistic ways. Dr. Parker told the audience that at a recent conference following the shattering and discrediting of much current evolutionary "evidence," the conference speakers exhorted the evolutionists to "keep the faith." So much emphasis was put on the fact that evolution was a theory and not a faith, Dr. Parker remarked, and evolutionists are not people who rely much on faith. Yet at that conference they were being exhorted to "keep the faith."

That's backward from scientific thought because evolutionists start with a theory and search for evidence to support it, yet our schools (except the Christian ones) teach it as truth!

This book is not intended to be an evolution versus creation book; there are plenty of good resources on that subject, but we do need to address this issue when we are considering *"In the beginning."* I personally believe in my own version of the *"Big Bang Theory."* I believe a *Big* God said it, and *"Bang!"* it happened. Fortunately for us, He did not have to operate within our mind box. (Oh, and by the way, He never intends to do that.)

You see, our mind is the biggest hindrance to our faith. Our mind is the box we try to fit God into. That is like the car trying to understand the automotive engineers. Just not possible!

I remember one time reading information from people who knew the Bible, yet denied the power of God in their lives. I cried out to God asking how someone could know the Word yet not tap into and even deny its power. God quickly answered me by saying, *"Because they are following the leading of their minds and not the leading of the Spirit. They have not renewed their minds* (see Rom. 12:2), *been transformed, and allowed the Holy Spirit to lead their minds; they are still letting their minds lead the Spirit."*

Romans 8:5 tells us:

> *Those who live according to the sinful nature have their minds set on what that nature desires; but those who live in accordance with the Spirit have their minds set on what the Spirit desires.*

We cannot understand everything about God with our fleshly minds because God is Spirit, and we can only understand these things as His Spirit reveals things to our spirits. Our minds need to take orders from the spirit and not from the flesh. *We cannot understand a spiritual God with the box He created to put our spirits in!*

We will talk more later about the renewing and transforming of our minds to better understand spiritual issues and to gain more revelation. I will give you a deeper understanding of the mind and its role in Chapter 20. Let us return to the issue at hand here.

"In the beginning God created the heavens and the earth" (Gen. 1:1). The heavens and the Earth were created at some point in eternity past, but apparently something unusual happened to mess up that creation. Genesis 1:2 tells us, *"The earth was formless and empty, darkness was over the surface of the deep."* The word *was* here is translated from the Hebrew word *hayah*, which means "to become" or "became." This means that God did not originally create it without form and void and in darkness.

Like the sandcastles we built as children on the beach or in the sandbox that were destroyed by the incoming tide or the local bully, the Earth had been vandalized. The passage further says that God's Spirit *"moved,"* or in the Hebrew *"brooded"* or *"hovered,"* on the face of the deep as we would stand over our destroyed sandcastle contemplating what was and wanting it to be excellent again. So we begin to build again, knowing full well the bully or the evil wave is still around. This is exactly what God did with this Earth, which had become without form and void, for we see in the next verse that the first thing God did after brooding was to turn the lights on. *"And God said, 'Let there be light,' and there was light"* (Gen. 1:3). He then proceeded to build again.

We will come back to this point in creation again, but what was it that ruined God's sandcastle so that He had to start all over again? We must contemplate all of Scripture, the words of prophets, apostles, and of Jesus Christ Himself to have an understanding of where this sandcastle bully came from, how he opposes us, and how he got himself on this beach where we children of God are trying to accomplish excellent things.

In the chapters to follow, we will continue to visit the things we have touched on in this chapter in greater detail to gain an understanding of these questions as well as others in understanding God's overall plan.

Chapter 2

The Sandcastle Bully

"In the beginning God created the heavens and the earth" (Gen. 1:1). Sometime during God's eternal preexistence, God was motivated to create a family He could love and who could love Him back.

The Alpha and Omega, the beginning and the end, started a process whereby He could create a family. He saw the whole picture, the beginning and the end; He saw you at that time as well and established a purpose for your life. He initiated a process still going on today to accomplish all He saw, to accomplish the desires of His heart.

He first began by creating a holy palace or throne in a spiritual heavenly city. He then spoke the word and created the heavenly hosts, beautiful creatures with different roles, to occupy that majestic city. We would refer to these wonderful creatures as angels.

God was not alone when He created these angels; someone was with Him from the "beginning." John 1:1-3 says:

> *In the beginning was the Word, and the Word was with God, and the Word was God. The same was in the beginning with God. All*

41

*things were made by Him; and without Him was not anything
made that was made* (KJV).

In this passage, the apostle John, who walked and talked with Jesus on
this Earth, refers to Jesus as the *Word* and tells us that He was there at creation and that *He actually was the Creator.* Jesus issued the creative Word!
Why was He there? He was there because He has always been part of the
triune God (Father, Son, and Holy Spirit). While on Earth, Jesus Himself
referred to being in Heaven during these early heavenly events.

The apostle Paul also testifies to this in his letter to the Colossians:

*The Son is the image of the invisible God, the **firstborn over
all creation.** For **in Him all things were created:** things
in heaven and on earth, visible and invisible, whether thrones
or powers or rulers or authorities; all things were **created by
Him and for Him. He is before all things,** and in Him all
things hold together* (Colossians 1:15-17).

Verse 17 says that Jesus was before all things, which means that He was
before the angels, the *"firstborn over all creation."* God manifested Himself in
Jesus first! He is the manifestation of the invisible God, creating the *seen* from
the *unseen.* Just as my spirit and your spirit are invisible and are manifested
on this Earth by the physical bodies they occupy, so Jesus is the manifestation or image of God. He is the part of God that can become visible to the
seen world. *Yes, Jesus **is** God, He is the Creator, and He always was! He holds
preeminence over all other creation. In fact, Paul tells us that it was created "for
Him"* (see Col. 1:17).

There you go again, trying to fit this concept into your "mind box." Understand that our limited minds cannot understand something that is unlimited.
Our minds were never created for that purpose; I will explain why they were
created later in this book. However, here is a hint: our minds were never intended to be used in the manner in which they are used, and that is why we

struggle with our minds as emotional battlegrounds! We will explore later in this book how the mind was intended only to be a processor of information from the spiritual realm to the physical realm.

Back to Heaven now.

God created the heavens and the Earth and put the Son over all of it (see Col. 1:15-17). Under the Son, the created angels were organized into three groups, and an archangel was put in authority over each of these three groups. *Arch* means "ruling," so there were three commanding or ruling angels. One group was led by Gabriel. This group served and carried out the affairs or the daily business of the heavenly spiritual *unseen* Kingdom (see Dan. 8–9; Luke 1). The second group, led by Michael, was charged with seeing that the will and Word of God were carried out in all of creation and that nothing would prevent that from being accomplished. They were the enforcers (see Jude 9; Dan. 10:13; Rev. 12:7-9).

The third group had the important job of leading worship and praise in Heaven and doing things that brought glory to God and to His Kingdom. They were responsible for carrying out the creative words uttered through the Son. This group was lead by an archangel who was more majestic than the others. A special light, the very light and presence of God, beamed in his countenance and shone around him brighter and more beautiful than around the other angels. He absorbed the "light" of the presence of God and beamed it upon all of creation. The name of the third archangel was lucifer. As an archangel, he was next in honor to the Son of God and was also known as *"the angel of light"* (see 2 Cor. 11:12). He was responsible for lighting the creation with the light of God and leading all creation in worship and in the praise of God the Father, God the Son, and God the Holy Spirit (see Job 38:4-7).

Lucifer, a powerful being in Heaven, was created with the free moral choice to complement a loving God's desire to love and be loved. Just as God wanted humanity to exhibit love by subordination and obedience as the created being, lucifer was to hold his position in the heavens out of love and obedience. God made him great in the Kingdom of Heaven, the most beautiful, with the greatest of archangel authority. There was no created being more beautiful than lucifer, for he was the reflection of the light of the eternal preexistent God.

We find a description of him in Ezekiel 28:12b-14. In this passage, the King of Tyre is being judged for the sin of pride, and in the prophecy, his fall is to be no different from the fall of the father of pride (lucifer) himself, as it is recounted here.

> *You were the model of perfection, full of wisdom and exquisite in beauty. You were in Eden, the garden of God. Your clothing was adorned with every precious stone—red carnelian, pale-green peridot, white moonstone, blue-green beryl, onyx, green jasper, blue lapis lazuli, turquoise, and emerald—all beautifully crafted for you and set in the finest gold. They were given to you on the day you were created. I ordained and anointed you as the mighty angelic guardian. You had access to the holy mountain of God and walked among the stones of fire* (Ezekiel 28:12b-14 NLT).

In lucifer's mind, there was none greater—or was there?

Oh yes, there was the Son, the manifestation of the invisible God, who was God Himself, ordained to receive the praise and worship that were due to Him.

In the light of Scripture, let us consider the following drama as it may have unfolded in Heaven.

The Creator of the universe and the heavenly host had called them to the throne room for a special meeting. In this assembly, He planned on conferring a special honor upon the Son. The Creator informed the heavenly host that by His (Father God's) authority, the Son would be equal with Himself and that whatever the Son said should be obeyed as if the Father had said it. Yes, the Son was in command of the heavenly host; He was the Prince of Heaven (see Acts 5:31; Gen. 23:6).

As the Prince of Heaven, the Son was to carry out the will and the purpose of the Father. He would do nothing of His own will, as the Scriptures tell us (see John 5:30), but only fulfill the will of the Father. The archangel Michael would be the enforcer to ensure that the commands were being carried out and that nothing would hinder them. Michael, Gabriel, and lucifer were all to report to and be obedient to the commands of the Prince of Heaven, the Son.

A celestial project was about to be launched, and the Son was to work in union with the heavenly Creator in the creation of a special place, a project perhaps known as the "Genesis Project"—yes, the creation of the Earth. *This Earth would be a physical place where the spiritual or the* **unseen** *could be manifested.* Hebrews 1:2 tells us that God created the universe through the Son. The Son was not only the heavenly foreman for the project, but would also be the authority over every living thing that would live upon the Earth. The creation would also be *"for Him"* (Col. 1:16). *The Son would send out the commands of God, the very Word of God, and the heavenly hosts would carry out that command and accomplish the purpose of the Word. God always carries out His Word through appointed agents, either through angels or through people. How that Word is carried out depends on the obedience of the appointed agent and the condition of the agent's heart.*

Why could not lucifer have been that manifestation, the *"exact representation of* [God's] *being"?* (See Hebrews 1:3.) After all, he had projected the light of God. What made the Son better than he? Lucifer, a free moral agent with the ability to choose, was envious of the Son. He wanted to be Him, to hold His position. When all the angels bowed to the Son to acknowledge His supremacy, high authority, and rightful rule, he bowed with them, but his heart was filled with envy and hatred (see Ezek. 28:17). Did not God bestow upon him majestic beauty, authority, and the ability to command the heavenly host? Did he not project the light of Heaven upon all of creation and bring the praises of the heavenly host day and night before the Father? Was it not the Creator Himself who gave him the name *lucifer*, meaning the "angel of light" or "morning star"? What was the Creator thinking?

In his own prideful mind, lucifer decided he would have to set things right.

The Genesis Project began at the direction of the Creator Father and the Prince of Heaven, His Son, whose commands concerning the perfect will of the Father were carried out by the heavenly hosts apparently under the leadership of the archangel lucifer. How do we come to that conclusion? Let's look at Ezekiel 28:13-14 once again:

> **You were in Eden, the garden of God.** *Your clothing was adorned with every precious stone—red carnelian, pale-green peridot, white moonstone, blue-green beryl, onyx, green jasper, blue lapis lazuli, turquoise, and emerald—all beautifully crafted for you and set in the finest gold. They were given to you on the day you were created.* **I ordained and anointed you as the mighty angelic guardian. You had access to the holy mountain of God** *and walked among the stones of fire* (NLT).

This refers to the fact that lucifer was on Earth before his fall and still had access to the presence of God. In fact, we find that he is referred to in Scripture as *"the prince of this world"* (John 12:31; 14:30; 16:11); perhaps he may have been the overseer or "mighty angelic guardian" of this Genesis Project, the creation and care of the Earth. That is what princes do; they are given charges. *He was to carry out the creative Words of the Son, the Prince of Heaven, who gave the Word according to the will of the Father.*

The passage reveals that God *ordained* lucifer (meaning, "to establish in a ministerial function and to empower") and *anointed* him (meaning, "to smear with ability") as well.[1] It was his charge, his dominion! He was to project the light of God's presence and His will on the *seen* creation and bring the glory and praise back to Heaven by overseeing the creative process (see Job 38:4-7).

That's one of those "make your hair go curly thinking about it" things again. So, what happened? Let's go back to the heavenly drama.

Lucifer left the presence of God after the heavenly meeting, but he left filled with envy in his heart against the Son of God. He began to discuss his favorite subject, *himself,* with the other angelic hosts. He began to convince some that they should only listen to him and not the Prince of Heaven who had, in his mind, usurped the position that rightfully belonged to lucifer. Why should he be the one on Earth receiving the directives from Heaven instead of being the one giving them? Perhaps he thought, *I will listen to what they say, but I am the one on site here; I know best, and I will do it my way—show them what I can do! I will accomplish God's plan my way.* Yes, pride raised its ugly head here.

How do we know? We know because in verse 18 of Ezekiel 28 we find God telling lucifer, *"By your many sins and your dishonest trade you have desecrated your sanctuaries."* The word *trade* is translated from the Hebrew as "dishonest or evil trade." We get the image here of a dishonest salesman who will do and say anything to persuade and accomplish his goals. Dishonest salesmen often resort to persistent plotting, slander, or tale-bearing in their efforts to persuade.[2] God knew that lucifer had been murmuring, conniving, lying, plotting, and manipulating to get others to follow him rather than to follow the leadership of the Father through the Son.

There was contention among the host of angels, and lucifer and his sympathizers sought to change the way things were done. They rebelled against the authority of the Son and thereby, the authority of God. They believed that their leader, the arch-deceiver lucifer, could be like God, so they sought to reform the government of God.

I can imagine that the angels, and more specifically Gabriel and Michael, sought to convince lucifer and his sympathizers of their error and also the consequences of their ways, but when they would not listen, these mighty archangels took word of the rebellious activity of lucifer and his sympathizers to the Prince of Heaven.

The first sin of pride led to more sins—disobedience and rebellion.

Lucifer's disobedience and plotting set a war raging in the heavens between Michael the archangel who was assigned to assure God's will and purposes were being carried out and the forces of lucifer (satan) and the one-third of the angels who fell with him (demons). Lucifer, a powerful being in Heaven, was created with the free moral choice to complement a loving God's desire to love and be loved. Lucifer was to hold his position in the heavens out of love, loyalty, and obedience. Instead, pride led to betrayal of that love and then to rebellion.

Whenever one begins to rationalize, it will lead to sin. Lucifer began to rationalize or think about the restrictions placed on him. *What is God holding back? God loves me, or does He? What is He trying to hide? Why would He bestow an honor on another that I believe rightfully belongs to me? Perhaps I can be like God, or maybe it is that I am like God, and this is how He controls me,* he thought. Once this questioning begins, then covetousness follows: "I can be like Him!" Covetousness is then overtaken by pride: "How dare He hold me back!" Pride leads to action and in lucifer's case, to sin, betrayal, disobedience, and a heavenly or spiritual rebellion.

Lucifer sought to discredit God in order to get others to rally behind him in his quest to "be like God"; he attempted to steal God's identity. Other heavenly beings under lucifer's leadership (angels) were tempted and joined him. The battle continued between those loyal to God and the disobedient. Evil had entered the heavens because of this disobedience and had to be purged. Lucifer and his host were cast out of Heaven by the archangel Michael and the forces of God, an event recalled by Jesus in Luke 10:18: *"I saw Satan fall like lightning from heaven."*

Jesus was there; He saw it, and when He later walked upon the Earth as a man, He recalled it and attested to it.

All of Heaven seemed to be in commotion as the crime of treason was committed against the government of God and the authority of the Son, the Prince of Heaven. The forces of lucifer were no match for the forces of God under the direction of the warring angel Michael because lucifer's purposes were not in alignment with the will and purpose of the Almighty God and because they would not ever succeed.

A great heavenly court was convened; the proud of heart were convicted, and their punishment was pronounced. First lucifer was stripped of his majestic beauty, and then he was cast out of the presence of God along with his sympathizers. Ezekiel 28:18 expounds further on lucifer's loss of the light of God's presence as he was cast down to the Earth: *"...So I brought fire from within you, and it consumed you. I let it burn you to ashes on the ground in the sight of all who were watching."*

Lucifer, like a meteor or a blazing comet, was cast down to the Earth, and as he fell, the glorious light of God's presence that he emanated began to flicker and grow faint; then like a flash of lightning, with the force of a comet hitting the Earth, the light went out!

Chapter 3

The Gap in Time

And the earth was without form, and void; and darkness was
upon the face of the deep... (Genesis 1:2 KJV).

Heaven was in mourning for the loss of lucifer and one-third of the angelic host who were cast out of Heaven with him. The praise of Heaven fell silent as lucifer and the others were cast down to the Earth or literally *"to the dirt,"* the focal point of creation, the place where lucifer had been given dominion to carry out the creative orders of the Son. It seems apparent from the Scriptures that it was then that the Genesis Project of Heaven fell into darkness and chaos.

The Word of God says in Genesis 1:1 that *"In the beginning God created the heaven and the earth"* (KJV). Then Genesis 1:2 says, *"And the earth...."* Notice that it does not say "the heavens and the earth," but only *"the earth was without form, and void; and darkness was upon the face of the deep..."* (KJV).

Most theologians today do not believe that God originally created the Earth in chaos. It is just not God's nature. Can you imagine God saying,

"Whoops, I made a mess of that on My first try; let's see if I can clean it up and get it straightened out a bit." Of course not! Sin creates chaos in the universe, as well as in our personal lives, and it is in God's nature to find a way to clean things up, just as He did with me and with many others when He found a way to cover our sins and bring us back into the divine order of things. Lucifer had sinned and made a mess of things, so in Genesis 1:2 we find the beginning of a re-creation process of the Earth.

This was a long-term process and project that is still going on today! God launched at that moment a master cosmic plan that would redeem the world out of the dominion of lucifer, restore it to its intended order, and finally populate it with God's children whom God would love, who would love Him back, and who would love each other as well. *God's quest for* **you** *began at this moment; yes,* **you** *were in His mind!*

Yes, you!

The quest for the physical manifestation of the Kingdom of Heaven with the Son of God as King started at this point. God saw all the events of the Earth at that time, which from our vantage point is the past, the present, and the future. He saw man's Fall and rebellion in Eden and all the events of humankind. In Genesis 1:2, He saw me bite my sister!

God created a perfect world, but it was a perfect world where the potential for evil existed and would ultimately manifest in rebellion. *However, God knew that the evil that would manifest in this early phase of creation would ultimately culminate in the perfect world of the Kingdom of Heaven, which from our vantage point is still in the future.* He would ultimately eliminate evil in the completed creative process, and in so doing, the end result would also eliminate the potential for evil in a great and final Kingdom of Heaven yet to be manifested on Earth. God had honored His Word or contract to give lucifer dominion, but He would have the final say in the world's future.

In the last chapter, we saw into the spiritual pre-creation world. In the light of Scriptures, we were able to put together a heavenly scenario regarding the fall of lucifer—the "sandcastle bully"—who, with his evil intentions, corrupted that which God intended for good, smashing Earth—God's sandcastle—into chaos. What about science? Is the world billions of years old as science tells us, or is it only thousands of years old as the literal creationist says?

Now over the years, I spent some serious "curly hair" time on this subject and would read whatever I could get my hands on regarding such subjects as creation, astronomy, geology, archaeology, evolution, and the age of the Earth. My father, George, had an interest in creation, evolution, archaeology, and geologic and astronomical information. I would sit on his bed looking at the pictures (I couldn't understand the words) in the books he was reading. When I was in high school, I went on geological research trips to help one of my teachers at the Delaware County Christian School in the Philadelphia area. Dr. Frank Roberts was a geologist who spent a lot of time studying geology and fossils in the Middle Atlantic States areas.

At Houghton College in upstate New York, I had the opportunity to sit at the feet of one of the great Christian scientists of our time, Dr. S. Hugh Paine, who had worked during World War II on the "Manhattan Project" (the atomic bomb that ended the war with Japan). I spent many hours with him on the roof of the science building at Houghton with a telescope, talking and postulating with him on many of these issues. In fact, the late Dr. Paine is one of the pioneers in the presentation of what has become known in theological circles as "The Gap Theory," which talks about that gap in time between Genesis 1:1 and 1:2. The Gap Theory postulates that there was a "first world" and a "second world" as scientists refer to them today, two separate and distinct periods of creation separated by a chaotic period of time that could have and most likely did span millions of years.

I sought the answers to the questions so many of us ask. What about the dinosaurs, the mammoth, and all those fossils of animals that obviously lived on the Earth, but according to science, *before* people? What about that strange prehistoric creature still in its preserved flesh that broke out of the ice cap and washed ashore in Alaska back in 1955?

These two gentlemen would get an amused smile on their face when they saw me coming. I always had a question about something I had just heard or read somewhere. I remember Dr. Paine teasing me that if anyone would ever figure it all out, it just might be me. Perhaps his teasing was prophetic, perhaps not. You can decide.

I continued with my curly-headed mind boggled with so much scientific theory and hypothesis that I began to study the Scriptures more thoroughly and quite frankly, only came up with more questions. I realized that until I got to Heaven, I may never understand.

Then something happened (I promised you I would get to this)!

"Something happened" were the words I would say to my wife, Andi, weeks and months after emergency surgery in 1995. The surgery was one I almost did not make it through, and at one point during it, I was resuscitated. When I came out, the doctor informed Andi and Ron Park, our pastor at the time, that I may not even make it through the night. Andi refused to receive that word, and the doctors forgot to tell me that, so I guess that's why I am still here! I am not certain why doctors think they can make such statements because, according to them, I am dead now over 15 years. God is in control of those decisions.

I was in the ICU and on a ventilator during that night and in the days to follow. In the ICU, I had a frequent visitor, but only when my nurse went out of the room. In the darkness and in my blurred vision, He was just a silhouette. He did nothing but lay His hand on me; I would feel such warmth, and the pain I was in would stop. As the days passed and I became more coherent, I began to believe I was imagining this visitor. I blamed it on the morphine, and silently asked for a confirmation from the Lord.

He then came to visit again, and as He left the room, my nurse came in and asked me if that was a friend of mine leaving. In the same breath, she said that no one was supposed to be in there with me without her permission, but my wife and my pastor. Wow! She did not know who He was, and she saw Him! I could not answer her because they had stuck the bathroom sink pipe in my throat, so realizing that I had just received the confirmation for which I had asked, I just nodded my head yes. Yes, He was a friend!

In the days to come, the Lord gave me further confirmations that the experiences I had during surgery did in fact happen. A week later, with the bathroom sink pipe now removed from my throat, a nurse entered into my room to talk to my nurse. I greeted her and told her that I remembered seeing her in the operating room. She looked at me somewhat startled and said, "Mr. Stephens, I have never seen you awake; how could you have seen me in the operating room?" I then realized that I saw her out of the body; in fact, she confirmed that she was there. I also remembered that the doctor who had put me under anesthesia had put me out before getting to the operating room, which he also later confirmed to me that he did. God is good; He honored my desire to know the truth.

I had my own gap in time.

It was during that experience that the Lord called me to the ministry that I am in. Those of you who have heard me speak or have read my previous book, *The Coming Financial Revolution,* know about the "near-death" experience I had, as well as my business meeting with the Lord, where He taught me things regarding finances that I taught in that book. At that time He told me that He would reveal much to me and that I would not only teach these things, but answer many questions of the world in preparation for His Kingdom. In fact, as it has become apparent, He downloaded revelations and a prophetic gift to me, perhaps during that time He or His angel stood by my bed. I, of all people, have been the most amazed at some of the things I have pre-known, said, or written down only to see them unfold at a later time.

There are a number of people now who have come to know and experience this gift of the Lord to them through me.

Now, before I lose some of you, let me tell you that all my friends know what a skeptic I was and still am. I challenge everything. I want to know the truth, and I never have accepted things unless I checked them out first. I was raised in a Baptist church and went to a Wesleyan college where I was a ministerial student, and it wasn't until the above experience that I was able to accept the Holy Spirit moving in me or to experience the supernatural in my life. Even then, it wasn't without a fight. The Lord was good though; He wrestled lovingly with me until I said, "Uncle!" (or in this case, "Lord!"). I had to swallow my pride and say, "Yes, Lord, I will let You out of that box I put You in and let You work in my life."

Now back to the subject at hand.

The Lord revealed to me that *"you cannot understand the literal or the physical, unless you view it through the overlay of the spiritual."*

"Now what does that mean, Lord?"

Much of what is *seen* is a result of what is happening in the *unseen* (see Heb. 11:1). Paul exhorts us to do as Abraham did and call those things that are not as though they are (see 1 Cor. 1:28), meaning that there is a spiritual side and a physical side to things, the *seen* and the *unseen. Remember these two words; they will be often used in this book straight through the final chapter!*

The Lord revealed that we cannot understand what has happened in the physical world unless we understand what has occurred in the spiritual world. *The spiritual existed before the physical, the **unseen** before the **seen**; one is a cause, and the other is an effect.* We will learn later that what is done in the *seen* can also affect the *unseen* world; it works both ways!

Thus, we cannot understand creation and the things that exist in our physical world unless we look at it through the spiritual world. *We can only* *understand what we **see** by looking at it from the vantage point of the **unseen.** The scientist tries to explain the physical world without the overlay of the spiritual, and the literal creationist tries to explain away science and only look at the facts as recorded in the Word of God!* However, if we understand the spiritual, we can see the footprints of creation in the physical, and we can see where God the Son and lucifer walked in this process.

Read again those last few paragraphs if necessary, but make sure you understand before we go on to the deeper things of creation. Put on your spiritual glasses of understanding from Chapter 2 on "The Sandcastle Bully" (or lucifer) to view what is *seen* in this world with more understanding.

Hang on—this is going to be a fun ride!

Chapter 4

The Genesis Project

———•———

We have already decided that we don't really know how long ago "the beginning" was; science says billions of years, and the literal creationist says thousands of years. The truth in the estimation of many good men and women of God who have studied this is that the truth is somewhere in the middle. But the most important thing about creation is that God did it; *we and the time we live in are still part of the outworking of His overall plan.*

One of the things we know from studying the Scriptures is that the amazing architect of our creation was the triune God—Father, Son, and Holy Spirit. Scripture mentions all of them as being there. (We will discuss this "triune God" or "Trinity" concept later to help you fit it in your "mind box.") The triune God spoke the Word, and it was carried out. Now remember that the heavenly host was responsible for carrying out the commands of God and seeing to it that His will was done, so it is biblical for us to assume that the entire heavenly Kingdom played a role in the creation of the heavens and the Earth. In fact, as we have discussed, Scripture seems to indicate that the one "ruler" member of the host who seemed to be given the dominion for the earthly creation was the sandcastle bully himself, lucifer. It seems he might have been the project manager, as we would think of it in today's terms. He, as the angel of light, would carry the presence of God and bring that presence (or light) to the seen physical creation.

When we look at the Genesis 1:1 part of the creation, we must overlay the activity of Heaven to gain a true understanding of what happened. We have already discussed that there appears to be a gap in time between Genesis 1:1 and 1:2, so we will refer to the first part as the first world and the second part as the second world!

Even God-denying scientists for years have referred to the first world and the second world. This is not a new concept I am postulating!

Scientists acknowledge that there appears to have been a world that was different from the world *as we now know it*, just as the first two verses of Genesis seem to indicate. It is interesting to also indicate here that the King James Version of the Bible was translated in 1611, before modern scientific thought began to develop and became accepted and used in the study of the Earth and its origins. The translators were, therefore, not influenced by current scientific thought in the translation. In fact, as we noted in the first chapter, the original Hebrew even more clearly indicates this concept of creation, restoration, and an actual re-creation of the world.

What are we talking about?

When we study the geology of the Earth, we find that there are three primary layers of rock or strata upon the Earth. These layers are known as the Palaeozoic, Mesozoic, and the Cenozoic strata or ages. In these strata or layers of rock, we find that the fossils of plants, animals, marine life, and insects in each stratum are distinctly different from the other strata layers.[1]

It gets even more interesting. In the second (Mesozoic) and third (Cenozoic) layers from the bottom and on top or after these strata, we have found bones of large creatures we have named dinosaurs, mammoths, and other forms of life that no longer exist upon the Earth.[2] In fact, we have found encased in ice at the poles, Siberia, and in chunks of ice that have broken off from the poles, perfectly preserved mammoths with fresh foliage in their stomachs and mouths. It has been reported that the Eskimos even ate some of these because the flesh was so well preserved. Then in 1955 in Alaska, as I mentioned previously, a huge carcass of an unknown creature, perfectly preserved, washed ashore in a large chunk of ice. Sixty feet of it were exposed above the sand and unfortunately, it decomposed before any real study could be made of it, but they do not have a clue as to what it was.

Something then must have occurred after the strata or layers of rock were put down to cause a sudden freeze to come upon the Earth, snuffing out all life and then creating what science refers to as the ice age. Again, the life-forms prior to this ice age do not exist in the second world. The studies of these creatures also indicate that where they lived was warm because of the fresh foliage found, perfectly preserved in their stomachs. It also indicates that their demise was sudden and violent and that they were immediately put on ice, and some of them remained that way at the poles until our time.

Subsequent to this ice age, we find on top of the layers the remains of the life-forms found today as well as an indication in the geology that the ice age may have begun in and ended the first world. The thawing of the ice spanned the Genesis gap between verses 1 and 2 as we discussed and ended in the very beginning of the second world as we pick up creation in Genesis 1:3. The *"deep"* of Genesis 1:2 appears to have been in a frozen state. Why? Because the lights were out (see Gen. 1:3). Science tells us that if for some reason the sun's light stopped shining, within 48 hours the world would be in a frozen state.

I must stop and observe that no remains or evidence of humans have been found in any of the three strata or in the ice age evidence. So we can conclude that humans did not walk upon the Earth until the second world. This was a good thing because many of these animals were so huge that, if humans had walked with them, they would most likely not be referred to as "human," but as "lunch."

Over the years, evolutionists have tried to put prehistoric people into this time, but let me recount again, as I did in Chapter 1, that they are taking a theory and looking for evidence to prove it. That is actually contrary to the scientific process of looking at the evidence and developing a hypothesis. All of their evidence over the years has either been proved a hoax or a real scientific "stretch."

Even as I write these words, one of the major news Websites reported the find of a human jawbone in Spain; scientists are referring to it as a possible prehistoric missing link because it is so deformed. On the same Website, the day before, was an article about a woman in England who had died because she had contracted a rare form of cancer that left her face and skull severely disfigured and protruding. I conclude that finding a disfigured jawbone is no proof of a prehistoric missing link, but the vain attempt to make something fit into a preconceived idea.

If you study evolution, it quickly becomes apparent just how desperate evolutionists are to prove their theory; yet we teach it in our "institutions of learning" as truth. My Bible says, *"The foolishness of God is wiser than human wisdom"* (1 Cor. 1:25). It takes more faith to believe what they do than what I do!

We must remember that, for us to have a proper understanding, we must look at what we see in the physical as a manifestation of spiritual activity; otherwise, we come up with falsehood.

Evolutionists try to explain the diverse life-forms of the different ages of the first world as part of the evolutionary process, but I tell you that it was part of a spiritual process!

I know, I know, you are getting anxious. "Tell us what happened!" you say. "What was it the Lord revealed to you in your near-death experience that helped you put all the questions you had into order?"

I will, but don't be tempted to jump ahead because you need this information to understand what I am preparing to tell you. You need to understand lucifer, who he was, what he attempted to do, and how that affected the creation process—how it still affects us today as we move toward the Kingdom.

I conclude that the evidence we find in the rock is the evidence of a spiritual battle in Heaven and is recorded in the astronomy and geology we study, a testimony to the ongoing battle of good and evil and the coming Kingdom of God.

There is no discrepancy between science and the Bible except in the vantage point from which we look at creation. The scientist only looks at the physical, and the literal creationist only looks at the literal. What I am proposing is that we look at the physical world and the literal Word through the eyes of the spiritual world as "cause and effect"; then we can understand.

Are you ready for this?

If we understand a *spiritually driven creation process*, we can also understand the Great Flood of Noah.

Let's go to the next chapter and look at how it all happened, taking into account the spiritual overlay.

Chapter 5

The Battle of Creation

---·---

We will now take a look at the physical world through the spiritual overlay of the events that occurred at the dawn of the creation of the Earth. We have explored through the revelation of the Scriptures in the previous chapters the spiritual activity of Heaven and the activity of lucifer and the one-third of the angels that were cast out of the heavenly Kingdom with him.

Every physical manifestation we see is the result of some spiritual activity in the past, the present, or the future. The **unseen** *activity reveals itself in the* **seen.**

The more skeptical among us should know that science is discovering evidence for the existence of an invisible world that is not bounded by the limitations of the physical world as we now know it. We will explore that in Chapter 22.

By the light of spiritual activity, the Church today is learning about spiritual warfare in understanding the events of the world, the coming Kingdom, and our own personal lives. *Spiritual activity can also be applied to those things we have not understood in the history of humankind and the world.*

Now I know to some of you, who tend to intellectualize everything, this is difficult; I know because I have been there myself. However, the more time I spend in the Word of God, seeking the Holy Spirit and His direction in life, the more sensitive I become to the spiritual side of things. Skeptics will always be skeptics until the Holy Spirit gets a hold of their minds. He did get hold of mine, and I want to give Him more of my mind so that I will walk around with the *"mind of Christ"* (1 Cor. 2:16).

The scientist or the literal creationist will never understand what he or she observes in the evidence without considering the spiritual, and the spiritually-focused person will not understand fully unless he or she takes a look at what is recorded in the dirt.

This book is not meant to be an exhaustive exposition on the scientific as it pertains to creation, so I will try to give you an understanding of the process as simply as possible without going into deep detail. I want you to see the whole picture without spending a lot of time focusing on each individual brush stroke of the picture. My purpose is to help you gain an understanding of how the physical world relates to the spiritual activity surrounding creation.

So, now let's think in the spiritual while we get our hands dirty and dig in the dirt of the Earth!

The Creation of the Heavens and the Earth

"In the beginning God created the heavens and the earth" (Gen. 1:1). In the last 50 years, numerous theories of the creation of the universe have come and gone; rather than get into the intricacies of each one, let me conclude that, however God's initial creation of the planet happened, there are some common elements. Violent explosions, gas, and molten material produced particles similar to the sun and the planets of our solar system. These bodies

were attracted to each other by gravitational or magnetic forces and began a never-ending trip into the expanse of an endless universe.

In the vast expanse of particles of molten materials and gas and dirt was one piece of dirt that caught God's attention, much as the mite given by the widow at the Temple caught Jesus' attention in Mark 12:41-42. God said, "Ah, there's something I can work with to lovingly build a place for My family." As I said earlier, I subscribe to my own Big Bang Theory: God spoke the Word, and Bang! It happened! From an *unseen* spiritual universe, God spoke the Word, and the *seen* universe came into being and began to organize itself.

According to the various theories, the Earth started as a collection of nebular gases and materials that, due to magnetic forces, assembled together; as a particle of the exploding stars; or even as a piece of the sun that broke off due to the gravitational pull of another star, which passed close to our current sun, pulling pieces off which cooled and formed into the planets of our solar system.

Whatever the cause, the fact remains that the original state of this Earth was a hot, molten body that began to cool as it fell into the orbit of our sun. Science verifies that it was very hot, as it still is at the core today, occasionally spewing its molten material to the surface through volcanic action. This volcanic action gives us a picture of the surface of the Earth at the initiation of the creative process. Due to this intense heat and the volatility of the surface of the Earth, vapors, gases, and materials were shot up and collected in orbit above its surface, forming four rings around the Earth. We can catch a glimpse of this worldwide volcanic activity recorded in the dirt when we look at Big Bend National Park in Texas.[1]

It is this type of activity that would have hurled gas and debris above the Earth and created the orbiting rings. These rings would be similar to what we observe encircling the planet Saturn. In early creation, the early Earth I saw in my experience resembled the planet Saturn as that planet appears now.

The first ring or layer to be cast off from the heat of the Earth was a vapor of hydrogen and oxygen forming a ring of water, followed by three more rings below it of material and gases from the volcanic action and heat on the surface. These rings also contained water vapor. These four rings became caught in the gravitational pull of the Earth and were suspended in orbit by centrifugal force around a spinning or rotating Earth. In between the Earth and the rings was additional water vapor that, as the Earth began to cool, settled as dew upon the Earth and watered it. If we study the planet Saturn, we find that the rings are held up by two opposing forces, centrifugal and gravitational. Our recent probes and studies of Saturn show that two things could cause the rings to collapse. The first would be a loss of intrinsic heat (the planet's own heat), and the other would be the slowing of the rotation of the planet. In addition, a study of our solar system shows that about one-half of the planets still have a covering of gaseous vapor ("atmosphere" or "canopy") we cannot see through with a telescope, but have been able to pass a probe through.

Keep this in mind as we begin to look at the process.

The fact that the foregoing could have taken millions or billions of years is not important. We will concede that to the scientists. Time is only important to people, for God and the spiritual realm are not bound by time, and as the Scripture says, *"…With the Lord a day is like a thousand years, and a thousand years are like a day"* (2 Pet. 3:8). The converse of that verse is also true. We usually think of the verse as illustrating God's patience as He takes time to complete something. However, the verse illustrates that God can also accomplish in a day what would take 1,000 years to complete! In my own gap in time, I recognized that I experienced what I refer to as "an ever-present *now.*" By that I mean that while I was in the presence of the Lord, time was not an issue, and it did not pass. What was but a moment on Earth for the doctors in that operating room frankly wasn't important in the spiritual realm. We had all the time we needed and accomplished all we needed to do in an Earth moment. For me, coming back was too soon!

With regard to time in the creation of the Earth, the fact is that the Earth may have been spinning or rotating faster in its early state; scientists might then make higher estimates of the age of the Earth since the rotation of the Earth and its orbit around the sun is the basis for our time. The processes to accomplish things that would take longer amounts of time during our present age would have taken less time in a faster rotating and orbiting Earth.

The point is that early in the creation process the Earth had rings; as the rotation slowed and the Earth lost intrinsic heat, the orbits of these rings would degrade. They would degrade to the point that their fate would become the same as many of the satellites and space junk that orbit the Earth today—they lose their orbit and come crashing in a fiery return to Earth. Recently, in 2006 the ArabSat 4A Commuications Satellite degraded in its orbit and, according to the Defense Department, the crashing satellite's course was altered and it was destroyed for safety reasons.[2]

This is important as we consider the rings and how they relate to the three strata or layers of rock found on the Earth's crust.

Some of you may be starting to get the picture. But why and how did this happen?

Let's stop and check in on the spiritual or *unseen* realm.

In Chapter 2, we looked at events in Heaven as God the Father in union with the Son launched a celestial project to create a *seen* or physical world. The heavenly hosts' responsibility was to carry out the commands of the Son. And it appears that lucifer, *"the prince of this world,"* was the foreman or, as the Scripture says, the *"angelic guardian"* (Ezek. 28:14 NLT), the *"anointed cherub that covereth"* (KJV) of at least the earthly creation; we will discuss that in further detail a little further on. The foreman of a project is responsible for taking the concepts of the mind provided by the architect and the developer and making it reality in the dirt. The Son gave the commands to prepare this one planet for the creation of physical life. Lucifer's jealousy and

pride were already beginning to infect him as well as the supernatural anointing he would need, as the superintendent of this project, to carry out the
Son's commands

The cooling Earth with its four rings encircling it began to be prepared
for the introduction of life. The life to be created was to be a manifestation of
the glory of God. The light of the presence of God in lucifer, the *"son of the
dawn"* (Isa. 14:12), gave him the anointing to carry out the creative orders
of the Son that were in accordance with the design of God the Father and
God the Spirit. The presence of God and His will and Word to create would
be carried out through lucifer, the prince of this world (see John 12:31). He
had been given dominion as the Creator's agent upon the Earth to beam the
light of God's presence upon the Earth. God works through His appointed
agents in the physical realm, just as He does today with people; lucifer was a
"tool" of God's creation to accomplish the will and Word of the triune God on
Earth. Unfortunately, he saw himself as more than just a "tool" in the hand
of the Creator.

The all-knowing Son began to plan life according to the will of the Father
while the project manager was on Earth making preparations and executing
the Word. Up until this point, he had done well with his responsibilities, but
the infection that had taken root in lucifer was ever growing. He began to
believe he could be like God, and since he carried the light of the presence
of the Father, it made him feel god-like. In his mind, he believed he really
did not need the Son to tell him what to do. He felt God's power, and he mis-
takenly thought it was his. As he acted on the Creator's Word, his pride and
jealousy infected it.

You might ask here how the all-powerful Word of God would not be carried out just as the Creator commanded it; after all, the prophet Jeremiah tells
us that the Lord watches over His Word to perform it (see Jer. 1:12 NASB).
However, lucifer's actions were very much in keeping with how God accomplishes and watches over His Word. Let's explore this before we go on.

Throughout Scripture, God uses His agents, both people and angels, to carry out His Word. We have numerous examples where God issued a Word and assigned an agent, often an angel, to not only carry it out, but to take action in order to enforce and to accomplish God's Word. Let us look at some examples with the prophet Daniel. In Daniel 4:13-17 we see that the *watchers* (another name referring to angels) carried out the decree of God against Nebuchadnezzar. Then again in Daniel 9:21-23 we see that Daniel's prayer for skill and understanding was decreed from Heaven and was delivered by the angel Gabriel, but we also see in Daniel 10:13 that this agent of delivery of the Word of God was also detained by the "prince of Persia" (satan) from delivering the Word or command of God. We also find that Gabriel had to wait for the help of another angel named Michael so that he could be released to carry out the command of God. This event also shows that the angels were assigned different roles because the messenger or delivery angel had to call on Michael, the enforcing angel, when confronted with opposition.

As we consider the creation scenario, we find through our studies that corruption and violence were found in the early creation. According to the passage in Ezekiel 28, God told lucifer that corruption was found in him (see Ezek. 28:15). If there is corruption in the created order, then we must conclude, among other evidence recorded in the dirt of the Earth, that this is the place where lucifer and his helper angels were carrying out the Word and that evidence of the corruption of the Word might also be found if we stop to look in the dirt.

What was the difference between these angels in our examples with Daniel and lucifer? Lucifer was a supernatural being of free moral choice, but infected with pride. The corruption growing within him was increasing and manifesting in how he carried out the creative Words.

However, just as God said in Jeremiah 1:12, He will watch over His Word to perform it, and that is exactly what He was doing. Soon in our timeline we will see Him step in and take corrective action.

As we once again consider creation and the role of God's agents in the creative process of His Word, let us pick up again on this possible scenario of our subject of creation.

The water between the first ring and the Earth began to water the cooling Earth, and as it did, lucifer began to carry out the will coming from the Father, calling forth life; however, it was not done exactly according to the commands of the Son. Colossians 1:16, speaking of Jesus, the Son, tells us that all things were created *"through Him."* After all, Jesus was the physical manifestation of the Father, and He, therefore, would be the one through whom the *seen* world would be created from the *unseen* world. Colossians 1:15 tells us that the Son is the *seen* image of the invisible or *unseen* Father.

The creative Word of the Son to be carried out by His agents was infected and corrupted by lucifer's prideful and jealous spirit. It is much like trusted teenagers, who find a sense of power and freedom in using your credit card, though they really are not using *their* authority to purchase, but *yours*—to the degree that you have given it to them. If they are alone though, they could abuse it and do some things with it that you did not authorize, and you would take corrective action. God trusted lucifer with His "credit card" until the bills started coming in!

Lucifer's pride corrupted the Word flowing through him from the Son as vegetation was prepared and grew in the warm environment. This occurs today as people distort the Word of God for their own purposes corrupted by their own desires and opinions. He also distorted the Creator's Word in the creation of things that would creep upon the Earth, insect-like creatures and marine life that would live among the vegetation. In his mind, it was not the Son who gave the Word, but it was he who called it out, using the power of the presence of the Holy Spirit working through him. Like prideful people who pray for the sick and see them recover might erroneously think they did the healing, lucifer thought in his mind that he truly was like God! He was infecting and distorting the Word of the Creator flowing through him with his own prideful lust and rebellion, distorting the power of the Almighty.

The Prince of Heaven, the Son, was not oblivious to all this, as the all-knowing mind of God was with Him. The Genesis Project was not going as planned by the Creator, but was twisted. Disapproving words were sent to the project manager or "angelic guardian" who had been given dominion over the physical Earth for the purpose of carrying out the commands of the Son. Unknown to the project manager, however, the Creator had built into the process a system for the correction of prideful errors or for holding all things together (see Col. 1:17).

The Earth continued to cool, and its rotation slowed to the point that the first ring of debris and water began to degrade in its orbit. We shall call this ring the Paleozoic ring, for that is what the geologists call it today. The project manager watched as the ring's orbit degraded to the point that it began violently to rain down upon the Earth, destroying and encasing in the sediment all the life-forms created when lucifer's pride had twisted the Son's creative Word. These failed life-forms were the *seen* evidence of a spiritual battle that was beginning to develop in the *unseen* world. Even today that is what lucifer (satan) does; he twists the Word and will of God to serve his own purposes and to deceive the people of the Earth.

We call this ring that came crashing down upon the Earth the Paleozoic ring because the ring put down the first layer of stratum or rock in which we find fossils of this life. Science refers to this layer of rock as the *Paleozoic Age* or stratum.

The sandcastle bully himself now had his own castle wiped out by a wave out of the heavens. The root of pride in lucifer began to bring forth anger at the Son. The collapsing of the first ring was part of the finishing touches of the creative process that had not yet been revealed to lucifer, which perhaps was placed in the creative process by an all-knowing God to deal with lucifer's rebellious, unauthorized creative act.

Undaunted, lucifer continued doing it his way in an effort to discredit God before his supporters and the rest of the heavenly host. The infection at this point began to fester into evil; the creative acts prematurely be-gan again, reflecting the mind and the pride of the earth-based creative tool and not that of the Father. Vegetation was created, but this time that which was called to creep upon the Earth reflected the growingly dis-torted, angry, and prideful mind of a created being with free moral choice carrying out the supernatural commands flowing through him from the will of the Creator. None of the vegetation fossilized from the early strata ever existed in exactly the same form in the present world. That which is created in this universe was created to reflect the mind of the Creator. The Creator's mind and will in this case were being distorted by His ap-pointed agent who infected it with his own will in much the same way as we can distort God's will for our lives by infecting and twisting it with our own will.

Pride growing within lucifer grew to anger; the infection now festered into evil, and creation manifested this evil infection. Lucifer would infect all of creation, and surely the Father would see that the Son, the Prince of Heaven, was not suited for the job to which lucifer wished to aspire.

Pride is not pretty, and neither were the creatures created, reptile-like be-ings that flew and walked upon the Earth—the dinosaurs! Studies show that evil must have been present at least in some of these creatures because they turned on each other for food and not just to vegetation, reflecting a confused and distorted creation of a confused and distorted creative plan.[3] They grew to enormous sizes, and science refers to this period as a time of violent life upon the Earth. This life was manifesting the angry spirit of the project man-ager of that creation and not the will of the Creator.

Remember that the angels' job is to see that the Word of God is carried out; they know what they are supposed to do, but this angel was not doing it. In fact, he may have whistled that Frank Sinatra song "My Way," a song reflecting an attitude in this world that has separated the creation from the Creator and twisted the Creator's plan throughout all history.

The Son, aware of the problem, also knew this violent creation would be taken care of as well by the plan of God already set in motion and orbiting the Earth. He called in the enforcer of God's Word, Michael the archangel, and dispatched him to confront lucifer and give him a warning for corrupting the Word of the Creator and for his rebellious, prideful attitude.

In the meantime, the Earth continued to cool and slow in its rotation, and the second ring, the Mesozoic ring, began to degrade, raining down on lucifer's parade of big creatures, plants, and marine life. All were violently destroyed and encased in the mixture of sediment and water, forming a second layer of rock and fossils that we know today as the *Mesozoic* stratum.

Pride is never rational, and *evil always oversteps itself,* whether it was in the creation of the *first world* or in the 21st century. Yes, you guessed it; lucifer began again with the corruption of creation. Again vegetation began to grow in a lush, tropical paradise that grew upon a warm Earth, but again the slowly cooling Earth caused the third ring, the Cenozoic ring, to degrade and rain down debris and water upon the Earth, wiping out the sandcastle bully's castle for a third time. This created the *Cenozoic Age* or stratum of rock we now see upon the Earth.

Back in Heaven, in the spiritual or *unseen* realm, Michael and his hosts reported lucifer's pride and unwillingness to submit to the authority of the Prince of Heaven, God the Son—something He already pre-knew and for which He had prepared. Lucifer just did not reflect the mind and will of God in this Genesis Project, but he was also letting his mind get in the way of God's will, much as people do today when they do not understand God.

Lucifer, in an effort to prove himself, was about the business of corrupting life-forms in his image, but a loving God was about the business of creating a family.

Something had to be done, but oh, how God loved lucifer and how hard it must have been for Him to instruct Michael to return to Earth to summon lucifer to the throne room of God for a hearing on these matters.

Michael returned to lucifer only to find that the corrupted creative process had begun once again. Perhaps it was Lucifer's irrational pride, or perhaps he realized that the three rings were now upon the Earth, and now only the ring of water vapor or the *"canopy"* remained encircled above the Earth. Surely nothing could destroy his castle this time. Michael looked about at the vegetation and the beasts that walked upon the Earth. There was some similarity to what God had intended upon the Earth, but it was not quite right. Lucifer had attempted to create more in line with the will and mind of God, but still there was evidence that his mind and the evil within him was now fully infected and about to burst. Michael looked about at the large beasts, the woolly mammoths, the saber-toothed tigers, and the rest of the land and marine life, then turned and informed lucifer, "You and your host are summoned to appear before the God of this universe and His Son immediately."

Lucifer, haughty and proud, returned to the spiritual realm to confer with and in his mind, confront God the Father and the Son. Surely he could convince God that he was His equal, as evidenced by his power to create, he thought—never realizing that he only carried the presence of God, which had the power to create according to His will, and that he did not possess it. He had abused God's credit card! It was not his, and he was about to lose it.

The heavenly tribunal began as Michael gave his report of the events of Earth and the Son challenged the actions of the *project manager,* lucifer. It was obvious that the root of pride had grown, then festered, and now oozed evil in the form of disobedience and rebellion against the authority of the Son and even against Father God Himself. One-third of the angels in his charge stood also in support of lucifer and defied the God of Heaven, pronouncing their support for their leader.

The great deceiver as we have come to know him first deceived himself! He was his own first victim.

God, in the witness of the heavenly host, pronounced a curse upon him, stripping him of his majesty, and in His wrath, He cast lucifer and his supporters out of Heaven and down to the Earth. Ezekiel 28:18 records what happened:

> *By your many sins and dishonest trade, you have desecrated your sanctuaries. So I made a fire come out from you, and it consumed you, and I reduced you to ashes on the ground in the sight of all who were watching.*

Remember, we discussed before that the word translated *trade* here has been translated in other places as *tale-bearing,* which means "slandering" (see Lev. 19:16; Prov. 20:19). In this passage, we find that the presence of God that lucifer carried is referred to as *"fire"* and that God made it come out of him and figuratively turned him to ashes. Ashes are what you find when a fire burns out, and lucifer found himself with the light of God's presence burned out upon the Earth, where God had previously given him dominion.

We have the words of Jesus in Luke 10:18 recalling this event: *"I saw Satan fall like lightning from heaven."*

This was a violent event as the "angel of light" and his host were cast out of Heaven, the light burning bright, then flickering, and then going out as the power of God's presence exploded with the force of a comet hitting the Earth. The Earth shook violently and was knocked on a different axis or angle, halting its rotation momentarily. The momentary loss of centrifugal force brought the final ring or water canopy down upon the Earth, covering it with water. Debris from the megaton impact and collapse of the canopy of water catapulted into the air in such quantity that the light of the sun was blotted out by the debris from the explosion. Now there was debris encircling the Earth as it began to rotate once again on a different axis.

Scientific research has taught us that if for some reason the sun's light and heat were blotted out, the entire globe would become a ball of ice. Scientists speculate that either a comet or a large meteor hitting the Earth would cause such an event. The Earth submerged under the deluge of water from the canopy was then quickly frozen as the light of the sun was blocked from shining. The light of God's presence had been extinguished as well from within lucifer. Plant and animal life were quickly drowned as they ate, and then they were immediately encased in ice by the intense cold that came upon the face of the Earth.

You might say that God not only cast lucifer and his host out of Heaven and down to the Earth, but that He also put them on ice!

In fact, He not only put lucifer on ice, but all the creation he had supervised as well. Mammoths, saber-toothed tigers, and all sorts of unusual creatures were suspended in time as they ate, some of them even preserved for centuries to be found in our time with fresh food in their mouths and stomachs.

What about the physical evidence of this spiritual battle? Let us take a look.

Evidence of a cataclysmic collision of a large meteor or even a comet strike has been discovered with the advent of satellite photography. Science has in fact determined that an impact of incredible proportions did occur prehistorically in the area of Central America known as the Yucatan Peninsula. This area was created by a large crater that eroded over time and mostly filled with water from the Gulf of Mexico. Scientists have determined that this impact would have created devastating destruction—not just in that area of the world, but also upon the whole Earth and could have been the catalyst for the ice age! Could we be looking at the very spot where the physical manifestation of an act in the spiritual realm hit the dirt, so to speak?

The cataclysmic explosion of lucifer's casting down also momentarily stopped the Earth's rotation, breaking the centrifugal force, which suddenly brought down the fourth ring or canopy of water with a splash of epic proportions, flooding the Earth. The loss of the light of God's presence and the debris from the explosion blocking the sun's light reduced the Earth to a frozen ball of ice, commencing the start of what we call the ice age!

Lucifer's domain was reduced to chaos, and he was in the middle of it with no ordained and anointed power to recreate because the creative Spirit of the presence of God was no longer within him. He had been stripped of his credit card, so to speak. The Earth was *"formless and empty, darkness was over the surface of the deep…"* (Gen. 1:2), a complete state of frozen darkness for who knows how long, perhaps a very long time, perhaps not so long.

The Earth hung rotating and revolving silently in space, covered in complete darkness from a catastrophic event of astronomical proportions. All life had ceased. The spirits of lucifer and one-third of the angels who fell with him were trapped upon a dark, frozen world.

Where had the creative Spirit of the presence of God gone?

Chapter 6

The Second World

———◆·◆———

The Spirit of God *"moved"* (KJV), *"was hovering"* (NIV), *"fluttering"* (YLT), over the waters (Gen. 1:2), or as the Hebrew implies, He *"brooded"* as a mother hen sits upon her eggs waiting for life to occur. The Spirit of God was hovering and fluttering, brooding above a ruined Earth, and as we might say with Hebraic appropriateness, about to "hatch" a new plan!

In the throne room of Heaven, *God pronounced a new plan, a new order for the world as it were, a plan that would take thousands of Earth years to complete.* The Son, understanding the will of the Father God, commanded the heavenly hosts to initiate the plan. There was more to be done here now than just the physical acts of restoration and new creation of the Earth. Something had been lost in the process. When lucifer was cast down to Earth, he not only lost his beautiful heavenly name, but also the beautiful light of God's presence that he had projected.

Even though he lost his heavenly name, we will continue to refer to him as lucifer, just so we don't lose track of who he is as we go through the events discussed in this book. We will also occasionally refer to him by his new names, "the devil," "satan," "the enemy," or "the deceiver."

God is a God of honor, and He had given dominion to lucifer to carry out His commands. When lucifer was cast down, heavenly dominion of the Earth was reclaimed in the heavenly realm. In the new world order about to be created, a plan was launched wherein the dominion taken back from lucifer would be given to a new overseer. The new overseer would gain dominion over the whole Earth and hold that position out of love, loyalty, and obedience to the will of the Father. The new overseer's obedience would override the disobedience of the one who had possessed the dominion. The Son would commune directly through the Holy Spirit with that new overseer as that overseer *subdued the earth* (see Gen. 1:28). This new overseer would once again project the light of God's presence upon the Earth. This presence also would be a holy fire burning brightly within him as it was originally in lucifer.

The First Day

The command of Heaven went forth, and the creative Spirit of God that hovered above the waters sprang into action. *Just as He has been revealed to us throughout the ages, God is a God of restoration, making new that which was ruined, fixing that which was broken through the Word of His Son, just as He does so today.*

God began to restore order out of the chaos; He took the Earth *"without form and void"* and began to re-form and refill it. The first thing that the Lord did in this restorative and recreation process was the same thing we do when we attempt to reorganize a room, garage, or shed—we put the lights on.

The Lights Go On

He took this dark Earth and said, *"Let there be light"* (Gen. 1:3). Nothing is said here about the sun being created, and that is because it already had been created. It was created as part of Genesis 1:1, when the heavens and the Earth were originally created. In verse 2, we find that only the Earth is *"without form and void."* The gas and dust that encircled the Earth from the cataclysmic impact had settled upon it, creating a layer of "dirt" upon the Paleozoic, Mesozoic, and Cenozoic strata of rock upon which new life could be created.

The sun's light was once again able to penetrate to the surface of the Earth, which, at this point, was still a frozen ball of ice in the height of the ice age. The Earth's rotation only allowed the sun to shine on one side at a time, so darkness was not totally eliminated, but now divided into night and day by the Spirit of God. However, as we shall see in day four, the light may still have contended with settling debris as it began to filter through. It may also have now been in a new position—due to the cataclysmic event of lucifer's fall, possibly at the impact crater at the Yucatan Peninsula—which knocked the Earth on its present axis. The first day and evening resulting from the rotation of the Earth created the first day.

Now let's talk about this "day" concept for a minute, since a day to us is a 24-hour thing. We also read in the Scripture that *"with the Lord a day is like a thousand years…"* (2 Pet. 3:8; see also Ps. 90:4), which has led some to adopt the "day-age" theory of creation. This theory accounts for the geologic age of the Earth by postulating that these are not literal 24-hour days in Genesis, but perhaps 1000-year periods or some other segment of time.

I believe, as it was revealed to me in my near-death experience, that these days are varying periods of time allowing the restoration and creative processes to be accomplished by God, who is not bound by time as we are. Remember I told you that I experienced an "ever-present *now*" when I was in His presence.

There has been a lot of speculation in recent years about the "near-misses" we have had when large meteors pass near the Earth. Astronomers speculate about what would happen if a meteor, a group of meteors, or even a comet struck the Earth. If you remember, in the revelation of creation that I am recounting for you, it was revealed to me that it was this type of an event that was the physical manifestation of the casting down of lucifer, bringing about the earthly chaos of Genesis 1:2.

In the speculations of scientists, if the Earth were struck with a cataclysmic impact of a heavenly body, it would be done with such force that we would measure the resulting explosion in mega multiples or megatons of the strongest bombs man has ever created upon the Earth. Our bombs would be comparable to a "firecracker"! It has been theorized that this would not only blot out the sun's light for a time, destroying all life as it apparently did with the *first world* at lucifer's fall, but that it could even knock the Earth off its present axis and *even stop its rotation for a period of time if the force of the impact were in the opposite direction of the rotation.* It has been noted that the impact crater in the Yucatan shows the impact's trajectory to be in the opposite direction of the Earth's rotation. If this type of thing would happen (and I do not believe God would let that happen in this present age), none of us would survive.

As the Earth recovered from this cataclysmic blast, the debris would settle and the sunlight would return as the Earth continued in its revolution around the sun. The Earth's revolution around the sun would start the Earth rotating again, very slowly at first, then increasing in the speed of its rotation until it reached its current 24-hour rotation. According to what the Lord has imparted to me, this serves as our explanation: the first day of creation was much slower than the days that followed, with each subsequent day being a shorter period of time as the Earth began to speed up in its rotation. I present to you that at the end of the seven creative "days," the Earth was rotating on a 24-hour schedule as the crowning acts of this new creation were completed.

This creative process, when combined with the time of lucifer's mishandling of the early creation, could actually have taken millions of years as the scientists say, yet still be a fraction of "time" in God's eternal existence prior to creation. I also believe that God could create in seven literal 24-hour days if He desired, but that God is an eternal, ever-existing, patient God who can take the time to "let things cook." God has all the time He needs since He is not bound by time. He has no need to hurry!

This is why we get impatient with Him. We think sometimes He is not timely, but He is always on time. You see, God not only created things, but He also created processes of re-creation and restoration. I have learned that He is never in the rush that I am. There is a process of healing, of growing crops, and of infants growing into men and women. He creates children today, but He allows His creative process to accomplish His creation, no matter how much Mama, especially in the ninth month, wants to get on with it. He's patient! That's why I believe abortion is akin to the sin of lucifer; you are interrupting and destroying God's creation process, taking matters into your own hands. And as we saw with lucifer, God does not like it, and He will take corrective action!

As the sun began to shine once again upon the frozen Earth, the ice began to melt first at the equator, and then moved north and south toward the poles as it melted. The ice traveled across the surface of the Earth as it melted, creating the evidences we have of glacial deposits of rock and landscape. Today we attribute them to the ice age and the resulting glaciers that moved upon the face of the Earth as they melted.

The core of the Earth was still hot from creation with molten material that began to push up mountains. Earthquakes were almost constant occurrences as plates shifted and pushed up and landmasses moved. This is why we find "first world" marine fossils in the rock of mountains. The strata put down by the rings in the original creation were bent and twisted into the manner in which we observe them today. Molten material moved to the surface of the Earth and spewed out of cracks, fissures, and mountaintops as volcanic activity began to heat the surface of the Earth and the deluge of water that was still upon it. The waters began to boil from the intense heat coming from under it as well as from the heat of the sun which shines on an Earth with no atmosphere to filter its heat.

The Second Day

We are now in the second day when the creative Spirit of God gives this command: *"Let there be a firmament in the midst of the waters, and let it divide the waters from the waters"* (Gen. 1:6 NKJV). Then the biblical account continues:

> *Thus God made the firmament, and divided the waters which were under the firmament from the waters which were above the firmament; and it was so. And God called the firmament Heaven. So the evening and the morning were the second day* (Genesis 1:7-8 NKJV).

What is meant by *"waters under the firmament"* and waters *"above the firmament"*?

What is a *firmament?* The *firmament,* according *Webster's Dictionary* is that expanse of sky between the surface of the Earth and the heavens, which is the area we would call today the atmosphere of the Earth.[1] Water was left on the Earth, but the Scripture tells us that there was water *above* the firmament or the atmosphere. We see here that the atmosphere is created once again, yet there is more that is sent back into the heavens by all the heat. What are we talking about?

Do you remember the fourth ring, that canopy of water vapor that collapsed at the time lucifer fell, deluging the Earth with water prior to freezing? Well, on this second day of creation, the restoring, creative action of the Spirit of God used the combined heat from the sun and the intrinsic heat from friction and molten lava from the Earth's core coming to the surface to vaporize much of the water upon the Earth. The vapor was again shot up, and it reestablished the atmosphere and the canopy of water vapor. Because there was so much water vapor encircling the Earth, the seas of the Earth were much smaller, and there was more dry land upon the Earth than there is now. We will discuss how that changed later.

We know the canopy was there in the early history of people because we find in Genesis 2:5-6 that *it had not rained upon the Earth,* but that God had watered the Earth with a mist or dew created by the waters below. We find that there was no rain upon the Earth from Adam's day to Noah's day. The canopy also served much like a greenhouse, allowing lush vegetation to flourish upon the Earth. It must have been a very humid environment.

Mountains continued to push up, lava was flowing, and valleys and basins were being created as the ice melted and carved out the landscape we see today. Waters were organized into seas, basins, lakes, valleys, and streams as the earth's surface began to change.

> *And God said, Let the waters under the heaven be gathered together unto one place, and let the dry land appear: and it was so. And God called the dry land Earth; and the gathering together of the waters called He Seas: and God saw that it was good* (Genesis 1:9-10 KJV).

This creative process is also recounted by David in Psalm 104:6-7: *"Thou coveredst it with the deep as with a garment: the waters stood above the mountains. At Thy rebuke they fled; at the voice of Thy thunder they hasted away"* (KJV).

While all this was occurring, additional water was accumulating in the canopy, and more dry land was appearing on the rotating and cooling Earth. Change was occurring everywhere with the exception of at the poles of the Earth, where the ice remained intact, still entombing specimens of lucifer's distorted creation. The poles were expanding and contracting in size as the

Earth traveled in its revolution around the sun. The Earth had assumed an axis or angle of rotation as the result of the cataclysmic event that lucifer's fall caused. This axis caused the temperature to vary on the Earth as the sun shined upon the Earth at different angles and distances as the Earth traveled in its somewhat elliptical revolution around it.

The Third Day

The dawn of the third day began, and again the Spirit of God called forth vegetation that began to grow upon the face of the Earth. We see that He also created the process of germination, as He specifically calls for vegetation that generated within itself the seed with which it would reproduce. God calls forth the trees, grass, fruit, and herbs. We see that God is not only creating originals, but also a process of reproduction in all that He is creating. The process that the Spirit of God had created would always be present on Earth, and He would not need to create again. Genesis records the events of this third day as follows:

> *And God said, Let the earth bring forth grass, the herb yielding seed, and the fruit tree yielding fruit after his kind, **whose seed is in itself,** upon the earth: and it was so. And the earth brought forth grass, and herb yielding seed **after his kind,** and the tree yielding fruit, **whose seed was in itself,** after his kind: and God saw that it was good. And the evening and the morning were the third day* (Genesis 1:11-13 KJV).

Notice that the seed also produced after its kind. Apple seeds don't produce tomatoes but apple trees, and grass seeds produce grass, not flowers, as they do to this day. Seeds only produce after their kind, held within the creative process or the DNA prescribed by the Spirit of God, not evolving and changing as the evolutionist says.

The Fourth Day

The Spirit of God continues with the restoration process of the chaotic world as it enters the fourth day of creation. We read,

> *And God said, Let there be lights in the firmament of the heaven to divide the day from the night; and let them be for signs, and for seasons, and for days, and years: And let them be for lights in the firmament of the heaven to give light upon the earth: and it was so. And God made two great lights; the greater light to rule the day, and the lesser light to rule the night: He made the stars also. And God set them in the firmament of the heaven to give light upon the earth, and to rule over the day and over the night, and to divide the light from the darkness: and God saw that it was good. And the evening and the morning were the fourth day* (Genesis 1:14-19 KJV).

The above passage in the King James Version implies that there were no lights in the firmament at that time until they were placed there on the fourth day. However, in Genesis 1:3, the Spirit of God commanded that there be light, and there was! The sun was already present and was allowed to filter through the debris that encircled the Earth after the cataclysmic event.

This account has caused some confusion over the years so it is important to look at the original language of the Scriptures. When we do that, we get a better understanding of what is going on. The original Hebrew text implies that the lights were already present, but perhaps not in the same order that they are today so that they might divide the day and the night, be used as signs and for seasons, to mark days and years. This has been the case with the sun, moon, and stars. We use them as the basis for our calendars, to mark seasons, and even our position on Earth.

Hebrew scholars have suggested that a better translation might be, *"Let the lights which are in the heavens,"* instead of, *"Let there be lights in the firmament of the heaven.*"[2] The Hebrew implies that the lights already existed at that time, but were given a new appointment or alignment in order to create the seasons and the signs and to be used as marks. Geologic evidence indicates that there were climate changes upon the Earth. Desert conditions exist where it is apparent the seas had once been, and other evidences indicate that the position of the sun may have changed. If it did, the magnetic pull of the sun would also change, causing the change of features, specifically the movement of waters upon the Earth.

God, on this fourth day of creation, appointed the two great lights to rule where they had not previously—or at least not in the manner in which they had been intended by the will of God. The stars were put in their place to adorn the night sky, testifying to the vast power and majesty of the Creator. The position of these heavenly lights, combined with the rotation of the Earth, divided the darkness from the light. The evening and the morning were now aligned differently as the Earth sped up toward the first 24-hour period of rotation here on the fourth day of creation.

Up until this point, we have seen the re-creation and restoration of the chaotic first world of lucifer's dominion properly orchestrated into the majestic second world—according to the will of God and without the original distortions. Creation this time was reformed and filled by the Spirit of God who now was given charge or dominion over creation.

The Fifth Day

God began to create all things new once again as we move into the fifth day of this glorious creation.

> *And God said, Let the waters bring forth abundantly the moving creature that hath life, and fowl that may fly above the earth in the open firmament of heaven. And God created great whales,*

and every living creature that moveth, which the waters brought
forth abundantly, after their kind, and every winged fowl after
his kind: and God saw that it was good. And God blessed them,
saying, be fruitful, and multiply, and fill the waters in the seas,
and let fowl multiply in the earth. And the evening and the
morning were the fifth day (Genesis 1:20-23 KJV).

The Spirit carried out the commands of the Son concerning the will of the Father upon the Earth, which now was covered with vegetation on the land and in the sea. The command to fill the waters with living creatures and the skies with an assortment of winged creatures or birds went out upon the Earth. As the waters and the air became occupied with beautiful creatures, the Spirit commanded them to use the reproductive process that He created within them, just as He had done with the seed of plant life. He then commanded them to be fruitful and multiply in order that they might fill the waters and the skies of the whole Earth.

The Sixth Day Dawns

The Spirit now looked upon the land and prepared for the sixth day of creation, the longed-for pinnacle day of creation when He would begin to create His family in the *seen* world. The sixth day would be the crowning glory of His creation.

As the sixth day of creation began, the Spirit of God, who *"calls those things which do not exist as though they did"* (Rom. 4:17 NKJV), ordered the land to be filled with creeping things, which included cattle, wildlife, reptiles, insects, and other forms of life that moved from place to place upon the dry land. The account in Genesis 1:24-25 reads:

And God said, Let the earth bring forth the living creature after
his kind, cattle, and creeping thing, and beast of the earth after

his kind: and it was so. And God made the beast of the earth after his kind, and cattle after their kind, and every thing that creepeth upon the earth after his kind: and God saw that it was good (KJV).

The Earth now resembled the wild kingdoms of our current day without the inherent violence that currently accompanies it. Animals, marine life, and fowl all existed in a natural habitat without the influence of a civilized world. The Earth was a beautiful, lush place, and creation was set to expand and multiply across the globe. However, something was missing! Who is the new overseer who would project the light of God's presence in this *seen* world? God, through the Son and executed by the Spirit, prepared for the crowning glory of their creation.

At this point you might stop and wonder, where is lucifer, the spiritual being, and what was he doing during this creation of the second world? He was only cast down, not destroyed! While we do not know exactly what he was doing, we know this—*he was upon the Earth!*

Chapter 7

Mudcakes!

Lucifer, a spiritual or *unseen* being, had been cast down to the Earth. He was stripped of his glorious ability to carry the light of God's presence as well as the creative ability that had flowed through him. Now the Holy Spirit carried out the commands of the Creator. Lucifer could not interfere. We read again the account in Isaiah 14:12: *"How you have fallen from heaven, O morning star, son of the dawn! You have been cast down to the earth...."*

Lucifer was cast down to the Earth, literally "to the dirt." *It was on this sixth day of creation that God would literally take the dirt that now was the symbol of lucifer's condemnation and "get in his face" with it.* Let's explore this further.

As children, most of us engaged in playing in the dirt at one time or another. I remember my mother "greeting" me at the back door and making me take off my clothes before entering the house because I was so covered with dirt.

Now, let me ask you a question.

What is it that you get when you mix dirt and water?

Yes, class, we get mud! (Smiles and nods for you for the right answer.)

Now what happens when we expose it to the air?

Right again! It dries, and we get a *mudcake,* which as children we usually formed into some type of figure or object.

Now, let me ask you another question.

What happens when God mixes dirt and water and then blows upon it with the breath of His Spirit?

No, class, He does not also get a mudcake like we did. The answer—*He got us! We are God's mudcakes!*

Science tells us that the physical makeup of the human body is primarily water and the elements of the Earth. This is why, when a body dies, the water and the flesh return to the Earth. It is true that we are but dust (see Ps. 103:14). Our bodies were originally created from dust in the wind of the breath of God, and when they die, they again become dust in the wind of the Earth.

God did something very different with this creation. Let's look at the account of it in Genesis 1.

> *And God said, Let us make man in our image, after our likeness: and let them* **have dominion** *over the fish of the sea, and over the fowl of the air, and over the cattle, and* **over all the earth,** *and over every creeping thing that creepeth upon the earth. So God* **created man in His own image,** *in the image of God created He him; male and female created He them* (Genesis 1:26-27 KJV).

God, here in the crowning of creation, recognizes all the creative parts of the triune God, as He says, *"Let* **us** *make man in* **our** *image…."* Father, Son, and Holy Spirit recognized that this creation would manifest each part of the triune God.

It is also important to note here that in the Hebrew there are numerous names for God, each of which recognizes a different attribute of the Almighty God. In English, we translate all these names as "God." When we consider the Hebrew, all the previous creation was done by *Elohim,* the plural form of God indicating the triune God, but it really gets interesting when we consider Genesis 2:7 in the light of this creation of man.

> *And the **LORD God** formed man of the dust of the ground, and breathed into his nostrils the breath of life; and man became a living soul* (KJV).

Notice that it says the *LORD God.* Literally in the Hebrew this is *Jehovah Elohim!* Wherever we see the name LORD in English in all capitals, it refers to Jehovah or the Hebrew *Yahweh.* Why is the name *Jehovah* added here? Jehovah was the covenant God of Israel, and the use of the double name meant that this creation from the dirt would be different from the other creation in that God, or *Jehovah Elohim,* the *covenant* triune Creator would make a covenant with this crowning finish to His creation. The Old Testament was originally written for the nation of Israel, and Moses the writer wanted Israel to know that the God of creation was also the covenant God of Israel. We will learn more about this covenant with Israel later.

It is also important to note here that the same LORD God who did the creating is the same LORD God who ultimately pronounces the curse on man and the Earth. It is also the same LORD God who is the only one who can ultimately lift that curse! We need to remember this point as we go forward in this book.

Now get this!

This mudcake was so special because this was *the only part of creation where God took the **unseen** and mixed it with the **seen!*** This mudcake was both physical and spiritual at the same time. Then the LORD God made a covenant with this creation.

God formed a mudcake from the elements of the Earth or the *seen,* and blew into it the breath of life and placed His Spirit or the *unseen within* the mudcake. Men and women are the only beings in the entire universe who are both physical and spiritual beings at the same time, possessing the *unseen* within the *seen*! We are unique in the heavens and the Earth!

Chapter 1 of Genesis finishes with a summary of the creation of the sixth day and the creation of these mudcakes that is picked up in greater detail again in chapter 2.

We read,

> *So God created man in His own image, in the image of God created He him; male and female created He them. And God blessed them, and God said unto them, Be fruitful, and multiply, and replenish the earth, and* **subdue it: and have dominion** *over the fish of the sea, and over the fowl of the air, and over every living thing that moveth upon the earth. And God said, Behold, I have given you every herb bearing seed, which is upon the face of all the earth, and every tree, in the which is the fruit of a tree yielding seed; to you it shall be for meat. And to every beast of the earth, and to every fowl of the air, and to every thing that creepeth upon the earth, wherein there is life, I have given every green herb for meat: and it was so. And God saw every thing that He had made, and, behold,* **it was very good.** *And the evening and the morning were the sixth day* (Genesis 1:27-31 KJV).

The sixth day ended the four days of restorative work of the *first world* and the two days of creative work of the *second world*. It is on this sixth day that God gave the command that these mudcakes should also be fruitful and multiply upon the Earth, but He also gave them a new command not given to any previous creation. God told them that creation was not only for them to use, but also to subdue and have dominion over.

As in the other creative days, God took an account of what He had done to be sure that it was good, but in the case of the sixth day, the Spirit of God stepped back and looked at what He created and determined that it was not only good but *"very good"* (Gen. 1:31).

The seventh day of creation now began, but we find no creative work being done, for the biblical account tells us that God rested. Perhaps He sat back and admired the work He had just completed. Perhaps He did as I often do after completing a project in the yard or in the house, taking the time to just look at it and study what I have done. Or perhaps, just as a father or mother stares at their newborn child, God watched His mudcakes, admiring quietly in love how wonderful they were!

You see, God loved His mudcakes, I mean, He really *lo-o-oved* those mudcakes!

Let me illustrate!

You see, I *love* people, but when it comes to my wife, my children, and my family, I *lo-o-o-ve* them! God just didn't love the mudcakes, but He *lo-o-oved* them! Yes, He *lo-o-oves* you! There is a difference between loving someone and *lo-o-oving* them! He would prove it more and more as time went forward. The Father's heart was in full flame, and He *lo-o-oved* His mudcakes!

They were His very image in physical form, possessing the mind of God and carrying the very light or presence of God. Awesome!

These Spirit-filled mudcakes now taking lucifer's place projected the light of God's presence upon all of creation. The light came from within, from the Spirit of the living God who lived within and in communion with their spirits.

Adam and Eve shone as the sun with light emanating from within their perfect bodies just as Christ shone on the Mount of Transfiguration. The light that shone from within them did away with their need for clothing. They were not naked, but covered with the light of God's presence, which emanated from within.

In my heavenly experience during surgery I wrote about in Chapter 3, one of the things I noticed was that everything I saw did not reflect light; instead, it gave light. Colors gave their own light, not because of the reflection of ultraviolet rays, but because the colors were projected outward from within everything I saw. Everything had its own light because the presence of God was within everything. In the heavenly spiritual Kingdom, there is no need for external light. Light, sound, and colors are not only seen, but they are also experienced. They flow to your very core with a feeling of warmth, unity, and intimacy with the Lord. When the Lord looked at me, I felt His gaze penetrate to every part of me. I felt His love. *He did not look at me with love in His eyes; He filled my very soul with the love that was projected into me from His eyes. I felt His look of love!*

Just wait until you experience it, for there is really no way to describe the things God has prepared for us. And by the way, if you are not certain you will ever experience this heavenly Kingdom, keep reading, because by the time you finish, those of you who do not know where you stand with this Creator will know how you can be sure. In the meantime, just remember—He *lo-o-oves* you!

Back to the Garden

The mudcakes walked in the flesh, with understanding of the mind and the will of the Father; His presence was within them and always with them, guiding them in all things. It was an incredibly intimate relationship between man and woman and their Creator.

We find, as we stated before, further details regarding the creation of humanity as we move on to the second chapter of Genesis.

The creative process of humanity by *Jehovah Elohim* is recounted here again, but now using the covenant name of God as we noted before. The first thing the LORD God did after creating man was to prepare a home for him: God planted a *"garden in Eden."* This apparently was *"east"* of Moses' location when he wrote Genesis. Most biblical scholars today place that location somewhere in southern Iraq.

Eden, as this garden is known, is a word synonymous with the Hebrew word for "paradise" and is also similar to the words for "bliss" or "delight." In that Garden, God placed trees that were good for food; then the text mentions that there were two specific and noteworthy trees there, the *Tree of Life* and the *Tree of the Knowledge of Good and Evil.* Matthew Henry, the great Bible commentator of the 1600s, gives a wonderful description of what this Garden and this time must have been like:

> The place appointed for Adam's residence was a garden; not an ivory house nor a palace overlaid with gold, but a garden, furnished and adorned by nature, not by art. What little reason have men to be proud of stately and magnificent buildings, when it was the happiness of man in innocency that he needed none! As clothes came in with sin, so did houses. The heaven was the roof of Adam's house, and never was any roof so curiously ceiled and painted. The earth was his floor, and never was any floor so richly inlaid. The shadow of the trees was his retirement; under them were his dining-rooms, his lodging-rooms, and never were any rooms so finely hung as these: Solomon's, in all their glory, were not arrayed like them.[1]

We have previously referred to the creation of man and woman, but we must realize that God first created the man, whom He named Adam. The name *Adam* appears to have been derived from *Admah,* the ancient word for "red earth," which gives us an indication that Adam may have had an earthy or red color to his skin, much like the people of that region of the Earth do today.[2]

God first gave Adam a home and a job before woman was created—good guidance for women considering a potential husband today! It was Adam's job to care for the Garden and to *"work it and take care of it"* (Gen. 2:15). He was also warned that he was not to eat of the *Tree of the Knowledge of Good and Evil*, for if he did eat of it, he would surely die. We will talk more on this later.

God recognized that it was not good for a man to be alone and that a "helper" was needed—not a servant, but as the Hebrew implies, one who was equal and comparable to him—a "counterpart."[3]

God brought all the created animals of the Earth before Adam, and Adam gave each of them their names. But none of them was a suitable helper to him, so God in His infinite wisdom created the perfect match for Adam. After Adam completed naming the animals, he lay down, and God caused a deep sleep to fall upon Him.

It is interesting to note that when God started His creation, He created something out of nothing. After the initial creation, it was His nature to take that which existed and make something new with the materials. In the Hebrew, the word *made* or *formed* was used to describe how Adam came to be. God literally made Adam from the dust of the Earth.

Now something different occurs here. This woman was going to be very special to this man, and God decided to create her from him. God performed a surgical procedure, took a rib from Adam, and then from it—are you ready for this, ladies?—according to the Hebrew text, He *built* the woman! A different word is used to describe the creation of woman. The Hebrew word *bara* used here means "to build!"[4] Man was *made,* but woman was *built!*

Man was *made* from dirt, but woman was *built* from quality, finished (albeit used) parts! Yes, she was created from out of the man and called "woman," meaning "from man."

I was sitting in a coffee shop as I wrote the above words, and as I did, the Holy Spirit spoke to me: *"God pierced Adam's side and took for him a bride; God pierced Jesus' side and took for Him a Bride."* The Holy Spirit was referring to Jesus, whose side was also pierced while on the Cross in the process of receiving His Bride, the Church. We will talk more about that later. We will see more and more parallels of what we call *pre-types* as we go on further in this book.

Adam was awakened to meet his forever companion, and in his excitement declared, *"This is now bone of my bones, and flesh of my flesh: she shall be called Woman, because she was taken out of Man"* (Gen. 2:23 KJV).

Adam was probably very excited as he admired this beautiful creature who was not like the others at all. If I were to paraphrase, perhaps he declared, "Look at what You built, Lord! She once was me; she has what I lost! Whoa, man, this is awesome!" Perhaps then God said, "Glad you like her, and OK, if you want, we will call her *'Wo-man.'*"

Well, maybe it didn't happen quite like that, but then again, I know men, and Adam was a man! The Bible tells us that *"He who finds a wife, finds a good thing…"* (Prov. 18:22 NKJV). Adam had just awakened to find a good thing. I think he had to be excited, don't you?

Now, you may ask, why did God use Adam's rib? Why did He just not grab some dirt and water, make another mudcake, and blow on it? Remember that this is the *LORD God* or *Jehovah Elohim* who is doing the creating here, a God of covenant. He knew Adam needed a mate, a helper, a covenant partner. By taking part of Adam, He was manifesting in the flesh the covenant of the spirits of the man and woman and God! Remember, the Spirit of God was united with the human spirit in the creation of man.

By splitting up part of Adam, God's intention was to bring the two together in what He now created as a covenant of marriage. The man and woman together now reflected the full image of God, both the male attributes and the female attributes. Yes, man and woman *together* reflect the nature of God. Man reflects the providing, protecting masculine, or what we would consider the father attributes of God, and woman reflects the nurturing feminine, or what we would consider the mother attributes of God. This is why God referred to them as *"one flesh,"* united together in constant companionship because their spirits are one with each other and with their God.

When a man and woman marry, they make a physical covenant with each other that creates a special covenant with God in which He joins the *seen* world with the *unseen* world to form the one flesh or the full image of God. So when we consider that man and woman were made in the image of God, it really means that they both together complete the image of God. Remember that when the LORD God created man, He said, *"Let **us** make mankind in **our** image..."* (Gen. 1:26). Therefore man and woman together with the Spirit of God within them reflect the image of the triune God—the Father, Son, and the Holy Spirit

In marriage, we still have our individual personalities, but that bond that has been formed in the Spirit creates a oneness that, as we walk with the Lord, gets stronger as we walk together in marriage with Him.

God did not just create a man and a woman in His image; He created a three-way covenant similar to the three-way covenant of the Father, Son, and Holy Spirit, a covenant with each other and with God, both the *seen* and *unseen* coming together. If we break a marriage covenant, we also break a covenant with God, for He was part of it originally. When we covenant before God to each other, we also covenant with Him.

God had formed a covenant with Adam and Eve and made them His agents upon the Earth to subdue the Earth and take dominion over it. He had given them all authority upon the Earth, which had originally been given to lucifer, and it was their responsibility to carry out the will of the *unseen* Creator in the world of the *seen*. They had become the prince and princess of this world as dominion over the Earth had been taken back from lucifer.

Dominion had been given to those made of the very thing lucifer had been cast down upon—the dust of the Earth.

Lucifer saw that God loved these mudcakes, and jealousy and hatred grew in his heart. God loved the mudcakes, but lucifer hated the mudcakes.

How dare God give dominion to this mud, he must have thought. *Who does God think He is? He destroyed my creation, so I will destroy His!* In quiet stealth, he waited and watched for his opportunity, hatching his own plan. He had fallen, but he had not lost the vision he had of himself, which in his case was self-deception. He knew, as long as these mudcakes were obedient, that he was powerless. He must deceive again; he must convince these mudcakes to give him allegiance through disobedience to God. He would show God; he would win, and he would have dominion over this Earth and defeat the forces of Heaven once and for all! *"…I will be like the most High"* (Isa. 14:14 KJV).

Chapter 8

The First Mudcake Rebellion

Adam and Eve had everything in the world to make them happy. There was no sickness, no disease, no conflict, no poverty, and no evil of any kind besetting them. Whatever work they did, following the direction of the Spirit of the Creator within, it was accomplished with all success, for there was no failure.

They most likely had no knowledge of the fallen lucifer and the hosts of fallen angels who had rebelled against God in the time prior to their creation, for it was a wonderful time of innocence and intimacy with each other and with their Creator.

*They possessed the mind of the Son and understood the will of God for their lives through the Holy Spirit within them. God's will was **communicated to them through their Spirit-controlled minds** as they carried out their dominion of the world as God's appointed agents on the Earth.* (This is important to remember when we visit this subject of the role of the mind and emotions later in this book.)

Whatever will in Heaven was to be done on Earth, these agents of the *unseen* Heaven were responsible for carrying it out upon the Earth. They were literally the physical manifestation of the *unseen* God in the *seen* world.

God only accomplished things upon the Earth through this physical arm of God known as man and woman. Adam and Eve would take dominion upon the Earth and subdue it.

They were to hold their position upon the Earth through loyalty and obedience. This obedience would stem from the love they had for the loving God who created them. God desired intimacy; He desired family, and these mudcakes would love Him of their own free will as He loved them willingly. A loving Creator does not desire a child who only loves because he or she is programmed to do so. We might ask, why did God give them the free moral choice?

Let me ask a question of those of you who, as a child, had a doll that, when you squeezed it or pulled a string, said, "I love you" to you. My question is, did the doll really love you? Of course not! It was not capable of loving; it was simply programmed to tell you that it loved you. God did not create a "Chatty Cathy" doll like the one that was out when I was a kid. He wanted true intimacy and love with His creation. In order to do this, He had to build into His real, live "Chatty Cathy" the ability to choose! These mudcakes would have the ability to choose to obey or not to obey, to love or not to love.

All was placed in the Garden for the mudcakes to enjoy, including fruit trees of every kind, good for eating. In the center of the Garden was the *Tree of Life*. It was this tree that sustained the life of the mudcakes, providing them with eternal life. It was the tree of choice, possessing the fruits of the Spirit of the Creator within it, fruits that allowed them to live in the midst of love, joy, peace, patience, kindness, gentleness, goodness, faithfulness, kindness, and self-control. (See Galatians 5:22-23.) All the good things in life were embodied within this fruit, and the choice to regularly eat of this tree would assure that these things would remain present in their lives—forever! No aging, no sickness, no death. Their mudcake bodies would be forever sustained by the *Tree of Life*.

In proximity to this tree was another beautiful tree, one that, according to the covenant they had with God, should never be eaten from. This tree was poisonous, leading to death, but remained in the Garden to ensure obedience out of love and loyalty. Understand this point: without the option of disobedience, there is no obedience—just a robotized response.

Let's review the instruction of God as He gave it to Adam in Genesis 2:

> *And the LORD God commanded the man, saying, Of every tree of the garden thou mayest freely eat: but of the tree of the knowledge of good and evil, thou shalt not eat of it: for in the day that thou eatest thereof thou shalt surely die* (Genesis 2:16-17 KJV).

If Adam and Eve chose to eat of the forbidden tree, the covenant of life the LORD God had made with them would be broken. *The **Tree of Life** was a covenant tree!* Their choice was simple; they could only eat from one of the trees—either the Tree of Life (obedience), maintaining the covenant, or the *Tree of the Knowledge of Good and Evil* (disobedience)—but not from both. *If they did eat from the forbidden tree, they would break the covenant with God and thereby create a covenant with another!*

Lucifer, whom we will now also know as *satan* or *the devil* from this point on, was aware of what was happening with these mudcakes and aware of the choices that they had before them. He hated these mudcakes, especially the one called woman. Yes, it is true that he hated women more than men. This has been evidenced in societies where satan has control: women are oppressed. He hated her because she was the one who would carry the seed of the man and produce even more mudcakes. He hated them both, but in particular this latest model of the mudcakes. We will see later another reason why his hatred for the woman increased even more! He was also aware that they both had the job that he had previously held, and he was jealous and angry at them. He was hatching a plan for which an opportunity now presented itself.

We find in chapter 3 of Genesis that he made his move as he took on the form of a serpent. Now most of us think at this point, *Yuck! A snake!* We must remember that the serpent had not yet been cursed, nor did it crawl on its belly. In fact, it must have been quite as beautiful as everything was in creation at that time. The Bible also tells us that it was the craftiest or shrewdest creature of all creation.

In any event, Eve was intrigued by this creature and encountered it by the *Tree of the Knowledge of Good and Evil.* It is not uncommon for the enemy to come in and appear very pleasurable, and he does so even today when confronting God's children. The things he tempts with today are often pleasurable. Eve was not aware that this crafty being was stealthily about the business of stealing God's identity and their identity as well. They were not aware that he was attempting to destroy God's creation and hold onto the dominion of the Earth, which he had lost and they had been given.

Perhaps the serpent spoke verbally as the Bible says, and as it did, proceeded to eat of the tree's fruit. Eve and Adam, who was by her side, watched the serpent continue to live even after eating of the fruit. Satan would not be affected, of course, because he already knew about good and evil; he had already disobeyed, and death was already in his future.

What did the serpent tell her? He told her that God was hiding something from them. He told them that God knew that if they ate of the tree, they would understand all things as God does. He told them that they would not surely die; as he did, he took another bite of the fruit and enticed them to do the same. Eve then reached out to take some of the fruit.

I wish to point out here that satan is often referred to as the *father of lies,* and I believe he could also be called the *master of half truths!* Satan often trips us up by telling us a half truth (which is still a lie), disguising the lie part in the half truth. This is what he did with Eve as he told her a half truth. He told her that her eyes would be opened (true), that she would understand good and evil (true), and that she would not die (true, she would not die at that moment, but she would eventually). The truth about what he told her hides within it the deception of the destruction it will bring on their lives. They would lose their identity, their intimacy, their innocence, their dominion, and so much more through their disobedience. It would break the covenant they had with the LORD God. The devil works the same way with us, and so many of us fall for it all the time.

If the devil desired to steal God's identity, why would he not try to steal yours? In my book, *The Coming Financial Revolution,* we have received the most comments about a chapter entitled, *"The Ultimate Identity Theft."* That chapter discusses the ways the devil tries to steal our identity today, and we will explore that topic again later in this book. We need to understand that it has its roots in this event here!

We have already discussed that an all-knowing God surely must have known in advance that lucifer was going to betray Him and rebel. Surely He must have known then that he would also deceive the mudcakes. Why did He allow that tree to remain in the Garden of Eden? Why would He plant such a tree? *We shall see that the* **Tree of the Knowledge of Good and Evil** *represented the potential for evil to exist in this newly created world and the potential for it to be released through disobedience, through a rebellion to the created order.*

Let me quote from my chapter in *The Coming Financial Revolution* regarding this tree and the revelation the Lord gave to me during my near-death experience.

> *How art thou fallen from heaven, O Lucifer, son of the morning! how art thou cut down to the ground, which didst weaken the nations! For thou hast said in thine heart, I will ascend into heaven, I will exalt my throne above the stars of God: I will sit also upon the mount of the congregation, in the sides of the north: I will ascend above the heights of the clouds:* **I will be like the most High.** *Yet thou shalt be brought down to hell, to the sides of the pit* (Isaiah 14:12-15 KJV).

Think of this…

If satan thought he could steal God's identity, do you think he might also try to steal yours?

The fact is, he did not steal God's identity but instead was cast out of Heaven. However, he then, given the chance, approached Adam and Eve, who did allow him to steal their identities. They had been given dominion, but they ceased to act like those with authority. Eventually, they ran and hid from God because of their sin.

Now, let me ask you this…

Who do you think planted that seed of the Tree of the Knowledge of Good and Evil in the Garden of Eden?

God?

I don't think so.

Consider this! James 1:13-14 tells us that God does not tempt us.

> Let no man say when he is tempted, I am tempted of God: for God cannot be tempted with evil, **neither tempteth He any man:** but every man is tempted, when he is drawn away of his own lust, and enticed (KJV).

The Tree of Knowledge of Good and Evil represented the temptation before Adam and Eve to disobey God. For many years, I believed that God had put the tree there to test His creation.

Then one day…

The Holy Spirit said to me, "I did not plant that tree!"

I said, "Of course You did, Lord. Who else would have?"

He then pointed me to James 1:13-14 and told me that if He indeed tempted anyone, they would be unable to resist His temptation because He, God, cannot fail in any effort. He said, "If I tempted you, you would submit to the temptation. You would be unable to withstand. But remember, it is I who provide the way of escape from that temptation." (See First Corinthians 10:13.)

I understood what He was saying. He went on to explain that He sowed good seed in the Garden of the Earth, but the enemy who had been cast out of Heaven down to the Earth, came and sowed tares among the good seed. "Hey, Lord," I said, "that sounds familiar." It did sound familiar to me, and I recognized it as the "Parable of the Sower."

> *Jesus presented another parable to them, saying, "The kingdom of heaven may be compared to a man who sowed good seed in his field. But while his men were sleeping, his enemy came and sowed tares among the wheat, and went away. But when the wheat sprouted and bore grain, then the tares became evident also. The slaves of the landowner came and said to him, 'Sir, did you not sow good seed in your field? How then does it have tares?' And he said to them, 'An enemy has done this!' The slaves said to him, 'Do you want us, then, to go and gather them up?' But he said, 'No; for while you are gathering up the tares, you may uproot the wheat with them. Allow both to grow together until the harvest; and in the time of the harvest I will say to the reapers, "First gather up the tares and bind them in bundles to burn them up; but gather the wheat into my barn"'"* (Matthew 13:24-30 NASB).

Then after a few verses, Jesus explained this parable to His disciples further…

> *Then He left the crowds and went into the house. And His disciples came to Him and said, "Explain to us the parable of*

the tares of the field." And He said, "The one who sows the good seed is the Son of Man, and the field is the world; and as for the good seed, these are the sons of the kingdom; and the tares are the sons of the evil one; **and the enemy who sowed them is the devil,** *and the harvest is the end of the age; and the reapers are angels. So just as the tares are gathered up and burned with fire, so shall it be at the end of the age. The Son of Man will send forth His angels, and they will gather out of His kingdom all stumbling blocks, and those who commit lawlessness, and will throw them into the furnace of fire; in that place there will be weeping and gnashing of teeth. Then the righteous will shine forth as the sun in the kingdom of their Father. He who has ears, let him hear"* (Matthew 13:36-43 NASB).

Hmm. I "thunk" about this hard and long....*and realized that the devil had access to the Garden prior to the fall (he was there to tempt Adam and Eve before they sinned), and ever since, the enemy has been continuously sowing tares in the garden of our lives.* Why? He wants to deceive us into disobedience. He wants what God has given us as joint heirs with Christ, that's why! He wants our authority! He wants our identity!"[1]

More on that later; now back to the Garden!

Doubt and questions entered the mind of Eve as she found her hand reaching out and taking the fruit. I can see the serpent continuing to eat; with great anticipation and curiosity, Eve took a bite and then passed it on to her husband. They were one flesh, one together, partners totally in love with each other, and he wanted to be part of what she was experiencing; he took and ate as well.

The serpent had told them the truth that their eyes would be opened: They realized that through their disobedience they broke their covenant with God, and suddenly they noticed that they were naked—so they quickly fashioned fig leaves to cover their bodies.

You mean they did not know they were naked before?

What were they in la-la land or something?

Do you remember that as God's covenant agents upon the Earth, the mudcakes carried the light of God's presence, which shone from within much as Jesus did on the Mount of Transfiguration? (See Matthew 17:2.) The light of God's presence from within covered them like a garment. They noticed they were naked because, when they broke their covenant with God, the light went out! God's presence within them left! Their garment was gone!

Adam and Eve truly were just mudcakes now, still possessing their human spirit, still part *seen* and part *unseen,* but the light of God's presence, the Spirit of God, was no longer within them. Fear gripped them for the first time as they ran and hid from the presence of the LORD God as He walked in the Garden. God noticed the break in the spiritual connection with the mudcakes and came looking for them because their communication with Him was suddenly broken. He confronted them about the knowledge that they possessed of their nakedness and asked that question for which He already knew the answer: *"Have you eaten of the tree that I told you not to eat from?"*

Adam replied in typical manlike style, *"That woman you gave me, gave it to me and I did eat"* (see Gen. 3:12). Now it sounds to me like he was working on those half truths of the new earthly master already, painting a picture to the LORD God that he did not know what he was doing. *"I mean Lord, she was truly the disobedient one. And after all, why would You hold me accountable for what she did since You were the one who gave her to me!"* Now isn't that what you think he was saying? I do!

However, if we examine the text, we will find that the whole time Eve was at the tree with the serpent, Adam was by her side, so Adam knew what was going on and did not do anything to stop it. Romans 14:22 says, *"...Blessed is the one who does not condemn himself by what he approves."* Adam condemned himself by passively approving what he did not initiate.

The Lord turned to the woman now standing before Him in the latest fig leaf designer outfit from Eden, and He asked her the same question He just asked Adam. Eve, in like manner, passed the buck and pointed to the serpent, blaming him. The serpent possessing the spirit of satan or lucifer was present, and the Lord not only spoke to the creature, but to satan himself, pronouncing a curse upon all creation. We read the curse in the Genesis account:

> *And the LORD God said unto the serpent, Because thou hast done this, thou art cursed above all cattle, and above every beast of the field; upon thy belly shalt thou go, and dust shalt thou eat all the days of thy life: And I will put enmity between thee and the woman, and between thy seed and her seed; it shall bruise thy head, and thou shalt bruise his heel. Unto the woman He said, I will greatly multiply thy sorrow and thy conception; in sorrow thou shalt bring forth children; and thy desire shall be to thy husband, and he shall rule over thee.*

> *And unto Adam He said, Because thou hast hearkened unto the voice of thy wife, and hast eaten of the tree, of which I commanded thee, saying, Thou shalt not eat of it: cursed is the ground for thy sake; in sorrow shalt thou eat of it all the days of thy life; thorns also and thistles shall it bring forth to thee; and thou shalt eat the herb of the field; in the sweat of thy face shalt thou eat bread, till thou return unto the ground; for out of it wast thou taken: for dust thou art, and unto dust shalt thou return. And Adam called his wife's name Eve; because she was the mother of all living. Unto Adam also and to his wife did the LORD God make coats of skins, and clothed them. And the LORD God said, Behold, the man is become as one of Us, to*

know good and evil: and now, lest he put forth his hand, and
take also of the tree of life, and eat, and live for ever: therefore
the LORD God sent him forth from the garden of Eden, to till
the ground from whence he was taken. So He drove out the man;
and He placed at the east of the garden of Eden Cherubims, and
a flaming sword which turned every way, to keep the way of the
tree of life (Genesis 3:14-24 KJV).

A two-part curse was put on the serpent, the first part on the creature who participated in the deception. He would no longer walk upright, but from then on would crawl on his belly and be cursed above all other creatures. Now let me ask you, is there any creature less loved in this world than the snake?

The second part of the curse was for the arch-deceiver himself as the LORD God warned him in verse 15 that this woman whom he hated and deceived would someday be the source of his downfall; he would be crushed as a result of the "seed of woman." This was the first messianic prophecy recorded in the Bible, referring to Jesus Christ. Adam and Eve heard this curse, and hope flickered in them, for they now longed to be restored to the original created order.

The woman then listened to the pronouncement of her judgment. It is a bit obscured in the English translation. She was told that as she produces children, it will be done with great pain; in the original order before disobedience, there would have been no pain, for the Spirit of the presence of God shielded them from it. Now the nerves would have to warn the body that something was happening within the body. The body was no longer controlled by the Spirit through the mind, but the mind, which was now disconnected from the Spirit, would get its signals from the body only. We use our minds today in a way they were never originally intended to be used, and the fact is that we only use a small part of their capability!

Then the Lord said that *"her desire would be for her husband."* Now isn't that nice? Every wife wants to desire her husband, right? But—in the Hebrew the word translated *desire* tends to mean "to dominate."[2] This might be better translated, *"She will be dominated or oppressed by her husband."* The NIV Study Bible also indicates that this relationship would cause her to experience trouble and anguish rather than unhindered joy and blessing. The curse goes on to say that her husband would *"rule"* over her. Now that word *rule* is bad enough when it hits a woman's ear, but let's once again put the light of the Hebrew language on it. This word translated *rule* in English literally means "to rule by crushing under foot."[3]

Now let me make an observation here. Throughout recorded history, man has been the dominant sex; in fact, the more godless the society, the more we see woman persecuted and her rights being violated. We have seen the double standards of the Islamic world in regard to men and women, the "honor killings," and the slaughter of unwanted daughters in parts of Asia. In many third world societies, women do the work of men because man has taken his curse and heaped it upon the woman. This has not just occurred today, but throughout the ages. The less influence godly principles have on a society, the more women are persecuted, dominated, and crushed! The serpent heard this curse and has seen to it that fallen men carried it out.

Now it was Adam's turn. The man was told that all his days would be spent in sweat and toil as he would work in the soil that the LORD God had also cursed with thorns and thistles (see Gen. 3:17-18). He told man and woman that instead of the covenanted eternal life He had intended for them, they eventually would return to the dust from which they were created.

Death now entered the world for the first time; in verse 21 we discover that the LORD God allowed some of His beloved creatures to be killed so that clothing could be made of their skins for the mudcakes. This is the first evidence of their sin causing death.

The Lord God now conferred with the other members of the Godhead, and the Father, Son, and Holy Spirit agreed together that evil must not be allowed to live eternally. A new celestial plan must be put in place to eradicate evil and the potential for evil from the universe. In the meantime, the mudcakes must be kept from the *Tree of Life,* lest they eat of it and propagate evil and rebellion eternally.

God's plan from the beginning had been to totally eradicate evil as well as the potential for evil from all creation. The **Tree of the Knowledge of Good and Evil** *was symbolic of the potential for evil to exist in the universe. This new celestial plan would not only be designed to destroy evil in the world, but also to destroy the potential for it ever to raise its head again.*

If the mudcakes had kept their original state and taken dominion over the whole world, lucifer would have been driven out by love and obedience into the hell God had prepared for him and his demons.

It must have been heartrending to God as He pronounced the curse, but He had to do so because His mudcakes had rebelled, breaking their covenant with Him. Of their own choosing they were now covenanted in sin with the arch-deceiver himself. Their covenant was no longer with God, but with lucifer, for they had disobeyed, eaten of his tree, bitten into the potential for evil, and allowed it to corrupt them. *They no longer carried the light of the presence of God's Spirit, but they carried the darkness of lucifer's sin—the sin of rebellion!*

Now the mudcakes must be left to die so they must be kept from the *Tree of Life* freely provided by the LORD God. We will not see the *Tree of Life* again until it appears in the last chapter of this book. The beloved mudcakes, Adam and Eve, were banished from the Garden; powerful warring angels were posted there so that they could not return.

And they never have!

Chapter 9

Mudcakes on the Run

Adam and Eve ran from the presence of the Lord and from the Garden. We must stop and think how they must have felt at that moment. We have all done something that afterward we wish we had not done; we wish we could go back and change it, but we cannot, and neither could they. Perhaps they pleaded with the Lord for a second chance as they looked at the entrance to the Garden now guarded by the cherubim, warring or guarding angels charged with enforcing the will of the LORD God.

Now I know that we have previously referred to the woman as Eve, but that is because we knew her name. She had no need for a name before this because she was *Adam,* the name that covered both man and woman as one flesh and one spirit united together in the Spirit of God. Now that the light of God's presence within them had gone out, they noticed their nakedness, their differences, and also the individuality of their personal wills. The "one flesh" of husband and wife would now struggle with that knowledge throughout history. Therefore, Adam, who had named everything, gave her the name of Eve. This name was appropriate, for she was to be the *"mother of all living"* (Gen. 3:20 KJV).

Adam and Eve, with no children born to them as yet, were alone outside of the Garden. They must have had quite a discussion about what had just happened to them, most likely a tearful time as they experienced failure and distress for the first time. They recalled the words that the LORD God had said, and suddenly an idea came into their heads. Perhaps it was Eve who said to Adam, "Did you hear what God said? He said that my offspring would crush that serpent's head. The man God will give me will defeat evil and restore all! We will then be returned to the Garden to eat of the *Tree of Life*. We need to have a child who will deliver us!" In a way, she was correct, but just as God does so often, He takes His time carrying out His promises. This would take place only after many generations had passed as God began to build His family.

We read in the opening phrase of chapter 4 that *"Adam made love to his wife Eve, and she became pregnant…"* (Gen. 4:1). The King James uses the word *knew*, which is an old term we might want to revive today since so many people today don't even really know the people they are sleeping with—a further perversion of the created order of marriage between a man and woman in becoming "one flesh."

Eve gave birth to a son, and they called him Cain. Can you imagine the excitement as this first baby entered the world through the natural process created by God to recreate life? On top of that, they saw him as their deliverer from the life sin had now created for them. How do we know? Back to the Hebrew once again to gain further insight into Eve's words regarding the birth of Cain. *"I have gotten a man from the Lord"* (KJV), or *"With the help of the Lord I have brought forth a man"* (Gen. 4:1). The Hebrew *eth Jehovah* has been rendered as "with the help of the Lord" by English translators, but comparisons to the use of these words in other Hebrew texts show that since God had not revealed His name *Jehovah* until the age of the patriarchs of Israel, it is unlikely that Eve would have declared this name. Instead, she used a broader term used by people prior to the time the names of God were revealed. The meaning, according to Hebrew scholars, is "the one who brings into being" or "the one who gives life" or even "the deliverer."[1] (See Exodus 6:3.)

When God makes a promise, we often expect it to happen right away, but we have learned that is not so. Abraham's 17 years in waiting for Isaac testifies to this. God's promises are fulfilled in the fullness of time, His time, and remember, He is not bound by time. In this case, about 4000 years passed before the promise was fulfilled. Jesus promised us a Kingdom, and it has already been over 2000 years since the promise. All in all, according to God's plan, it will take about 7000 years to bring things full circle back to Eden again! In God's eyes, 7000 years is but a microcosm of eternity, a flash in time—something our "mind box" cannot comprehend.

We think with finite, limited minds, but God is not confined in His thinking. He still does it His way, no matter how or what we think. So it was natural for Eve to think Cain was the promised deliverer; after all, he was her seed, and that was who God said would crush the serpent! She was the only woman at that time, so why would she think that the promise would be fulfilled by another woman named Mary, a distant daughter of hers, 4000 years and 60 generations later?

"I have brought forth a deliverer!" Eve exclaims. Imagine their disappointment when Cain instead turns out to be a murderer of their second son, Abel. The first death of a human occurred, not naturally, but viciously, a premeditated murder spurred on by jealousy. All this came from the evil that had infiltrated the hearts of the mudcakes due to their new covenant with the *"prince of this world,"* as lucifer is also referred to in Scripture (see John 12:31; 14:30; 16:11).

After murdering Abel, Cain fell into further degradation, causing another curse to fall upon him and his toil upon the Earth. He would not have success as he worked the fields, causing him to wander, seeking the place of success as a nomad, a "drifter." Such is sin today, making the lost one wander about seeking success, love, and fulfillment everywhere but where it can be found. When confronted with the truth, the lost one then refuses to take responsibility for his own behavior, making excuses, wanting to do it his way, and not submitting to the rule of God for his life. Pride ultimately prevents him from seeking the face of God.

Today this type of behavior has been referred to as "the way of Cain." In "the way of Cain," Cain chose to bring vegetables instead of an animal sacrifice. It is apparent that Adam had received instruction on when and how to prepare a sacrifice. The opening words of Genesis 4:3 indicate that there was an appointed time, and since God is a just God, we know that both Cain and Abel must have been instructed by Adam and known how and when the sacrifice should be done. When God killed animals in the Garden of Eden and made clothing out of them for Adam and Eve, He was showing that sin means death and that innocent animals must die in order for the sacrificers to be pardoned. These blood sacrifices conducted by the early patriarchs would later be formalized into the law given to Moses for the nation of Israel. The sacrifice pointed to Christ and looked forward to the provision of the deliverer. Only the death of the innocent could bring forgiveness of sin (see Heb. 9:22), not the smashing of a nice pumpkin or the squashing of an unblemished tomato. This was not what God had prescribed so that people could approach Him with their sins covered. Abel had brought the appropriate sacrifice; Cain did it his way.

Only a sacrifice of innocent blood would provide for atonement since death was the pronounced curse for sin. Cain, jealous of his brother who had been accepted by the Lord in his sacrifice, now sought to vent that jealousy, which had further turned to anger. He made plans, deceived his brother, and denied it when confronted by God; he refused to take responsibility and allowed the evil in his life to master him.

God exhorted Cain to do what was right and warned him that sin was crouching by his door and desired to have him. He exhorted him to master it; if he was obedient and did what was right, he would indeed master it (see Gen. 4:7). Cain instead followed his own anger and the ravings of his mind, and he killed his brother. He initiated "the way of Cain." How greatly sin and evil had worked in just one generation in the history of human-kind! Five generations later in Cain's line is another murderer, Lamech, who killed again, the result of what we refer to as a generational curse. (See my teachings on "Breaking the Curse of Poverty" for more information on that one.)

It was also at this point that two distinctive groups of people began to develop. The one group would develop into a group that would become totally godless and be wiped out in the Flood. No descendant of Cain is alive today. The other group, the descendants of Seth, would survive and repopulate the Earth. Because of Cain's curse, the first child born upon the Earth would be father to a society of iniquity and be wiped out. Sin became deeply rooted in this line of Cain. Since Adam's son Abel was dead, the line of Adam's son Seth would instead seek God, and it is from this line that all people alive today descend. We are all descendants of Adam and Eve through their son Seth. However, as we shall see, evil was about to take on a new dimension as satan (formerly known as lucifer) gained control of more and more mudcakes.

During a trip to Israel, a couple of years after my "near-death" experience, we stood in the ruins of the Philistine city of Beth Sheen. I asked our guide what he knew about the Nephilim who populated the world and whether Go-liath the giant killed by David was suspected to have been one. (The Philis-tines have been thought to be influenced by these Nephilim, which we will discuss in the next chapter.) I remember that our guide did not recognize the term and did not have an answer for me. It was at that moment that I realized that the Lord had downloaded some information in me because the revelation from beginning to end suddenly leaped from the Spirit to my mind. Without a word being spoken, I suddenly knew who they were and how it had all happened.

I wanted to share it with the group, but the Lord suddenly spoke to my mind and said, "No, it is not for now." Of course, I thought it was for later on in the trip, but no, it was for such a time as this, over ten years later as part of this work.

Come to the next chapter, as I share with you what has been revealed.

Chapter 10

The Nephilim

———◆———

We discussed in the last chapter that Adam and Eve recalled the words of the Lord that it would be the *"seed"* of woman who would crush the enemy's head and restore things to their former created order. Of course, the couple thought it would be their immediate seed, not a seed thousands of years later. I am sure that they knew Cain, their murderous son, was not that seed. With Abel gone, Eve gave birth to yet another son, and they knew in their hearts that this one had to be their deliverer. In a sense, they were right because it would be from this son, Seth (his name means "appointed"[1]), that the deliverer would ultimately come.

Seth and his brother Cain would be the fathers of two lines of humanity that would develop in the antediluvian, or pre-Flood, world. However it would be Seth's line that would survive. How and why did that happen? Let's take a look at the Scriptures again.

In Genesis chapter 4, we read an account of Cain being driven from his family and from the presence of the Lord. He became a fugitive and a vagabond, struggling to make a living because the Lord had cursed his success in tilling the ground. The Lord, however, placed a mark on Cain and pronounced that if anyone killed him, vengeance would be taken on that individual sevenfold.

"Then Cain went out from the presence of the Lord and dwelt in the land of Nod on the east of Eden" (Gen. 4:16 NKJV). Since Eden is thought to be somewhere in the area of modern-day Iraq, Nod must have been somewhere in the area of modern-day Iran.

It was there that Cain built a city named Enoch in the land of Nod, a city he named after his firstborn son, Enoch. Now, I do not want you to be confused; both Cain and Seth had a descendant named Enoch. Cain's Enoch was a much different person than the one we will speak about shortly. Cain also had a descendant, as did Seth, named Lamech—again, two different people.

Genesis chapter 4 gives us the genealogy of Cain. His line starts with his son Enoch and ends with four children, Lamech's three sons and daughter. Lamech was also a murderer like his great, great, great, great-grandfather Cain, and Lamech boastfully pronounced an even stronger vengeance than God had pronounced for Cain on anyone who would take vengeance on him. Thus the genealogy of Cain is as follows:

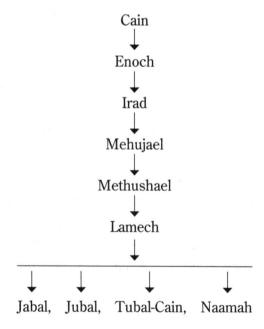

Cain
↓
Enoch
↓
Irad
↓
Mehujael
↓
Methushael
↓
Lamech
↓
_____
↓   ↓   ↓   ↓
Jabal, Jubal, Tubal-Cain, Naamah

The occupations of Lamech's sons are specifically noted here and seem to indicate that the Cainite civilization had become an advanced civilization agriculturally, industrially, and culturally. It was, however, a civilization that excluded God and was facing judgment for its moral state. This civilization appears to have been advanced due to supernatural influences, as we shall see later.

Unlike Seth's genealogy, the Cainite line ends with Lamech and his children, who were contemporaries with Noah, a descendant of Seth.

Seth's genealogy continues, including Noah and beyond the Flood, and as we shall see, his genealogy is also prophetic and tells us a lot about what is going to happen. Chapter 5 of the Book of Genesis gives us the genealogy of Seth over a period of time that spans about 2000 years. During this time, the effects of sin were just beginning to set in; the gene pool was still strong so people lived longer and were able to not only enjoy their grandchildren but also well beyond that generation.

Seven generations after Adam, we find in Seth's line a very significant individual by the name of Enoch, the *other* Enoch. Enoch was the father of another significant individual by the name of Methuselah. Methuselah is significant to most people because, in recorded history, he is the oldest person to have ever lived, living to the ripe old age of 969 years. While that is an accomplishment, we shall see that there was something even more significant about his life—and his death! Even upon Methuselah's birth, his father Enoch received a revelation of what was to come upon the Earth, and it changed his life significantly. Enoch became the first of four generations of preacher-prophets and is regarded as the first prophet recorded in the Bible. He and the three generations to follow would begin to preach God's pending judgment upon the Earth for the evil that was occurring.

You see, evil was growing on the Earth just as fast as the population. The fallen angels were upon the Earth with their leader, lucifer, and they were seeing to it that evil would grow to a point that would bring God's judgment upon the Earth and God's creation would be destroyed. That was lucifer's goal! The serpent of the Garden of Eden had heard the pronounced curse that the *"seed"* of woman would crush his head.

The woman's seed would be his destruction! Lucifer understood that.

The pride that had led lucifer to judgment and being cast down to the Earth welled up in him, and again, he thought he could undermine God's sovereign plan.

He hatched a plan of self-preservation.

He needed to pollute this seed and bring about God's judgment on His creation because the creation had become evil. He had to pollute and destroy this seed in order to prevent his own destruction!

"How can I corrupt the seed of the woman and cause God Himself to destroy it?" lucifer asked himself.

Let's consider the curse pronounced upon the serpent, lucifer, again. Read Genesis 3:15 carefully again.

> *And I will put enmity between thee and the woman,* **and between thy seed and her seed;** *it shall bruise thy head, and thou shalt bruise his heel* (KJV).

God was talking to the serpent lucifer here. What does He mean by *"thy seed"*? Again, we must look to the original Hebrew word to gain understanding. The Hebrew word translated *seed* here is *zera,* which means "offspring"![2]

Lucifer has offspring?

According to the Scriptures, God is acknowledging that fact when He pronounces the curse! The New International Version translates Genesis 3:15 as follows:

> *I will put enmity between you and the woman, and between* **your offspring** *and hers; he will crush your head, and you will strike his heel.*

What offspring of lucifer's is God referring to? Let us explore this further.

We will come back again to the genealogy of Seth, but let's skip ahead to Genesis chapter 6 to gain a fuller understanding of what was happening during the 2000 years between Adam and Noah. One thing we learn in studying ancient Hebrew texts is that things are not always recorded in chronological order, so let's step ahead to Genesis chapter 6 and then we will step back again to chapter 4 before going on. This is very intriguing, so go slow and grasp the concepts I am teaching here.

> *Now it came about, when men began to multiply on the face of the land, and daughters were born to them, that the* **sons of God** *saw that* **the daughters of men** *were beautiful; and they took wives for themselves, whomever they chose. Then the Lord said, "My Spirit shall not strive with man forever, because he also is flesh;* **nevertheless his days shall be one hundred and twenty years***."* **The Nephilim** [literally "fallen ones"] **were on the earth in those days,** *and also afterward, when the* **sons of God** *came in to the daughters of men, and they bore children to them.* **Those were the mighty men who were of old, men of renown.** *Then the Lord saw that the wickedness of man was great on the earth, and that every intent of the thoughts of his heart was only evil continually* (Genesis 6:1-5 NASB).

Let's examine this passage in detail to gain an understanding of what was happening on the Earth between the time of Adam and the time of Noah and the flood.

The command of God to be fruitful and multiply was being carried out, and we see here that the mudcakes were multiplying upon the Earth. It has been mathematically estimated that by the time of the Great Flood there must have been close to 1 billion people upon the Earth. Women, *"the daughters of men,"* were also multiplying, and apparently they must have been, as they still are today, *"beautiful."*

Now it says that the *"sons of God"* noted their beauty and took for themselves wives from this group of beautiful women. Now the question is, "Who were these guys, anyway?"

The study of the Hebrew text tells us that the term *"sons of God" (bene elohim)* always in the Old Testament refers to spirit beings, specifically "angels,"[3] those who are a *direct creation of God* rather than a result of a creative process of God. In Scripture, the term was used for Adam, who was made from nothing or the dust and was a direct creation of God (see Luke 3:38). As we discussed previously, Eve was "built" from Adam, and of course, everyone else descended through the reproductive process created by God from these two individuals.

The term *sons of God* is used three other times in the Old Testament (see Job 1:6; 2:1; 38:7). In each case, it clearly means "spirit beings," and twice it refers specifically to those "fallen spirits" who accompanied lucifer in his periodic visits to the throne room. So as we shall see, from the Scriptures and from ancient Hebrew tradition, these sons of God who had intermarried with the daughters of men were actually the fallen angels, and they produced a corrupted seed or DNA with the women. The DNA originally created by the Creator was altered through these evil unions.

I will first address the skeptics here, and then we will develop this evidence further.

Many believe that the *sons of God* refer to the descendants of Seth, the godly line that split off from Adam and Eve. This was a concept that developed around the fifth century. In reality, many in the Church found it so offensive (and it is!) to think of angels and women cohabitating and having sexual relations that produced an evil offspring of giants that a new theory was developed just so they would not have to deal with such an offensive thought. Jewish tradition and the early Church, as we shall see, held to this view that the *sons of God* were angels. But first, let's discuss why these *sons of God* were not the godly descendants of Seth marrying the ungodly women who descended from Cain, as has been suggested by the proponents of this view. Let me list some reasons.

First of all, if the descendants of Seth were so godly, why would they marry ungodly women? After all, would they not subscribe to the philosophy, *"I don't drink smoke or chew, and I don't run with women who do"?* No, the descendants of Seth would marry women from the godly line. That's what godly men would do.

Second, when godly and ungodly people produce offspring, they do not produce giants. We can all think of God-loving people who are married to people who have little or no regard for God. They do not necessarily produce a family that looks like an NBA basketball team!

It has also been argued that angels are sexless based on Jesus's words in Matthew 22:30 that at the resurrection we will be like the angels and will not marry or be given in marriage. This simply refers to the fact that marriage will not be needed. It is clear that we will still have our individuality, and there will not be a need for procreation within the marital bonds.

In addition, the fact that the angels are incapable as spirit beings of engaging in sexual activity is not supported by Scripture. We see numerous places where angels took on human form. The two angels who visited Lot in Sodom and Gomorrah not only came in human form, but the people pleaded with Lot to send them out so that they could have sex with them (see Gen. 19). These angels also ate and slept at Lot's house. They engaged in human activity and had a need for sleep.

I had previously stated that this view developed around the 5th century, but history shows us that the translators of the Septuagint and early Hebrew tradition held to the view that the *sons of God* were the fallen angels, a view that was also repeated in the New Testament in the Books of First Peter and Jude.

It is apparent that angels have the ability to assume human form, and we find them doing so often in the New Testament as well. Hebrews 13:2 warns us not to forget that when we entertain strangers, we may be entertaining angels unaware. Let's consider my experience in the Intensive Care Unit that I shared earlier. Who was that visitor anyway? I saw him as flesh and blood, not as an ethereal spirit that hovered in my room. My nurse saw him that way as well, and he greeted her. He seemed to come and go as he pleased in a restricted area, and no one knew who he was. But let me tell you, I sure liked his visits! I know now that He was imparting to me additional skill, knowledge, understanding, revelation, and prophetic understanding, much of which I am sharing with you in this book.

The point is that angels were created to be ministering spirits with the ability to perform human tasks; they are not indulging spirits. These fallen angels had left their creative purpose, and in their evil nature lusted after women. *It was satan's purpose to corrupt the seed of humanity by replacing God's Spirit in humanity with the corrupted evil spirit of the fallen ones.*

Satan wanted to corrupt the seed of women so he had "his seed," the one-third of the angels (now demons) who fell with him, reproduce with the women of the Earth. They produced a corrupted human seed just as lucifer had corrupted and distorted creation before. *God had destroyed that creation through the collapsing rings that encircled the Earth, so lucifer knew that if he corrupted God's mudcakes, God would have to destroy them as well!*

Lucifer's goal from the beginning of time was to destroy God's creation. He wants to destroy you!

It appeared at this point that his plan was working because God said in Genesis 6:3: *"My Spirit shall not strive with man forever, because he also is flesh; **nevertheless his days shall be one hundred and twenty years"*** (NASB).

Many people think that God was reducing the longevity of people's lives to no more than 120 years here as a result of their evil, but that is not what is meant. At the time these words were spoken, there were exactly 120 years until the Great Flood.

Now let's look some more at our passage in Genesis chapter 6. The Nephilim, as the giant race was known, walked upon the Earth; they were corrupted half-human, half-demonic beings. Their genetic makeup was a DNA from mixing human flesh with the evil spirit of a fallen one, corrupting the spirit God had placed in Adam and Eve.

"...*Those were the mighty men who were of old, men of renown*" (Gen. 6:4 NASB). Moses, the author of Genesis, was referring back to an understanding of the Jews that had been passed down from generation to generation. Generational teaching was characteristic of the Jews, and there was a teaching among the ancient Jews that taught that giants lived upon the Earth, giants who were terrible in battle and in every other way. In fact, all of ancient mythology refers back to a race of "giants" or "titans." Near Jerusalem, there is a valley that is referred to in the current day as the "Valley of the Titans." The extent of these giants' depravity was mind-boggling, yet God tarried, longsuffering in His mercy. He showed His mercy by causing the line of Seth to begin warning all of humankind of a pending judgment through four generations of prophet-preachers in the line of Seth. However, except for this one family line, the world tumbled into their pursuit of evil, and the corruption of the Nephilim was reproduced among the mudcakes descending from Cain.

Now I told you that there was one individual in the line of Seth who played a significant role in prophesying the pending judgment upon the Earth, not only for this ancient time, but for a time to come, and still to come. There is a part one and a part two to his prophecy; the same prophecy applies to our present day as well as to Enoch's day.

Enoch's mission began with a significant event in his life, the birth of a child—his child, his son!

Chapter 11

The Prophecy of Enoch

Eve believed that Seth, her son born after the death of Abel, would be the deliverer that God spoke of in the Garden, as we have previously stated. She had seen the evil path that her son Cain had taken. She and Adam, therefore, named this next child born to them *Seth,* which means "appointed." She must have watched him grow to be a man and was pleased that he had a heart toward God. Surely he would deliver them and restore their life in the Garden that, day by day, was becoming a fading memory.

Time continued to pass as she perhaps witnessed the birth of her grandson Enos and perhaps even the birth of her great-grandson Cainan. We do not know how long Eve lived, but perhaps she lived as long as Adam who, according to Genesis 5:5, lived until he was 930 years old. The DNA of these ancient parents and their pre-Flood descendants had not yet been affected by generations of the effects of sin; radiation from the sun, unprotected by the canopy as it is now; and sickness and disease, which would have gradually over time degraded the genetics of humankind.

Eve and Adam's hopes must have declined over the years as they saw their hard lives go on with no sign of the promised deliverance and restoration to the Garden. It must have been discouraging, but according to

Jewish tradition, which has proven to be incredibly accurate, Eve held on to her faith in the promised deliverer. According to the same tradition, Adam walked less and less with God, and there is some doubt that he was among the faithful who would be ultimately released from "Abraham's bosom" by Jesus Christ after His death on Calvary. According to the Jewish Mishnah (book of rabbinical teachings), the worship of idols began to take place upon the Earth in the days of Enos.[1] Perhaps that is why Enos, whose name means "mortal," named his son Cainan, which means "sorrow." These names have great significance; keep this in mind as we go forward in this book.

Life continued on and so did the family line as Cainan also had a son. The name he gave his son, *Mahalaleel,* indicated the reverence he held for God, for it means "the blessed God." As Cain's family line became more and more evil, Mahalaleel's wife gave birth to a son he named Jared, which means "shall come down." Jared was to be the father of a very significant man. We will talk much about Jared's son, Enoch, who was born seven generations from Adam. He became the first of the four preacher-prophets who would begin warning humankind of a coming judgment upon the earth. His name indicated the significance of his occupation as a preacher, for the name *Enoch* means "teaching."

The first of four generations of preachers, Enoch would father Methuselah, the oldest living person in recorded history, who lived 969 years, outliving both his father and his son. We all know his name because the name *Methuselah* has become synonymous today with anything old. Actually his name comes from three Hebrew words: *meth* or *met* means "to die." The word *u* means specifically "his death," and the word *shelach* means "to send forth" or "to initiate or bring."[2] We will see the significance of this name when we get to the Flood. It was his birth that also brought about a change in his father. Genesis 5:22 tells us that Enoch was 65 (sounds young, doesn't it?) when Methuselah was born. It says from the day Methuselah was born, Enoch, all his life, walked with God.

It appears that according to this Scripture, the birth of this baby boy was a life-changing event for Enoch. God Himself at that time must have revealed something to Enoch, for he started to preach the pending judgment of God upon humankind. Methuselah became a preacher as well and *begat* (to use the King James Bible word) his son Lamech. Now how would you like your father to name you a name that means "despairing"?[3] We would not do that today because it might cause damage to our son's self-concept, but to the Jews, names were significant and told something about the circumstances of the time in which the child was born. These must have been despairing times into which Lamech was born.

Lamech would also continue the line of preachers himself and father a very significant preacher-prophet. Lamech's son was not only a preacher-prophet, but also a master craftsman in the ocean-going marine industry. He would name this prophetic, preaching, boat-builder son a name that would mean "comfort." Lamech's son was Noah!

Before we talk specifically about Enoch a bit more, let's take a look at these generations of the godly line from Adam to Noah, a time that spanned about 2000 years. Here are the generations from Adam to Noah:

Adam

Seth

Enos

Cainan

Mahalaleel

Jared

Enoch

Methuselah

Lamech

Noah

I am sure you have heard it said that "God knows the end from the beginning," and you will see this as we summarize the events of this world from a spiritual perspective in this book. I have studied the Word of God all my life, and the older I get, the more I cannot leave that book, the Bible, alone. It amazes me more and more that about 40 authors, over a period of thousands of years, with no collaboration with each other, relying only on the Holy Spirit's inspiration, should record things with such accuracy and continuity. With the benefit of hindsight, we can see how the Spirit of God has been directing every step of humankind and working out a master plan since the beginning of recorded time. We can only expect Him to continue to do that as we move forward into our future. The few things prophesied in the Bible that remain unfulfilled must surely come to pass with the same accuracy. His master plan started before the foundation of the world, and it will prevail and accomplish *His* purpose.

With that said, let me tell you something amazing! I will never forget how this affected me when I discovered the meaning of these men's names in the generations of Seth years ago as a Bible student. God orchestrated it so that the names these fathers gave their sons over a period of 2000 years would tell the story of what God was going to do in the time between the Fall of humanity in the Garden of Eden and our subject in the next chapter, the Flood of Noah!

We now know that from the days of Enoch until the days of Noah God began to warn humankind about the coming judgment for the evil that flourished upon the Earth and the corruption of the "seed" of people through their reproduction with the "fallen ones." Not only did God warn them with preachers, *He told the whole story of what would happen through the names of these men!*

Let us take the meaning of the names of the men in Seth's line and include Adam, Seth's father in the beginning. Then let's put them in a sentence and just add three little English words (*is, and, the*) to complete the sentence for easy reading in English. Then just for our reference, let's put a slash between the meanings of each man's name as they appear in the sentence in the succession of their birth.

This is what we get:

Man / (is) appointed / mortal sorrow, / (the) blessed God / shall come down / teaching, / his death shall bring judgment / (and) (the) despairing / rest (and) comfort.

Got chills?

I do every time I read it. Read it again!

Man / (is) appointed / mortal sorrow, / (the) blessed God / shall come down / teaching, / his death shall bring judgment / (and) (the) despairing / rest (and) comfort.

Go ahead; talk amongst yourselves!

I did not name these people, nor did these men confer among themselves over a 2000-year period to create a sentence with their son's names, which would not only foretell the coming judgment upon the Earth at the time of the Flood, *but outline the whole plan of God to redeem humanity!* In fact, we could consider it the outline for this book!

Yes, the sentence using the names of these men outlines the whole plan of God to redeem the mudcakes and to defeat evil and its potential to exist for eternity!

Amazing? Naw…that's our God!

Let me paraphrase this sentence, filling in some facts with the ability of hindsight and knowledge of the Scriptures and history for those of you who may not quite get it. You may not completely understand if God's plan of salvation for the world is not yet clear to you.

Here is my paraphrase:

Because people sinned, they are appointed once to die a mortal death, but Jesus, the Son of God, will come to Earth and teach and redeem us through His death, which will bring rest to those who are despairing and judgment upon those who reject so great a salvation.

Hmm...and you thought the Bible was boring! It is tempting to read quickly over a chapter that lists genealogy, but *when we read carefully, we hear God's voice of love shouting His adoration for His mudcakes!*

Just like Andrea, my wife, likes to say, *"Studying the Bible is like peeling an onion; the more layers you pull off, the more potent the onion becomes as you get closer to the center."*

Yes! The more we understand the Bible, the louder God yells, **"I love you!"**

What an awesome God! Do you know Him? Now is the time to get to know Him better and start peeling off those layers of what He is revealing to us in these days. If you have never made Him Lord of your life, we will help you find Him in the pages of this book (or please visit the section in the back of this book entitled "The Secret of Eternal Life" so you can know this secret for yourself).

Let's get back to our journey of the first 2000 years of humanity.

Perhaps you are thinking that we have spent a lot of time so far expounding on the creation of the Earth and the first 2000 years of human existence, the pre-Flood history of the world.

I want you to understand that just as we saw with the names of the generations of Seth, in the creation of the world, and the first 2000 years of man, God clearly laid out His master plan for redeeming and restoring the mudcakes and His original creation to their originally created purpose and order.

I also want you to see that the purpose of your life now, this brief moment in your eternity, is to determine your place in that restored eternal creation. This book will help you understand why things are the way they are, why you are you, and what your eternal purpose is.

OK, mudcakes, let's look at what is written about Enoch in this fifth chapter of Genesis.

> *And Enoch lived sixty and five years, and begat Methuselah: and Enoch walked with God after he begat Methuselah three hundred years, and begat sons and daughters: and all the days of Enoch were three hundred sixty and five years: and Enoch walked with God: and he* **was not;** *for God took him* (Genesis 5:21-24 KJV).

Enoch, as we previously stated, had a life-changing experience when Methuselah was born, for Genesis says that he walked with God *"after he begat Methuselah."* God revealed the end from the beginning to him in the 365 years that he lived, and unlike the other men of Seth's line, his death was not recorded. The Scriptures simply says that Enoch *"was not"!* Actually in the original Hebrew, it says that *"he not."* (See the King James Version of Genesis 5:24.) The word *was,* you will notice, in most Bibles is italicized because it was added by the English translators so the sentence would make some sense. What it actually means is that he *disappeared!* One moment there and then, poof—gone! Literally Enoch *was;* then he *was not!*

"God took him." Of every other man in this line, the Scriptures say that they *"died,"* but Enoch *"was not,"* and his family knew why they did not have a body to bury; God had him!

This happened one other time in the Bible, to the prophet Elijah, as recorded in Second Kings chapter 2. Only two people in all of recorded history did not taste death. Jesus was resurrected after He died on the Cross, but Elijah was taken up in a whirlwind and disappeared! Why?

This is part of the master plan we will discuss more toward the end of the book. In an event that has not yet happened, more people will disappear in the same manner as Enoch did. Actually, here's a hint for you: Some theologians believe that Enoch may not be done walking with God on the face of the Earth. His work was not done, and his prophecy was not only for his day, but for a day to come, a day still in our future.

What was Enoch's prophecy?

First of all, Enoch prophesied of the coming judgment of the world for its evil of that day—but there may be more. Let's talk about an obscure book that was not included by the early Church fathers as part of our Bible.

The leaders of the early Church met to finalize what books of the Bible should be included in what we refer to as the canon of Scripture; only those books that showed signs of divine inspiration and a clear connection to the named author of the book as well as some other stringent criteria could be included.

There were a number of other works that bore the name of a biblical character, but the writing was inconsistent with the teaching of the apostles or other inspired Scripture so they were not considered to be part of the Bible.

The Book of Enoch was one such manuscript, which was not included because it could not at the time be verified as being written by Enoch. In this ancient writing, there is a clear account of the pre-Flood world, a prophecy about the coming judgment on the Earth for humanity's evil, and a reference to a future, final judgment. Its teaching was consistent and accepted in Jewish tradition, but it just could not be verified as truly recording the prophecy of this man Enoch, so it was not included.

Today, many theologians increasingly believe that the Church leaders made the proper decision to not include the Book of Enoch in the Bible based on their set criteria. There are also many, however, who feel that the decision was an error because more information has come to light about this manuscript and the passage of time has attested to its accuracy. The finding of a manuscript of the Book of Enoch in the caves of Qumran in 1948 with other ancient manuscripts of included books has given more credibility to this book. These ancient manuscripts, known as the Dead Sea Scrolls, have validated the veracity of the translated Scriptures as we have them today, and the Book of Enoch was among them!

Probably the biggest endorsement of the book comes from two of the biblical authors themselves as Peter makes reference to Enoch's prophecies in the Book of First Peter. Jude, in the penultimate book of the Bible, makes extensive reference to the Book of Enoch as well.

Our purpose here is not to argue whether the book should be included, but to consider whether it sheds some light on what happened during these 2000 years and what will occur in the future. If Peter and Jude had no problem referencing and accepting it as inspired, then I will have no problem referencing it to enhance our understanding.

Let's look at some of the things recorded in the Book of Enoch as it relates to our discussion so far.

In the first few verses of this book, the writer (who we will assume is Enoch) says that he was living in a wicked and godless tribulation where all the godless were to be removed. He further states that the vision he had was not only for this generation, "but for a remote one which is to come" (Enoch 1:2). Then he launches into verses that seem to talk about a future godly King who shall rule at this later time on the Earth.

In the second part of the prophecy, he steps back and begins recounting the events of Genesis chapter 6:

> The angels, the children of the heaven, saw and lusted after
> them [daughters of man], and said to one another. "Come,

let us choose us wives from among the children of men and beget us children" (Enoch 6:1-3).

Enoch tells us that this occurred during the days of Jared with the daughters of Cain. He also names the fallen angels who were involved and calls them the "Chiefs of Ten." Let's read some of the narrative:

> And all the others together with them took unto themselves wives, and each chose for himself one, and they began to go in unto them and to defile themselves with them, and they taught them charms and enchantments, and the cutting of roots, and made them acquainted with plants. And they became pregnant, and they bare great giants, whose height was three thousand ells: Who consumed all the acquisitions of men. And when men could no longer sustain them the giants turned against them and devoured mankind. And they began to sin against birds, and beasts, and reptiles, and fish, and to devour one another's flesh, and drink the blood (Enoch 7:1-6).

The passage echoes the passage in Genesis where these "fallen ones" lust after the daughters of men and take them as wives, having children who became giants or "Nephilim." These giants also became a drain on the social systems of the day so that when people could no longer sustain their great needs, they began to kill the people.

Not only that, but these fallen angels introduced things like witchcraft, bestiality, cannibalism, and the drinking of blood.

But there is even more. Let's read further:

> And Azazel [one of the fallen angels according to the text] taught men to make swords, and knives and shields and breastplates, and made known to them the metals of the earth and the art of working them, and bracelets, and ornaments,

and the use of antimony, and the beautifying of the eyelids, and all kinds of costly stones, and all coloring tinctures. And there arose much godlessness, and they committed fornication, and they were led astray, and became corrupt in all their ways (Enoch 8:1-3a).

Earlier I told you that Cain's civilization was an advanced civilization and that they may have had supernatural help. Here is a possible explanation: These supernatural beings not only introduced them to enchantments, witchcraft, and the macabre, but also taught them other skills.

Azazel taught them how to work with metal and fashion weapons of warfare. He taught them how to make jewelry and how to work with precious gemstones and antimony, a metallic ore used in all kinds of preparations from mirrors to cannonballs!

In the 1970s there was a bestselling book entitled *Chariots of the Gods,* authored by a man named Erich Von Däniken. While the book for the most part was sensational fiction, building upon some mysterious archaeological findings throughout the world, it brought to light some of the mysteries of the ancient world. I remember as a student at Houghton College being intrigued with the book and reading it. Because of my relationship with my professor and renowned scientist, Dr. S. Hugh Paine, I shared the book with him, and he read it as well. I wanted Dr. Paine's comments on what I had been reading because I knew he was extremely knowledgeable in these things.

We then sat down and discussed what we read over coffee. He agreed that the book was sensational, drawing conclusions from a godless perspective that the Earth had previously been visited by aliens from another planet and that this was why archaeologists found signs of advanced technology in the ancient civilizations. We have long been aware of some of the achievements of the ancients, such as the building of the pyramids with technical precision and without the aid of modern-day equipment. In addition, we have unearthed what archaeologists believe to be batteries and other electronic and technical equipment. Von Däniken built on this and supported his hypothesis that aliens had visited the planet and taught people these things. We most certainly can conclude that something more advanced did visit these people.

I shared my thoughts with Dr. Paine that it could possibly have been these fallen angels—risking his laughter—but he agreed with me. He warned me that I would get resistance from many to this idea, mainly because people did not like to accept the idea that fallen angels could and did have sex with humans. He also postulated that since it was closer to the Fall, and genetics were better, humanity's mental capacity was also greater in those days. Dr. Paine pointed out to me that studies show that we only use a small part of our brains. He then added that he thought he had had some students who did not use them at all—present company excepted, of course. He laughed and told me I made him use his even more and encouraged me to share my thoughts with him more. I only wish I could share with him my near-death experience and the revelations it gave me. But Dr. Paine, now with Jesus, already has all the information. I wonder if he is sitting in glory chuckling at me the way he used to do as I write out these words.

Further along in this passage in Enoch, we read that some of the other "fallen ones" taught the people of the Earth other things as well.

> Semjaza taught enchantments, and root-cuttings, Armaros the resolving of enchantments, Baraqijal taught astronomy, Kokabel the constellations, Ezeqeel the knowledge of the clouds, Araqiel the signs of the earth, Sharmsiel the signs of the sun, and Sariel the course of the moon. And as men perished, they cried and their cry went up to heaven (Enoch 8:3).

Well, I have one thing to say here. *"New age" thinking ain't new! It's as old as time itself!*

New Age is just an old trick of the devil that he uses today to deceive many and get them to look elsewhere than to God. It doesn't take a rocket scientist to realize that some of the things taught to these ancients were astrology, witchcraft, and other New Age and occult practices that the enemy uses to entice people away from the truth. Sadly, many even in the Church today are intrigued with it themselves and call it entertainment. We will discuss this more in Chapter 20.

It is recorded that as people perished, they recognized they had been deceived and cried out to God. A number of years ago, a client of mine who was a nurse cared for a well-known scientist who was a prominent New Age advocate and atheist. He believed the Earth had been visited by extraterrestrials. She cared for him in the ICU as he was dying. She shared with me that in his last hours, he would cry out, "God, where are you?" He would continually call out God's name in distress up until the moment he died. Is it possible that as he lay dying, he recognized that he, such an intelligent man, had been deceived? Did he know enough at that point to make Jesus Lord of his now very short life, accept the gift of salvation, and enter into eternal rest, or did he follow the deceiver, satan to his final destination of hell? His books are still on the shelves of the local library; I wonder what he thinks of his entire hypothesis now?

The Bible says that the wisdom of this world is foolishness to God. When some people cannot understand it with their minds, they will not open up their hearts in faith and thereby gain the understanding. In spiritual things, the heart comes before the head, the spirit before the flesh. If we try to put the head first, we can be deceived and end up as the Scriptures say, *"The fool hath said in his heart, there is no God..."* (Ps. 53:1 KJV).

Somber minute here, folks. Some of you need to take the time to get it right now. If you are such a one, take a minute, go to the back of the book, and read the section entitled, "The Secret to Eternal Life." Then come back and join us in the next chapter. Do it now; don't wait until the end of the book. You never know how short life can be.

Chapter 12

The Flood

———•———

Genesis chapter 6 and the Book of Enoch record that evil had become so great upon the Earth that, from lucifer's perspective, God appeared to be falling right into his plan to destroy creation. *Satan's plan was to corrupt humankind so that God would destroy His mudcakes, just as He had previously destroyed the creation that was unacceptable to Him.* God revealed to Enoch, Methuselah, Lamech, and Noah that He was about to destroy evil humankind. Men and women in the 2000 years between Eden and Noah had degenerated so much that they had become useless to God. They could never have a relationship with God in their current state. Unless a redeemer would come, as promised to Eve, and create a change in these creatures, they would pose no value to their Creator and must be destroyed.

Before we go on, let's step back to Genesis chapter 4 for a few moments to a verse that has caused some confusion, for this verse seems to indicate on the surface that the hearts of people were changing and that God was ignoring their cries. This is not the case.

We read in Genesis chapter 4, *"And to Seth, to him also there was born a son; and he called his name Enos:* **then began men to call upon the name of the Lord"** (Gen. 4:26 KJV).

How do we know that God was not ignoring the cries of people? We must again consult the Hebrew language regarding the last verse of Genesis chapter 4: *"...then began men to call upon the name of the Lord"* (KJV). The proper translation of the Hebrew implies that the mud-cakes began to call out the name of the Lord in a profaning way. The Hebrew words *chalal qara* translated to "call upon," in Hebrew mean to "call upon with profanity"![1] God's name was being used in a cursing way. Sound familiar? People so easily use God's name in their profane language, and as we see here, it is a serious thing. It's not funny and not to be taken lightly.

Let's pick up the text again in chapter 6.

> *And God saw that the wickedness of man was great in the earth, and that every imagination of the thoughts of his heart was only evil continually. And it repented the Lord that He had made man on the earth, and it grieved Him at His heart. And the Lord said, I will destroy man whom I have created from the face of the earth; both man, and beast, and the creeping thing, and the fowls of the air; for it repenteth Me that I have made them.* **But Noah found grace in the eyes of the Lord***. These are the generations of Noah:* **Noah was a just man and perfect in his generations, and Noah walked with God.** *And Noah begat three sons, Shem, Ham, and Japheth. The earth also was corrupt before God, and the earth was filled with violence. And God looked upon the earth, and, behold, it was corrupt;* **for all flesh had corrupted his way upon the earth***. And God said unto Noah, The end of all flesh is come before Me; for the earth is filled with violence through them; and, behold, I will destroy them with the earth* (Genesis 6:5-13 KJV).

Here we have the account of the Lord's judgment upon the corrupted creation as He looked to a remnant of creation, the family of Noah.

Now I want you to notice that God was going to carry forward His master plan through a small group of people, a remnant. *As we look at God's master plan throughout this book, you will notice that every time God wants to do something significant at a transitional point in history, He raises up a "remnant" of people to accomplish His purpose. This will be true even in the last days before the manifestation of the heavenly Kingdom on Earth as we shall see.*

Almost all of humankind (nearly one billion people) and animals on Earth at that time had become corrupted through the sins of the Nephilim, except for a small remnant who had continuously walked with God from the days of Enoch and Seth. They had not intermarried or corrupted themselves with the *fallen ones*. We see that *"Noah found grace in the eyes of the Lord"* (Gen. 6:8). Grace means *"unmerited favor."* Noah still had the sin nature that he had inherited from his distant grandparents, Adam and Eve. He did nothing on His own to merit this favor; God gave it to him because Noah sought the Lord and was willing to obey Him. Such is the case for us today.

Our text says that Noah was a just man, that he was *"perfect in his generations,"* and that he *"walked with God"* (Gen. 6:9). The phrase *"perfect in his generations"* means that Noah's genealogy was unblemished by the marriage of the *"sons of God"* (fallen ones) and the *"daughters of men." This small remnant of people was all that remained of creation that had not been corrupted by the fallen ones!* Humankind had come to a point where they could not be redeemed because of these corrupted genes so God acted to bring about His *long-term* plan of redemption. No quick fix here, but then again time does not matter to God, only to us. Remember, it's not our plan; it's His!

When the Lord's call came to Noah to begin to prepare an ark to lift them above the floodwaters, his father Lamech had been dead about seven years. Noah's family consisted now of his wife, his three sons and their wives, and one other person—his grandfather Methuselah. Methuselah, Enoch's son, whose name means *"his death shall bring judgment"* or *"when he dies it shall come"* was still alive upon the Earth! If we do the math, we find that Noah was about 480 years old at the time he received this assignment to build an ark, and he was given 120 years in which to build it, as we learned in Genesis 6:3. This concept is further confirmed by the fact that Genesis 7:11 tells us that Noah was 600 years old (480 +120 = 600) when the floodwaters came upon the Earth. This means Grandpa Methuselah was 849 years old, and he was just given another 120 years to live.

Can you imagine 120 years of ridicule while you build an ocean liner in your backyard—and on top of that, you live nowhere near the ocean? Can you imagine the laughter and the jeers every time you gave your sermon of judgment to the people of the world for not repenting? Can you imagine the difficulty of Noah's continued obedience despite how things appeared to the natural eyes?

Keep in mind that while Noah and his boys were male bonding with this incredible backyard family project, they were also about the business of collecting and protecting an unblemished stock of animals to take with them on this voyage. Also, it had never rained upon the Earth up until this point in history, as we learn from the Scriptures. The Earth was watered by a mist that came up from the Earth and the moisture created by the *canopy of water which had and **still** encircled the Earth!*

Do you remember that?

Let me go back to Chapter 6 for a moment and review again what I wrote there so that you will gain an understanding of what was about to happen 2000 years after the creation of the second world. Back in Chapter 6 of this book we read:

Do you remember the fourth ring, that canopy of water vapor that collapsed at the time lucifer fell, deluging the Earth with water prior to freezing? Well, on this second day of creation, the restoring, creative action of the Spirit of God used the combined heat from the sun and the intrinsic heat from friction and molten lava from the Earth's core coming to the surface to vaporize much of the water upon the Earth. The vapor was again shot up, and it reestablished the atmosphere and the canopy of water vapor. Because there was so much water vapor encircling the Earth, the seas of the Earth were much smaller, and there was more dry land upon the Earth than there is now. We will discuss how that changed later.

We know the canopy was there in the early history of humanity because we find that in Genesis 2:5-6 that it had not rained upon the Earth, but that God had watered the Earth with a "mist" or "dew" created by the waters below. We find that there was no rain upon the Earth from Adam's day to Noah's day. The canopy also served much like a greenhouse, allowing lush vegetation to flourish upon the Earth. It must have been a very humid environment.

Mountains continued to push up, lava was flowing, and valleys and basins were being created as the ice melted and carved out the landscape we see today. Waters were organized into seas, basins, lakes, valleys, and streams as the Earth's surface began to change.

> *And God said, Let the waters under the heaven be gathered together unto one place, and let the dry land appear: and it was so. And God called the dry land Earth; and the gathering together of the waters called He Seas: and God saw that it was good* (Genesis 1:9-10 KJV).

This creative process is also recounted by David in Psalm 104:6-7: *"Thou coveredst it with the deep as with a garment: the waters stood above the mountains. At Thy rebuke they fled; at the voice of Thy thunder they hasted away"* (KJV).

While all this was occurring, additional water was accumulating in the canopy, and more dry land was appearing on the rotating and cooling Earth. Change was occurring everywhere with the exception of at the poles of the Earth, where the ice remained intact still entombing specimens of lucifer's distorted creation. The poles were expanding and contracting in size as the

Earth traveled in its revolution around the sun. The Earth had assumed an axis or angle of rotation as the result of the cataclysmic event that lucifer's fall caused. This axis caused the temperature to vary on the Earth as the sun shined upon the Earth at different angles and distances as the Earth traveled in its somewhat elliptical revolution around it.

Yes, a canopy of water still encircled the Earth, and over the 2000 years it created a greenhouse effect, protecting people from the harmful rays of the sun that could cause harm to their bodies and decrease the longevity of life. It also kept the climate constant as it watered the Earth.

In the 2000 years since Eden, evil increased upon the Earth, and all the while the Earth continued to revolve around the sun, rotate on its axis, and cool!

Do you see where this is going? You got chills again? I do! Yeah, right now, class, it's OK to wiggle in your seats!

Back to the biblical account in chapter 7 of Genesis.

And the Lord said unto Noah, Come thou and all thy house into the ark; for thee have I seen righteous before Me in this generation. Of every clean beast thou shalt take to thee by sevens, the male and his female: and of beasts that are not clean by two, the male and his female. Of fowls also of the air by sevens, the male and the female; to keep seed alive upon the face of all the earth. **For yet seven days, and I will cause it to rain upon the earth forty days and forty nights;** *and every living substance that I have made will I destroy from off the face of the earth. And Noah did according unto all that the Lord commanded him. And Noah was six hundred years old when the flood of waters was upon the earth. And Noah went in, and his sons, and his wife, and his sons' wives with him, into the ark,* *because of the waters of the flood. Of clean beasts, and of beasts that are not clean, and of fowls, and of every thing that creepeth upon the earth,*

There went in two and two unto Noah into the ark, the male and the female, as God had commanded Noah. **And it came to pass after seven days that the waters of the flood were upon the earth.** *In the six hundredth year of Noah's life, in the second month, the seventeenth day of the month, the same day were all the fountains of the great deep broken up, and the* **windows of heaven were opened.** *And the rain was upon the earth forty days and forty nights. In the selfsame day entered Noah, and Shem, and Ham, and Japheth, the sons of Noah, and Noah's wife, and the three wives of his sons with them, into the ark; they, and every beast after his kind, and all the cattle after their kind, and every creeping thing that creepeth upon the earth after his kind, and every fowl after his kind, every bird of every sort. And they went in unto Noah into the ark, two and two of all flesh, wherein is the breath of life. And they that went in, went in male and female of all flesh, as God had commanded him: and the Lord shut him in* (Genesis 7:1-16 KJV).

The remnant of nine people, out of about one billion, went to work following the Lord's command to fill the ark with the beasts, fowl, and other creeping things of the Earth. The four generations of preachers from Enoch to Noah saw no one except the remaining members of the family of Seth receive their message of warning. The mocking continued as Noah loaded the complete zoo of animals they had collected upon a massive, seaworthy vessel sitting on dry land many miles from a sea.

Then when the animal passengers were fully loaded, we read in verse 7 that the crew, Noah, his wife, and his sons and their wives, entered the ark. Verse 10 further tells us that *"after seven days"* the rain that lasted 40 days and

40 nights began to fall upon the Earth. The account goes on to say that the Lord then shut the door when the rain began to fall.

The question is raised here as to why the Lord waited seven days to shut the door after the crew and the passengers had been loaded on the ship before allowing the rains to come. Some have speculated that it was just a merciful God allowing ample opportunity for last-minute decisions of those who were outside. Perhaps there is an element of truth in that, but I want you to notice here in the Bible's account who else beside the members of the animal kingdom went onto the ark. Let's count the crew:

Noah and his wife: 2

Shem and his wife: 2

Ham and his wife: 2

Jepthah and his wife: 2

Total: 8

Wait, were there not nine people in our remnant? Who's missing?

Yes, class, you're right. Grandpa Methuselah did not board the ark. Why?

It is not recorded here, but the seven-day wait of the Lord before closing the door and sending the rain was most likely due to His honoring of a Hebrew tradition of a seven-day period of grieving over the death of a loved one. When we put two and two together here, we not only get how many of each unclean animal was put on the ark and how many in each little family went on the ark, but we also understand why God waited seven days.

When we add the fact that Methuselah's name meant "*when he dies, it will come*" to the fact that Noah and the family would have had a seven-day period of grieving over his death, we see the purpose of the Lord's loving wait.

Remember, *"Man / (is) appointed / mortal sorrow, / (the) blessed God / shall come down / teaching, / **his death shall bring judgment / (and) (the) despairing / rest.**"*

You see, Methuselah was not to be a passenger on the ark, but as prophesied, his death would signal the judgment to come and the dawning of a new day, a new start in the world. His death would parallel Jesus's death, which would instead signal redemption and the start of a new day in the world.

Again, we must remember that all the while for 2000 years the Earth continued to revolve and rotate and cool! As the Earth began to go through a period of global cooling, the canopy of water that had encircled the Earth, orbiting since the creation of the second world, began to degrade in its orbit as it had done once before.

Just as a satellite can degrade in its orbit to the point that it comes crashing to the ground, so this canopy of vapor began to "rain" down upon the Earth as it degraded in its orbit. The Earth with its suspended canopy of water had cooled enough so that now the gravitational forces were slightly greater than the centrifugal force of the rotating Earth; the orbit of the canopy began to degrade, and the water began to fall first gently, then heavily upon the Earth.

For 40 days and 40 nights the canopy rained down upon the Earth. The seas and rivers overflowed their banks; the water caverns of the Earth bubbled over onto the surface of the Earth as the deluge of water vapor fell to the Earth. The ark with its passengers, creaking on its supports, rocked, shook, rumbled, and soon began to float, its massive hull rocking and yawing on the waves and rising ever higher as the water rose to the levels of the mountaintops. I suppose there were some who clung to the side, pleading to be pulled on board only to be swept away into eternity.

Once again, life was destroyed upon the Earth in a cataclysmic event. Only those unblemished and uncorrupted by the fallen ones, the remnant, heard the creaks and the groans of the ark as it rolled and rocked upon the waters.

Evidence shows us that there was a complete submergence of all things. Caves in the mountains throughout Europe have been found to be full of animal bones. These are bones that belong to the age of people, not fossils that belong to the Cenozoic, Mesozoic, or Paleozoic layers that we have discussed in earlier chapters. Evidence of a panic in the animal world is clear as they sought safety in the higher elevations as the waters rose higher and higher, even to the mountaintops (see Gen. 7:20). According to the biblical account, the floodwaters were upon the Earth 150 days. Let's return to Genesis for a full summary of what was occurring during this time:

> *And God remembered Noah, and every living thing, and all the cattle that was with him in the ark: and God made a wind to pass over the earth, and the waters assuaged; the fountains also of the deep and the windows of heaven were stopped, and the rain from heaven was restrained; and the waters returned from off the earth continually: and after the end of the hundred and fifty days the waters were abated. And the ark rested in the seventh month, on the seventeenth day of the month, upon the mountains of Ararat (Genesis 8:1-4 KJV).*

The canopy of water now rested upon the face of the Earth, and this great volume of water would have caused convulsions and upheavals. New basins, valleys, and mountains created new resting places for all this water.

Geologists tell us that although the Earth is now three-fourths water, it was not always so. The area of the Bering Strait between Asia and North America was at one time dry land, and evidence of civilization has been found submerged deep below the surface of the waters. First thought to be mythical, recently discovered evidence of submerged architecture has seen a resurgence of the claims concerning the lost city of Atlantis. Atlantis, written about by Plato, was an ancient city that was destroyed by "floodwaters" according to tradition. Perhaps it did exist. It becomes even more interesting when we consider that the city derived its name from "Atlas" the Titan. Remember that *titan* was also another name for "giant," or in the Hebrew, "Nephilim."

Go ahead and again talk amongst yourselves, but not too long because we have a lot more to talk about—like the ark.

We read in the account that after the 150-day voyage of the ark, it came to rest on Mount Ararat, which is located in the modern-day nation of Turkey. The Armenians, who live near that ice and snowcapped mountain today, consider themselves the direct descendants of Noah. In the 1950s, some interesting things began to develop regarding this mountain. A French explorer named Navarro, encouraged by stories of a sighting of a large wooden structure on the mountain by locals at various times when the ice would melt and glaciers would move, began to explore the mountain. He too saw what appeared to be a large wooden structure partially exposed from the ice and snow, which would have had the capability of preserving the wooden ark for 4500 years.

Then in 1959, a Russian pilot photographed what appeared to be a large wooden structure on the mountain. The photographs were subsequently reported lost, but according to accounts, were destroyed by a communist government not wanting anything to give credibility to the Bible. Since that time, numerous expeditions have been attempted. The famed Christian archaeologist Ron Wyatt also claimed to have viewed the structure and the petrified timbers. Even a NASA astronaut, the late James Irwin, was involved in attempts to verify that the ark was still on the mountain. However, to this day, no conclusive evidence has been able to be established due to the treacherous terrain and conditions as well as the political, anti-Semitic, and anti-Christian climate of the area. An explorer risks his life in any attempt to verify the authenticity of the preservation of the ark upon the mountain where it came to rest after the waters receded.

I cannot help but think that perhaps the discovery of conclusive evidence for the ark and even for Atlantis is not far off as God may use them as a warning to humankind of another coming judgment upon the Earth.

Of course, perhaps they will just mock it again, *"as it was in the days of Noah"!* (See Luke 17:26.)

It was from Mount Ararat that all animal and human life was once again reintroduced upon the Earth. The Earth was a changed place with the canopy now gone and the sun now shining unfiltered and creating areas of high and low pressure as air currents begin to flow upon the Earth. Conceivably, Ararat at this time was not snowcapped because of the greenhouse effect that was upon the Earth, but temperatures began to vary at different elevations due to air currents freely flowing in the atmosphere. For the first time upon the Earth, seasons were known. Seed time and harvest, cold and heat, and summer and winter were experienced without the protective canopy. The life span of people began to reduce due to the loss of this protective canopy and the disintegrating effects of the sunlight's radiation upon human tissue.

> *And Noah went forth, and his sons, and his wife, and his sons' wives with him: every beast, every creeping thing, and every fowl, and whatsoever creepeth upon the earth, after their kinds, went forth out of the ark. And Noah builded an altar unto the Lord; and took of every clean beast, and of every clean fowl, and offered burnt offerings on the altar. And the Lord smelled a sweet savour; and the Lord said in His heart, I will not again curse the ground any more for man's sake; for the imagination of man's heart is evil from his youth; neither will I again smite any more every thing living, as I have done. While the earth remaineth, seedtime and harvest, and cold and heat, and summer and winter, and day and night shall not cease.*

And God blessed Noah and his sons, and said unto them, Be fruitful, and multiply, and replenish the earth (Genesis 8:18–9:1 KJV).

And God promised to never completely destroy His creation, His mudcakes.

Why? This was the desire of the enemy—to get God to destroy creation as He had done before, but God promised He will not destroy the fallen creation. As He had promised Eve, He would provide a way of redemption and restoration. He had a plan to redeem them from the eternal death sentence they were currently facing and to destroy all the power of the enemy who held creation hostage. In the process of redeeming His mudcakes and all creation, God would also destroy evil and its potential to exist in an eternal Kingdom.

Yes, God had a plan, and despite the frustrations it would experience, eventually His plan would prevail, and it would be very good!

Chapter 13

Ten Generations

———◆———

The thing that hath been, it is that which shall be; and that
which is done is that which shall be done: and there is no new
thing under the sun (Ecclesiastes 1:9 KJV).

In the ten generations from Adam to Noah, the Earth grew to a population estimated to be 1 billion people; in just one day, it was reduced to eight people, Noah and his family, the unblemished remnant or seed preserved by God. It was this remnant, unblemished by the interbreeding with the *"fallen ones"* or with their offspring, who were once again given the task to be fruitful and repopulate the Earth.

We will see as we go along in our study that God is a God of order and that numbers are very important to Him—the numbers 3, 7, 8, 10, 12, 14, and 40 seem especially important. This is not an exhaustive list either. Our creative God is very precise in what He is doing; as we study history, we see this precision coming through.

Numbers seem to be a signature or a fingerprint from the hand of God to verify that His hand is still on His creation. You have probably already noticed that the number seven has played a major role so far.

There were *"in the beginning"* seven creative days; we also see the number seven in the created order, like seven notes in music and seven colors of the spectrum, for example. God made a big display of this color spectrum after the Flood as the sunlight beamed through the vapor in the air creating a rainbow. God used this as a sign of His covenant with His post-Flood mudcakes. The canopy of water that had previously encircled the Earth was now upon the Earth, and He promised that a catastrophic flood would never occur again. This spectrum of seven colors, as the sun shone through the vapors, was the sign of His promise.

We even see that God told Noah to take seven of the clean animals upon the ark. Of the unclean animals, he only took two each into the Ark. However, I am sure by the end of the 150-day voyage, Mrs. Noah did not think of any of them were very clean!

We could fill a whole book on the number seven as used by God throughout the history of Israel and the Scriptures. In fact there are 391 verses in Scripture that reference the number seven a total of 463 times. We cannot divert too much from our path to explore that now, but it is important for you to know that the number seven is commonly referred to as the "perfect number" because it means "all things being done and in order, or completely satisfied," or "complete." Literally it is referred to in the Hebrew as the *"sacred full one."*[1]

Enoch was the seventh generation from Adam, and he was caught up to Heaven because *"God took him."* and we will see the significance of the symbolism of this later on. Methuselah was the eighth generation, and the number eight in the Hebrew world symbolizes "new beginnings." The eighth day of the seven-day traditional Jewish "Feast of Tabernacles" is known as *Shimini Azeret,* meaning "new beginnings." We will see as we go along that the eighth generation in the genealogies frequently is someone who is the grandfather of a significant person in a pattern of ten generations, which also emerges in the Scriptures. In genealogies listed in the Bible, "Grampa," as we saw with Methuselah, often signals a significant change or event that is about to occur, a significant person who comes on the scene, or both! We tend to skim over these genealogies that occur in Scripture, for they make for dry reading, but they are there for a purpose and, when studied, can be quite intriguing.

What is God doing in all this?

He likes to smear events and history with His fingerprint of exactness and order just so we know that He is behind it all, working out His plan to redeem humankind and establish the eternal Kingdom.

God often makes events of the history of the world symbols or "pre-types" of a future event. As Scripture says, *"The thing that hath been, it is that which shall be; and that which is done is that which shall be done: and there is no new thing under the sun"* (Eccles. 1:9 KJV), or as translated more literally from the Hebrew, *"What has been will be again, what has been done will be done again; there is nothing new under the sun."*

Keep this Scripture in mind as we go forward because the past will give us a glimpse of the future. Even Jesus referred to a time to come as being *"as it was in the days of Noah"* (Luke 17:26). We will gain an understanding of the times leading up to the establishment of the Kingdom of Heaven on Earth by looking at those events of the past, specifically in regard to the nation of Israel.

We will look more at the numbers 12 and 14 later, but now we will see how the number ten is significant. Understand that numbers have meaning in antiquity and to God as we look at the number ten, which means *"divine order"* or *"perfection."*

So far we have seen that Enoch was the seventh generation from Adam, and Methuselah, his son, the eighth generation, was the grandfather of Noah, who was the tenth generation from Adam. Noah is a very significant person because his family repopulated the Earth following the Great Flood. Noah carried out the "new beginnings" signaled by the life of Methuselah.

Noah had three sons, Shem, Ham, and Japheth. In these three sons, God immediately went about working out His plan, looking for His next remnant based on the characters of these three sons. These sons would be the fathers of three different groups of people who would scatter throughout the world and populate it.

It was at that time that an incident occurred.

The Earth's canopy was now gone, and the sun was allowed to shine unfiltered upon the Earth, not only reducing the longevity of people, but also causing produce to spoil more quickly and to ferment. So it was with the grapes that Noah planted in his vineyard. We find that one day as Noah was enjoying, literally, the fruits of his labor, he had too much of the fermented kind and fell asleep in a drunken stupor, naked in his tent.

Ham, and also apparently Ham's son Canaan, discovered him and announced it to Ham's brothers. Seeing the drunk and naked Noah accidentally would not have been a crime, but the implication of the Hebrew words coupled with ancient Hebrew tradition tell us that Ham and Canaan were amused with the sight and announced it in a scornful, deriding manner. There is even the implication of lewd behavior involved, a type of behavior seen among the descendants of Ham and Canaan later on in what we know as the Canaanite civilization.

The eldest brother Shem and his brother Japheth treated their father with respect; they did not join in with Ham's levity and lewdness, but took a garment and, hiding their faces, backed into the tent and covered their father.

When Noah awoke, he was angry with Ham and pronounced a curse upon Ham's son Canaan:

"Cursed be Canaan! The lowest of slaves will he be to his brothers." He also said, "Blessed be the Lord, the God of Shem! May Canaan be the slave of Shem. May God extend the territory of Japheth; may Japheth live in the tents of Shem, and may Canaan be his slave" (Genesis 9:25-27).

We see that *God is already beginning to build a remnant again as He did through Seth in the pre-Flood civilization!* Ham's son Canaan is cursed to be the slave, not only of Shem, but also of Japheth. Not only that, but ultimately the land of Canaan would be handed over by God to another future remnant of people (Israel) whom God would choose to carry out His plan.

Shem's descendants were called Semites. The nation of Israel would ultimately come through the descendants of Shem. He was, we might say, the post-Flood Seth. Abraham, David, and Jesus would all come from the line of Shem. Not only would the Hebrews (Israel) descend from Shem, but also the Chaldeans, Assyrians, Persians, and Syrians. These groups of people were destined to rule the ancient world, fulfilling both Noah's curse upon Caanan and the prophetic word he spoke at that time.

Ham's descendants settled in Canaan (modern-day Israel), Egypt, and Africa. He would father the most evil, satanic civilizations of this ancient world, for he would father the Canaanites, Egyptians, Philistines, Hittites, and the Amorites. These people and their descendants have been the historical enemies of Israel. Giants like Goliath lived among these people, indicating that the *fallen ones* were likely after the daughters of men again. Yes, lucifer was once again about his attempt to corrupt the "seed" of the woman in his effort to thwart God's plan of redemption. This is why God forbade the Israelites to intermarry with these people. He did not want them to have their genetics corrupted with the DNA of the Nephilim. It is also why God decreed that when Israel conquered Canaan, they were to destroy all the people—something He has been much criticized for over the years. These people's genetics were corrupted by the *fallen ones,* and

God wanted them destroyed to protect the mudcakes from their genetic corruption.

Japheth's descendants settled mostly in Europe and Asia Minor and the area of modern-day Russia. He would father such civilizations as the Greeks, Thracians, and Scythians.

It would be through Shem's descendants that God would begin to carry out His plan to redeem His mudcakes, and it would be Ham's descendants that satan initially would use to try to stop this plan.

Before we go on with our next generation of ten, I would be remiss if I did not stop here to tie into this picture the story of the Tower of Babel. You see, the world was growing at a rapid rate, and as people spread out over the Earth once again, so also was evil spreading. Pride in the hearts of people drove them to want to be like God.

These post-Flood people were not much better than the pre-Flood people, except that God had a plan to develop His new remnant and use them to carry out His redemptive plan.

Cush was the son of Ham, and Cush's son Nimrod became one of the most famous figures in antiquity. Nimrod was also known by his throne name *Sargon,* and he was feared throughout the world as one of the mightiest of all warriors. He battled his way to the lands east of the territories settled by his Uncle Canaan, where he founded a city known as Babel. This area would later become known as Babylon, which is now in the area of present-day Iraq.

At Babel the pride of people became so great they began work to build a tower high enough to reach to Heaven in a conquering way and, *therefore, be like God!* You see, ever since Eve and Adam ate of the fruit in the Garden, mudcakes have been driven, like the deceiver lucifer, to achieve the same status as God. Yes, Nimrod believed that if he could get to Heaven by building a tower, that he could conquer that as well. The Scripture account in Genesis 11 tells of this first skyscraper project.

The Tower of Babel

Now the whole world had one language and a common speech.

As men moved eastward, they found a plain in Shinar and settled there.

They said to each other, "Come, let's make bricks and bake them thoroughly." They used brick instead of stone, and tar for mortar.

Then they said, "Come, let us build ourselves a city, with a tower that reaches to the heavens, so that we may make a name for ourselves and not be scattered over the face of the whole earth."

But the Lord came down to see the city and the tower that the men were building.

The Lord said, "If as one people speaking the same language they have begun to do this, then nothing they plan to do will be impossible for them.

Come, let us go down and confuse their language so they will not understand each other."

So the Lord scattered them from there over all the earth, and they stopped building the city.

That is why it was called Babel—because there the Lord confused the language of the whole world. From there the Lord scattered them over the face of the whole earth (Genesis 11:1-9).

Babel means "confusion," and instead of becoming like God, their pride caused them to be scattered even further into the entire world, becoming subject to God's overall plan. Even today, people who are wise in their own eyes don't feel they need God. They have this inward desire to be God, living according to their own beliefs and not according to the commands of God. Even some of our New Age people say, "We are like God." I even heard a famous New Age actress tell how she loves to stand on the beach and yell, *"I'm God...I'm God!"*

That's tantamount to an ant standing on the sidewalk yelling, "I'm a man... I'm a man!" while a man unknowingly walks up from behind and squashes it on the pavement. In the same way, God came down and scattered these people like ants from their great big anthill!

While the ants were scattering, the plan of God was being worked out in the descendants of the chosen remnant, the descendants of Shem. Like Noah, who was the tenth generation from Adam, we see that in ten generations from Noah, another significant man emerges in this remnant group. After Noah, we see the descendants of Shem in this order:

1. Shem

2. Arphaxad

3. Shelah

4. Eber

5. Peleg

6. Reu

7. Serug

8. Nahor

9. Terah

10. Abram

Number ten is Abram, also known as Abraham, "the father of many nations." We need to stop and take a look at this man as God begins to define

His remnant even further and sets the stage for His long-term plan to redeem His mudcakes.

It is important to note that Abram, renamed Abraham by God, was a man who sought God all his life. He was not born in the area of the future nation of Israel's "promised land," but in the area of the world now known as Iraq. Early in his life, God spoke to him, and he began the long journey of moving his family back into the area of the world where God would establish the nation Abraham would father. Up until this point, the people of the Earth were mostly nomadic, grouped together as families or tribes, but things were beginning to change. Nations that would rule and remain in a geographic area were beginning to develop.

Genesis chapter 12 gives us an account of how Abraham was called to the area of modern-day Israel to begin to lay the groundwork for a remnant nation who would be used of God to carry out His mudcake redemption plan.

The Call of Abram

The Lord had said to Abram, "Leave your country, your people and your father's household and go to the land I will show you.

"I will make you into a great nation and I will bless you; *I will make your name great, and you will be a blessing.*

"I will bless those who bless you, and whoever curses you I will curse; and all peoples on earth will be blessed through you."

So Abram left, as the Lord had told him; and Lot went with him. Abram was seventy-five years old when he set out from Haran. He took his wife Sarai, his nephew Lot, all the possessions they had accumulated and the people they had acquired in Haran, and they set out for the land of Canaan, and they arrived there.

Abram traveled through the land as far as the site of the great tree of Moreh at Shechem. **At that time the Canaanites were in the land.** *The Lord appeared to Abram and said, "To your offspring I will give this land."* *So he built an altar there to the Lord, who had appeared to him* (Genesis 12:1-7).

God called Abram to go to a land He would show him. We find in verses 6 and 7 that the land God showed Abram was the land where the notoriously wicked Canaanites lived (descendants of Caanan who were cursed by Noah).

God then made an incredible promise to him.

God told Abram that He would bless him and make Abram's offspring into a great nation and that *whoever blessed this nation would in turn be blessed and whoever cursed this nation would be cursed.* He also told Abram that all the peoples of the Earth would be *blessed through him!*

What does God mean by *blessed through him*?

A new promise and a new covenant were being made, different but related to the promise God made to Eve in the Garden of Eden. This new covenant promised Abram that redemption would be provided for the world through his seed, that the nation he would father would produce the seed of the woman who would crush satan's head as Eve had been promised. *Yes, out of the nation of Israel would come the redeemer who would deliver the world from the curse pronounced upon the mudcakes in the Garden of Eden.*

Abraham would have descendants as the stars or the sands of the beach, but there was one problem. Abraham and his wife Sarah were not young, and at the time of this promise, they had no children. Time continued to pass, and Sarah and Abraham decided to come up with their own plan since God had not delivered on His promise. Sarah persuaded Abraham to have a child by her maidservant, Hagar. Abraham at the age of 86 did father a child named Ishmael, whose descendants would become the modern-day Arabs. Throughout all recorded history, they have opposed the remnant, the nation of Israel. If Abraham had waited for God's promise to be fulfilled, perhaps the nation of Israel today would be known as the nation of Abraham. God continued to work His plan and established the nation through Abraham's grandson, Jacob, also known by the name *Israel*.

God did make good on His promise 14 years later when Sarah became pregnant. Abraham was 100 years old. She gave birth to Isaac, and because of the jealousy that developed between the two mothers of Abraham's sons, Ishmael and Hagar were sent away from the tents of Abraham out into the desert. It was at this time that the hatred that we still see today between these two groups of people, the descendants of Ishmael (Arabs) and the descendants of Isaac (Israel) began to develop. The turmoil we see in the Middle East today is rooted in these ancient events. Both groups claim Abraham as their father, and the descendants of the scorned son carry on with great hatred toward the descendants of the favored son.

At this time we see an event that provides a *pre-type* of the one who would deliver the mudcakes and redeem them. It had been a long wait for Abraham for the son through whom God would provide this deliverer. Now he finally was here, and Abraham loved and delighted in this boy, Isaac.

Then one day, God made another strange request of Abraham. Let's pick it up in the biblical account in Genesis.

Abraham Tested

Some time later God tested Abraham. He said to him, "Abraham!"
"Here I am," he replied.

Then God said, "Take your son, your only son, Isaac, whom you love, and go to the region of Moriah. Sacrifice him there as a burnt offering on one of the mountains I will tell you about" (Genesis 22:1-2).

Now this is where I would have said, "Now wait, this can't be You, God. You told me I would be the father of nations; in fact, You even changed my name from Abram, which means 'father,' to Abraham, which means 'father of multitudes!' This can't be You. He is my only son, and I waited so long for him. If he is dead, this does not work out the way we planned. This can't be You!"

Yes, that is what most of us would have probably done, but this great man of faith had developed such trust in his ability to hear from God that he trusted God even when God did not seem to make sense. So what did he do? Let's read on:

> *Early the next morning Abraham got up and saddled his donkey. He took with him two of his servants and his son Isaac. When he had cut enough wood for the burnt offering, he set out for the place God had told him about. On the third day Abraham looked up and saw the place in the distance. He said to his servants, "Stay here with the donkey while I and the boy go over there. We will worship and then we will come back to you."*

> *Abraham took the wood for the burnt offering and placed it on his son Isaac, and he himself carried the fire and the knife. As the two of them went on together, Isaac spoke up and said to his father Abraham, "Father?" "Yes, my son?" Abraham replied. "The fire and wood are here," Isaac said, "but where is the lamb for the burnt offering?" Abraham answered, "God Himself will provide the lamb for the burnt offering, my son." And the two of them went on together.*

> *When they reached the place God had told him about, Abraham built an altar there and arranged the wood on it. He bound his son Isaac and laid him on the altar, on top of the wood. Then he reached out his hand and took the knife to slay his son* (Genesis 22:3-10).

(Let's stop it here again for a moment. Now if I were Isaac, it would not have taken me long to figure out what was going on here, and ya know what, I could have outrun that old boy Abraham all the way down the mountain, yelling for that servant we left behind to help me 'cause the old man had stripped his gears!

But Isaac didn't, did he? He trusted his father and was obedient to him—even if it meant his death. Wow, Abraham was not only a man of faith, but he also fathered a man of faith and obedience. So what happened? Let's go on.)

> But the angel of the Lord called out to him from heaven, "Abraham! Abraham!" "Here I am," he replied. "Do not lay a hand on the boy," he said. "Do not do anything to him. Now I know that you fear God, because **you have not withheld from Me your son, your only son.**"
>
> Abraham looked up and there in a thicket he saw a ram caught by its horns. He went over and took the ram and sacrificed it as a burnt offering instead of his son.
>
> So Abraham called that place The Lord Will Provide. And to this day it is said, "On the mountain of the Lord it will be provided."
>
> The angel of the Lord called to Abraham from heaven a second time and said, "I swear by Myself, declares the Lord, that because you have done this and have not withheld your son, **your only son,** I will surely bless you and make your descendants as numerous as the stars in the sky and as the sand on the seashore. Your descendants will take possession of the cities of their enemies, **and through your offspring all nations on earth will be blessed,** because you have obeyed Me" (Genesis 22:11-18).

Now I told you this event was a *pre-type* of God's redemptive plan. Here a man was willing to sacrifice his **only son,** and the son was willingly allowing the sacrifice because of his love for and trust in the father.

But wait, there is more! Do you know where this took place?

Yes, class, on Mt. Moriah, specifically on a rock there which many years later became the Temple Mount where the Temple was built. The rock became the place where the Holy of Holies was built. It was here that the nation of Israel worshiped and made sacrifices of animals for the atonement of their sins. One can even see the rock today. The enemies of Israel, the Arabs, have taken possession of it, however, and it can be observed within the walls of the Dome of the Rock shrine, which was built upon the Temple Mount in A.D. 8th century, after the Temple was destroyed in A.D. 70. This possession, despite what the Arabs believe, is temporary, according to prophecy. Bible prophecies tell of a new Temple being rebuilt again on this mountain by the nation of Israel, and plans currently are underway. More on this later.

The need for the Temple as a place of sacrifice would ultimately be replaced by a sacrifice where a Father on a mount nearby Mount Moriah would sacrifice His only son who would bless and provide redemption for the mudcakes.

You see where this is going, don't you? God would sacrifice His only son at Calvary and provide redemption for the mudcakes—but not yet. The plan was still in the development stage as was the remnant nation of Israel. The descendants of Abraham would also produce another remnant of people through whom this redemption would be provided, just as Abraham on that mountain that day prophesied, *"The Lord will provide."*

Yes, a pre-type of the coming redeemer is seen here, and we will see another pre-type in (yes, class, you guessed it!) another ten generations when the next significant individual in God's redemptive plan arose.

But first, let's discuss further the development of the remnant nation through whom this redemption would be provided. Abraham, as we previously noted, had two branches of offspring, those who descended from Ishmael and those who descended from Isaac. Ishmael's descendants became the Arab nations of today. Isaac, like Abraham, had two sons—named Esau and Jacob. Perhaps you remember the story of these two brothers who were actually twins. Esau was born first and thereby entitled to the birthright as the eldest, but there was Jacob, literally hanging onto Esau's heel.

Isaac's wife Rebekah noted that the two boys seemed to struggle with each other in the womb, and the Scriptures tell us that she inquired of the Lord about them. The Lord revealed to her that there were two nations of people within her and that the eldest would serve the youngest.

We see that this must have played a part in her helping Jacob trick his father Isaac in his old age into giving the blessing of the birthright to Jacob. Perhaps you recall the story of how a very hungry Esau returned one day from hunting to find his brother Jacob with a bowl of red stew. He asked Jacob to give it to him, and Jacob said he would if Esau would give him his birthright. Esau shortsightedly and foolishly agreed—and so it was with Rebekah and Jacob's trickery of Isaac, the birthright was given to Jacob. The word of the Lord to Rebekah that the eldest would serve the youngest was fulfilled, and Esau's descendants also became known as the Edomites who are also considered Arabs today, along with the descendants of Ishmael.

Out of all these descendants of Abraham, God would refine the remnant even further. It would only be the descendants of Jacob, also known as *Israel,* who would become the remnant nation through whom God would bring forth His plan to redeem the mudcakes.

The "brothers" of two successive remnant generations, Esau and his uncle Ishmael, would become the nations of people who would be used by satan in the generations to come to oppose the descendants of Jacob or Israel.

In their opposition, they would attempt to destroy the nation of Israel many times.

Lucifer believed that in so doing, he would destroy the plan of God to redeem the mudcakes. His strategy—destroy the plan by destroying Israel! Throughout history we see satan's attempts to eliminate Israel, most notably in recent times through Adolf Hitler and the Nazis. Even in current days, the president of Iran declares openly his desire to destroy the nation of Israel. Perhaps you wondered why there has been so much hatred of the Jews and the nation of Israel historically. Perhaps you have even joined in yourself. If so, remember God's promise to Abraham to *"bless those who bless you and curse those who curse you."*

I like getting blessings better than curses, don't you?

Yes, the remnant nation to carry out the plan in the *seen* or physical world would be the descendants of Jacob known as the nation of Israel, and in the establishment of this nation, we see the fingerprint of God in numbers again, this time the number 12.

The number 12 is considered the "number of government"[2]; there were 12 tribes or families at the foundation of Israel who were the descendants of the 12 sons of Jacob/Israel. Israel was a representative physical nation or pre-type of the coming heavenly Kingdom, and it was founded by 12 individuals— the 11 sons of Jacob, with Joseph receiving a double portion as promised by God for his faithfulness. Joseph's two sons Ephraim and Manasseh would make up two of the 12 tribes.

It is also interesting to note that Genesis chapter 25 reveals that Ishmael also was the father of 12 rulers or tribes and nations. Satan is the great counterfeiter, mimicking the plan of God in order to deceive and lead as many mudcakes as possible away from the truth. This is why lucifer became known as satan, because the word means "adversary."

*We will discuss later how the coming heavenly or **seen** Kingdom of redeemed mudcakes on Earth was also founded by 12 individuals, the disciples, who were the **spiritual** descendants of another significant "number ten" in the line of generations—Jesus!*

Now back to Israel, the pre-type of the coming heavenly Kingdom.

Jacob and his sons founded the nation of Israel because 12 tribes developed from them, but these tribes were held captive as Hebrew slaves for many years in the nation of Egypt. God's plan does not develop quickly because He is not bound by time or space as we are. We are three-dimensional beings, bound by time, while God is a supernatural, multi-dimensional being who lives in an *"ever-present now,"* as I experienced in my near-death encounter. Because of the sin of these brothers in selling their brother Joseph into captivity in Egypt and lying to their father about his death, they planted a seed of captivity in their own lives. Later when that negative seed sprouted, their descendants were held captive as slaves to the pharaohs of Egypt, the descendants of Canaan, who almost destroyed these peoples by overworking them and then trying to kill them when they fled the country under the leadership of Moses.

Moses would be called out of Egypt to be prepared by God to confront Pharaoh and to lead the Israelites out of captivity. They then wandered in the wilderness for 40 years before settling in the land of Canaan, just as the Lord had promised Abraham long before Isaac was even born.

The number 40 was important to Moses; he was 40 years in Egypt before fleeing to Midian where he lived for 40 years before returning to Egypt to demand that the Hebrews be let go. Then Moses spent his final 40 years wandering in the wilderness with the Israelites in preparation for the establishment of the earthly remnant kingdom. Moses spent 40 days on Mount Sinai where he received the law from the Lord.

Jesus also spent 40 days in the wilderness where He was tempted by the devil in preparation for His earthly ministry to establish the spiritual Kingdom. There are other examples where the number 40 played a significant role: rain fell for 40 days and 40 nights bringing the Flood upon the Earth. My point is that the fingerprint of the Lord appears all throughout the history of humankind as He works out His plan of redemption; numbers and precise plans are one of the ways He leaves His fingerprints.

*God is an awesome and loving God; He cries out for us to listen, to look for Him working out a plan in our lives, but so many of us just go on never giving Him a thought, never reading His Word. We live our lives as if this is all there is, when this **life is just a temporary thing, a brief moment in eternity for the purposes of our redemption.** So many leave this life never knowing the purpose and plan of God for their lives—their lives fully spent with God's fingerprints of love and redemption all around them. They have never learned the secrets of this life or the secrets of the coming eternal one-world order!*

We have been discussing His fingerprints in numbers, and I want to return to the fingerprint of the ten generations now. We have seen so far that number ten counting from Adam produces a significant individual in the history of God's redemptive plan. Our first two number ten individuals were Noah and Abraham. We now should look at the next ten generations to see what develops in God's plan in the nation of Israel.

The Kinsman Redeemer

The next ten generations from Abraham produces another pre-type, in this case a pre-type of the Messiah, the redeemer promised to Eve long ago in the Garden and longed for by Israel since the birth of their nation. Let's look at who makes up these generations:

1. Isaac

2. Jacob

3. Judah

4. Phares

5. Esrom

6. Aram

7. Aminadab

8. Naasom

9. Salmon

10. Boaz

Boaz is our number ten this time, and Boaz makes his appearance in the Book of Ruth in the Bible.

God frequently has used times of distress to prepare or position people for the outworking of His plans for their lives and for His overall purposes. This should be an encouragement to us when we go through difficult times in our lives and economies. Many have found new life with God because of difficult circumstances that cause them to seek joy and peace. We need to remember that God's plan is still at work. Such is the case here as God uses difficult times to bring together the man and the woman who would become King David's great-grandparents, Boaz and Ruth.

The story of how this couple came together gives us another pre-type of Christ and His relationship with the Christian Church, which He calls His Bride.

First of all, we need to understand that the Hebrew law as instituted by God through Moses provided for the care and support of a widowed woman whose husband died without leaving her a son to care for her. We see this custom known as the *kinsman-redeemer* described in the Book of Deuteronomy:

> *If brothers are living together and one of them dies without a son, his widow must not marry outside the family. Her husband's brother shall take her and marry her and fulfill the duty of a brother-in-law to her* (Deuteronomy 25:5).

In the case of Ruth, not only had her husband died, but also his father and brother, so no one was under obligation to marry her to provide for her. A kindly man named Boaz, who was of the family of Ruth's husband, noticed her and was kind to her in her need. Although he was not the closest of kin, he was willing to take someone else's place and to "redeem" Ruth, take her to be his bride and to provide for her.

Boaz redeemed a bride lost in death to be his own bride, just as Jesus Christ did for the Church, those who have accepted his offer of redemption. This is the reason the Church is called "the Bride of Christ."

Boaz and Ruth then had a child named Obed, the grandfather of the great King David, the man to whom God promised to raise up a king from his lineage whose Kingdom would be forever, the *Kinsman Redeemer*, Jesus Christ.

It is at this point that we see another important number come to prominence—the number 14. Besides the number 10, God uses the number 14 to point to Jesus. God uses these two numbers to smear Jesus with His fingerprints, proving that it was He who is the promised deliverer and that it is God who is behind all of this, working out His long-term plan.

King David marks a significant point in God's overall plan of redemption, for the promise is made to David that one of his descendants would forever sit on the throne. The eternal Kingdom promised to Abraham is established at this point with the promise to David, who is of the tribe of Judah, one of the 12 tribes of Israel. This Kingdom would commence as an earthly kingdom, which would rise and fall and then rise again, eventually becoming the eternal *seen* Kingdom ruled by a descendant of David, one who would reign forever. In God's plan it will be the nation of Israel who in the end will rule the world from Jerusalem with a descendant of David upon the throne who will rule eternally.

It is at this point also that the remnant is refined even further to the tribe of Judah—a remnant of a remnant (Israel/Jacob) of the remnant (Abraham) of the remnant (Shem, Ham, Jepthah) of the remnant (Noah) of the remnant (Seth). And there will be more remnants that follow the remnant of the 12 tribes of Israel.

You see, when we count back now from the establishment of the pre-type of the promised Kingdom that shall never fail, from David to Abraham, we get 14 generations. Is that significant? Yes, it is! We will see how God marks Jesus with both the number 10 and the number 14! God is very organized in His plan, and that organization confirms that a mighty God is behind all that is happening in this world as He works out His plan.

We find in the Bible in the books of First and Second Kings and First and Second Chronicles that after the reign of David's son Solomon, the Kingdom of Israel is split in two, with the tribe of Judah separating from the other tribes. It is this new remnant that King David's descendants would lead and from which, ultimately, the *"seed of woman," "kinsman redeemer,"* and promised *"deliverer"* would descend—but only after some difficult times for this earthly pre-type kingdom of Israel.

Disobedience to God's commands prevailed in both parts of this divided kingdom. God remembered His promise to King David, and as Second Kings 8:19 tells us, *"Yet the Lord would not destroy Judah, for the sake of his servant David, as He promised him to give a lamp to him and his sons forever"* (NKJV).

So God, eight generations from Boaz, rose up in Judah a *"new beginnings"* king named Jehoshaphat. He would be the grandfather of our next number ten, Uzziah. Jehoshaphat began to restore the kingdom to God's prescribed ways only to have it undermined by his son Jehoram, who returned to the evil ways and formed an alliance with Israel (or the other 11 tribes). Second Chronicles 21:19 tells us that the Lord struck down Jehoram with a disease in his intestines, and he died a painful death for his evil.

Then the Lord raised up his son Uzziah (also known as Ahaziah) to reign in his place. Uzziah, our next number ten, was a great king in Judah who restored Judah to greatness and godliness. He reigned 52 years, defeating the Philistines and the Arabs. The Ammonites paid tribute to him. He built cities and towers in Jerusalem and in the desert, digging many cisterns. Judah, under his reign, became mighty, prosperous, and powerful again, with a second-to-none army. At the end of his reign, however, he became prideful and tried to assume the role of the priests. Kings were never to take on the role of a priest under Jewish law and vice versa. The priests withstood him, and Uzziah was stricken with leprosy. The work of this number ten, marred with disobedience, planted the seeds for a return to unfaithfulness on the part of the subsequent kings and the nation of Judah.

The nation of Israel, including the tribe of Judah, forgot their God and followed their own thinking and desires, much as people in our time are doing. They did not listen to the words of the prophets sent by God, who called them to repentance and foretold the consequences if they did not change their ways. God's ways and plans became less important to them; as a result, the protective hand of God came off of the nation. Babylon invaded and captured this earthly God-ordained kingdom—14 generations after the reign of King David!

While the physical kingdom was defeated, and its people dispersed throughout the world, the tribe of Judah, though displaced and scattered, has never disappeared. The other 11 tribes have been scattered and have come to be known as the "lost tribes," but the tribe of Judah has made its presence known throughout the generations and within the nations of the world through all the ages to come. These people since that time have come to be known as the *Jews,* deriving that name from the name *Judah.*

The remnant of the nation of Israel now is broken down even more. The remnant through which God continues to work out His plan is now specifically the tribe of Judah or the Jews. It would be through the Jews from the tribe of Judah that Eve's promised deliverer will come, the one the Jews call the Messiah.

I want you to understand this remnant thing, so let me summarize it another way:

1st Remnant…Descendants of Seth

2nd Remnant…Noah and His Family

3rd Remnant…Descendants of Shem

4th Remnant…Descendants of Abraham

5th Remnant…Descendants of Israel/Jacob

6th Remnant…Descendants of David

7th Remnant…The Tribe of Judah, the Descendants of David, the Jews

Fourteen generations after David, King Jeconiah became the last king to physically reign over the kingdom of Judah, as Babylon defeated and dispersed the nation just as the prophets in Israel had warned.

Now the prophets' message takes on a new direction, foretelling the coming redeemer and eternal Kingdom as well as the restoration of the nation of Israel, whose people were scattered and whose land had been given to another. The land of Israel was now occupied by the enemies of Israel, those under the influence of satan. Worship in the Temple of Jerusalem ceased.

We learn of these 14 generations in Matthew chapter 1, a chapter we tend to gloss over when reading the Bible, but it is all important as it shows the hand of God working out His plan, making good on His promises as we move to a new phase, a new day, and a new Kingdom for the mudcakes.

Matthew tells us that there were 14 generations from Abraham to David, 14 from David to Jeconiah when the Jews were carried off in exile into Babylon, and 14 generations from Jeconiah until Jesus. (See Matthew chapter 1.) It is during this last group of 14 that the prophets begin to give us some insight into the coming Kingdom and God's continuing plan, despite the scattering of the Jews, to redeem all of creation.

Let's now consider the road map laid out by the prophets to this redemption, the future of the Jews, and toward the coming eternal Kingdom.

Chapter 14

The Kings Who Never Were

———◆———

Lucifer leapt with glee as King Zedekiah watched his sons, heirs to the throne of Israel, killed before his eyes. It was the last thing Zedekiah ever saw before the killers put out his eyes, bound him, and took him to Babylon.

With the remnant kingdom in exile and the heirs to the throne destroyed, lucifer believed this was the destruction of God's plan to provide a "deliverer" through King David's descendants. Now surely God would destroy these mudcakes and all of creation in His anger! The ones He had chosen to redeem humankind had failed Him. Surely God would now realize that lucifer had won. Yes, *he would be like God!*

The exile into Babylon marks the last time that the Jews would live in Jerusalem under their own rule until 1948.

It is amazing to me that mere people think they can match wits with God when over and over a spiritual being like lucifer fails. You see, Nebuchadnezzar had invaded and captured Jerusalem under the previous King Jehoiachin, who was a direct descendant of David. Jehoiachin, also known as Jeconiah, had been carried off to Babylon, and Nebuchadnezzar had appointed his uncle as king in Judah. So if Zedekiah was Jehoiachin's uncle, that meant that the sons who were killed were his cousins!

The rightful heirs to the throne of Israel, the descendants of David, were alive and well in Babylon!

Shealtiel, Jehoiachin's son, is our next number eight, the father who signals a new beginning in God's unfolding plan. During the life of Shealtiel, Persia had conquered the kingdom of Babylon. The nation of Israel remained in Babylon, and was now under the rule of the kingdom of Persia while their homeland still lay in ruins. King Cyrus, king of Persia, issued a decree that provided another "new beginning." He decreed that the Temple in Jerusalem should be rebuilt. He therefore allowed a remnant of Jews under the leadership of a man named Zerubbabel to return to Jerusalem for that purpose. Zerubbabel was the son of Shealtiel, and the grandson of the last rightful king to the throne of Judah, Jehoiachin. You see, had the kingdom of Judah not been conquered, these men would have become King Shealtiel and King Zerubabel. Zerubbabel and a high priest named Joshua, along with two prophets, Haggai and Zechariah, led a remnant of Jews back to Jerusalem where the Temple was rebuilt.

The son of Zerubbabel is our next number ten. Abiud took over the leadership of the Jews in Jerusalem for many years after the Temple was rebuilt under his father's direction. Under Abiud, the practice of daily sacrifices and worship resumed, and the culture of Israel was restored in their own land, although not under their own rule, but under the rule of the king of Persia. This worship and activity in the Temple would continue in Jerusalem from the 6th century B.C. up until after the time of Jesus.

Ten generations after Abiud, another significant individual would emerge. This individual would also be 14 generations from the carrying off of the Jews into Babylon, which was 14 generations after King David, who lived 14 generations after Abraham. Our next number 10 and number 14 would become known as the *second Adam* who would begin the transition of the *earthly* kingdom Israel into a *heavenly* Kingdom manifested on the Earth. He also would be responsible for the restoration of the worship of God, restoring man's intimacy and oneness with the Creator.

The other 11 tribes of Israel had now disappeared into obscurity, and the remnant of the tribe of Judah began to scatter all over the world as the Persian Empire was conquered by the Greeks under Alexander the Great, and then as the Greeks were conquered by the Romans. However, God continued to work through His remnant of the Jews wherever they were and especially through their prophets.

The Jewish prophets continued to foretell of a promised redeemer, one who would set up an eternal Kingdom that would *"crush…all the others"* (Dan. 2:40). The Jews who continued to live in captivity never lost their identity wherever they would go, and they never stopped looking for their promised *Messiah*, the *"anointed one"* who would come and deliver them from their captors.

OK, class? Here's the plan! God's plan, not theirs!

The prophets foretold of a coming King, who would be rejected, despised of men, and beaten, who would suffer much in order to restore the spiritual bond of people with their Creator by overcoming evil and defeating death. (See Isaiah 53.) The Jews, however, looked toward a deliverer who would defeat their enemies, gather them back into their land, and rule the world from Jerusalem. They believed their Messiah would be an earthly military leader. They could only see their circumstances, and they wanted deliverance from them. They did not have a spiritual deliverance in mind. They were thinking in the here and now and not with eternity in view. In the Jews' plan, evil and the potential for evil would still exist because lucifer, the purveyor of evil would still be upon the Earth attempting to stir it up!

You see, by delivering humankind from spiritual death, God would also deliver them from a physical, eternal death. That is what God really was up to in His plan of redemption: first, restore the spiritual link with the Creator, and then the *seen* creation would be restored to its original created order, which also included eternal life free from the presence and the potential for evil. This physical restoration would be accomplished by a physical battle fought later on by an army of the spiritually restored mudcakes led by King Jesus. Only then would the redemption of the spiritual and the physical creation be full and complete. God always has a bigger picture in mind! *We can be so focused on the temporal things of life that we lose sight of the eternal things upon which we should really focus.*

What happens in the physical or **seen** *world is a manifestation of spiritual activity.* When we see evil in this world occur, it is a manifestation of the activity of demonic spirits; good is a manifestation of the activity of the Spirit of the living God. As I have heard the evangelist Oral Roberts say many times, "God is a good God; the devil is a bad devil."

God knew that by restoring the spirits of people to intimacy with Him, the physical world be restored to its originally created order. Eden would be restored when intimacy was restored. Eden then would become known as *"the Kingdom of our God."*

So, if you are one of these people who asks, *"If God is a loving God, how can He allow evil in this world?"* the answer is—He doesn't! He is going to destroy evil, but He has first provided a way of escape for humankind through redemption by a *second Adam* who, in what we could call a "reverse rebellion," would restore what was lost in Adam's rebellion.

He tarries to give *you* time!

As I stated before, **your life is a brief moment in eternity for the purpose of your redemption.** *How you live your life and whether you have accepted this redemption determines where you will spend that eternity, in the Kingdom of our God, or in the kingdom prepared for lucifer known as hell. Perhaps it is time, if you have not already done so, to visit that part in the back of the book entitled, "The Secret of Eternal Life."*

Now back to the Jews and their prophets.

One of the most important events described by God in the *Tanakh,* (the Old Testament) for the faithful Jew, is the coming of Messiah to Earth to redeem His people and to establish the authority and rule of God among the peoples of the world.

Throughout the *Tanakh,* the Lord gave pictures or "pre-types" of how this redemptive package He was putting together would work. Take, for example, the story of Joseph in the last chapters of the Book of Genesis. Joseph's brothers tried to kill him, and he ended up enslaved in Egypt. He was falsely accused, and after a time in prison, he was exalted and became a leader in Egypt. When his brothers went to Egypt because of the widespread famine, *they failed to recognize Joseph as he provided a way for them to be saved.* The parallel of this event to the events of Jesus's life is stunning.

We have already discussed the parallel of Abraham, who was willing to sacrifice his son, *his only son* (see John 3:16), as a remission for sins upon the very rock where the Temple would one day be built many years later. It is also at the very place from which God, through His Son Jesus, will rule His eternal Kingdom.

We also discussed the parallel of Boaz and Ruth and the *kinsman-redeemer* law in Israel, and there are other types of this redemptive plan throughout the Old Testament.

Yes, fingerprints of a loving God are all over the place! *He left us a road map to redemption, restored intimacy with God, and eternal life.*

God knew that the mudcakes would need some help in recognizing the redemption He was about to provide. He, therefore, provided a way for those who were truly seeking the Messiah to recognize Him when He came.

God always spoke to His people Israel through His prophets, whose writings appear in the Tanakh (Old Testament). These prophecies told of the fate of unrepentant Israel, the coming Messiah, the restoration and gathering of the Jews back to their land, and the coming Kingdom on Earth ruled by this Messiah.

Unequivocally, Jesus Christ fulfilled each and every prophecy given regarding the coming Messiah, including the very first one given to Eve in the Garden of Eden!

Remember, God said to the serpent, *"I will put enmity between you and the woman, and between your offspring and hers; He will crush your head, and you will strike his heel"* (Gen. 3:15).

Let us take a look at what these prophets foretold about this coming Messiah and how Jesus fulfilled each and every one of these prophecies. The prophecies in regard to the future Kingdom have yet to be fulfilled, but the ones that are signs of that coming Kingdom are being fulfilled and can be seen in the news every day. Because the prophecies of these prophets have proven so accurate, we can only expect that the others in time will be fulfilled as well.

There are so many prophecies regarding the coming Messiah that it appears humanly impossible for one individual to fulfill them, yet Jesus did. Author and speaker Josh McDowell took a closer look at the probability of such a feat. The task of calculating the probability of one individual fulfilling *every* prophecy was so immense that they decided instead to have mathematicians calculate the probability of one individual fulfilling only *eight* of these prophecies. The resultant probability was 10 to the 17th power for you mathematicians. The number would look like this:

One chance in 100,000,000,000,000,000. You can't even say it, can you?

They also calculated that the probability would be equivalent to covering the entire state of Texas with silver dollars two feet deep, marking one of them, mixing them up, spreading them all over the state, and then having a blindfolded person select the marked one at random on the first try.

You see, multiple prophets over a long period of time without contact with each other laid out an improbable scenario that could only be met by one under heavenly, supernatural power. Some of the same prophetic qualifications were given by more than one prophet. No imposter could ever accomplish such a feat.

Let's take a sampling of just some of these prophecies and their fulfillment, not even looking at the ones in the Book of Revelation in the New Testament. This is not an exhaustive list, but I am sure you will get the idea.

I will give a list of the prophecies, including where they are found, and where the fulfillment is recorded. I will not endeavor to comment on each of these lest we end up with one of the longest books written.

Ready? Let's go.

Prophecy, OT Reference, and NT Fulfillment

The Messiah would:

1. Be a descendant of David (see 2 Sam. 7:12-13; Matt. 1:1,6; Luke 3:31).

2. Be eternal, without beginning or end (see Mic. 5:2; John 8:58).

3. Be the only Son of God and God Himself (see Ps. 2:7; Prov. 30:4; Matt. 3:17; Luke 1:32).

4. Be a prophet like Moses (see Deut. 18:15; John 7:40; Acts 2:19-20).

5. Be in a ministry according to Isaiah 61:1-2 (see Isa. 61:1-2; Luke 4:18).

6. Be in a healing ministry (see Isa. 35:5-6; Matt. 11:5; Luke 17:12-19).

7. Begin ministry in Galilee (see Isa. 9:1; Matt. 4:12-17).

8. Be without sin (see Isa. 53:9; 1 Pet. 2:22).

9. Bear reproach and sin of others (see Isa. 53:12; Rom. 15:3).

10. Be a priest (see Ps. 110:4; Heb. 5:5-6; 6:20).

11. Be riding a donkey entering Jerusalem (see Zech. 9:9; Mark 11:1-11; John 12:12-16).

12. Be in authority entering the Temple (see Mal. 3:1; Matt. 21:12; John 2:13-22).

13. Be known by God's name, *Mighty God, I Am* (see Isa. 9:6; Jer. 23:6; Luke 22:70; Phil. 2:9).

14. Be born of a virgin (see Isa. 7:14; Matt. 1:23; Luke 1:26-35).

15. Be preceded by a "messenger," John the Baptist (see Isa. 40:3-5; Mal. 3:1; Matt. 3:1-3; Luke 3:2-6).

16. Be pierced in hands and feet during execution (see Ps. 22:16; Zech. 12:10; Luke 24:39; John 19:34-37).

17. Be put to death with no bones broken like a Passover lamb (see Exod. 12:46; Num. 9:12; Ps. 34:20; John 19: 33-36).

18. Be raised from the dead (see Isa. 53:9-10; Matt. 28:1-20; Acts 2:23-36).

19. Ascend to Heaven to sit at the right hand of God (see Ps. 16:11; 68:18; 110:1; Luke 24:51; Acts 1:9-11; 7:55).

20. Be born in Bethlehem (see Mic. 5:2; Matt. 2:1; Luke 2:4-7).

21. Be adored by great people (see Ps. 72:10-11; Matt. 2:1-11).

22. Have the anointing of the Spirit of God (see Isa. 11:2; 61:1; Matt. 3:16; John 3:34; Acts 10:38).

23. Be rejected by His own people, the Jews (see Isa. 53:2; 63:3; Ps. 69:8; Mark 6:3; Luke 9:58; John 1:11).

24. Be hated (see Ps. 69:4; Isa. 49:7; John 15:24-25).

25. Be plotted against by both Jews and Gentiles (see Ps. 2:1-2; Acts 4:27).

26. Be betrayed by one close to Him (see Ps. 41:9; 55:12-24; Matt. 26:21-25; John 13:18-21).

27. Betrayed for 30 pieces of silver (see Zech. 11:12; Matt. 26:16).

28. His price, the 30 pieces of silver, then used to buy a potter's field (see Zech. 11:13; Matt. 27:7).

29. Be executed 483 days (69 weeks) after the walls of Jerusalem rebuilt (see Dan. 9:24-26; Luke 23:33).

30. Be forsaken by the disciples (see Zech. 13:7; Matt. 26:31,56).

31. Be struck on the cheek during trial (see Mic. 5:1; Matt. 27:30).

32. Be spit on (see Isa. 50:6; Matt. 26:67; 27:30).

33. Be mocked (see Ps. 22:7-8; Matt. 27:31; 39-44).

34. Be beaten (see Isa. 50:6; Matt. 26:67; 27:26,30).

35. Ask for a drink during execution (see Ps. 22:15; John 19:28).

36. Given vinegar to quench His thirst (see Ps. 69:21; Matt. 27:34).

37. Be considered a criminal (see Isa. 53:12; Matt. 27:38).

38. Be buried with the rich (see Isa. 53:9; Matt. 27:57-60).

39. Be followed by Gentiles as well as Jews (see Isa. 11:10; 42:1; Acts 10:45).

40. Be received by the Gentiles (see Isa. 11:10; 42:1-4; 49:1-12; Matt. 12:21; Acts 10:45).

Whew! Have I made my point? Better yet, have I made *His* point?

The fact is that there are more prophecies than I have taken the time to record here. Remember, there is only a one in 100,000,000,000,000,000 chance that any one individual could and would fulfill only eight of these prophecies.

Jesus's supernatural fulfillment of these prophesies confirms that God is responsible for His existence! Yet most of the world does not even know who He is and lumps Him together with others who lived and died and are still in their graves! *Why? It is because they have never investigated the unsearchable and unexplainable Jesus Christ.*

How about you? Do you know this Jesus?

In the next chapter, we are going to look at the life of this *second Adam* a bit more closely so you can get to know Him better. All of the history of the world has been building to this point, to this coming *deliverer who will change the course of humankind and restore intimacy with the Creator once again.*

Let's trace these Jewish men listed in Matthew chapter 1, these *kings who never were kings,* and see how we get to this point in the history of the world and the plan to create a *new world order.* Let's also see how we get to this point in God's plan to redeem His mudcakes who were lost in the first mudcake rebellion.

God does so by creating a second mudcake rebellion! This rebellion would be used to counter the effects of the first mudcake rebellion. This is that "reverse rebellion" I mentioned earlier.

Praise eternal God! I long to worship You at Your throne!

If you recall, we left Jerusalem in the hands of Abiud, our last number ten and the fourth generation from the "carrying off" of the Jews to Babylon, which means we need to look ahead another ten generations from Abiud and 14 generations from Jehoiachin to see where this leads. I think you already can guess. Let's start counting these kings who never were, but who would have reigned as kings had the nation of Judah/Israel been obedient to God's commands. God continued to track these kings in order to fulfill His promise to David that his heirs would sit on the eternal throne in a Kingdom that would never end. We will start with Abiud's son and next king who never was, Eliakim, the first in our next list of ten and the fifth in our list of 14 (see Matt. 1).

1. Eliakim—5 of 14

2. Azor—6 of 14

3. Zadok—7 of 14

4. Achin—8 of 14

5. Eliud—9 of 14

6. Eleazar—10 of 14

7. Matthan—11 of 14

8. Jacob—12 of 14

Let's stop here for a moment. I want to point out that our *"new beginnings"* Grampa (remember our first was Methuselah) just so happens to have the same name as the patriarch who was the grandson of Abraham. Jacob, who was also known as "Israel," was the one from whom the remnant known as the nation of Israel descended and began. This later Jacob is signaling a "new beginning," a new nation of Israel, a spiritual Israel, one founded by a King who would reign eternally in a Kingdom that would never end, just as God had promised King David. I for many years skipped over this part of the Book of Matthew, never seeing this, as I am sure most of you have done. In fact, God just revealed this to me as I listed this group of ten!

God's fingerprint here is so big—it's unquestionable! He really wants you to notice here that it is His hand working all this out. Why? Just watch!

So then who is this son of this "new beginnings" Jacob anyway? It is:

9. Joseph—13 of 14. The husband of Mary; yes, the Joseph of your nativity scene would have been King Joseph of Judah had the kingdom not been conquered!

Sorry, readers, I heard some of our skeptics say, "All right now, just a minute here. If you say that Jesus was born of a virgin, then Joseph cannot be Jesus's father, but maybe only his 'stepfather.'" It is true; Joseph was not Jesus's biological father. Jesus was instead the seed of the Spirit of God in the womb of Mary, the mudcake Jesus's biological mother.

That's no problem here for a number of reasons!

First of all, Mary also was a descendant of David as shown in Luke 3:23-38. In Hebrew society, the mother's lineage was also important. In fact, today you are eligible for Israeli citizenship if you are the child of a Jewish mother or grandmother. But here is where it really gets interesting!

Let's time travel back to the Garden of Eden where Adam and Eve just had eaten of the *Tree of the Knowledge of Good and Evil*. God is talking to the serpent and judging him because of his deception of this first couple. In this first prophecy regarding the promised deliverer, God says, *"I will put enmity between you and the* **woman,** *and between your offspring and* **her** *offspring. He will bruise your head, and you will bruise his heel"* (Gen. 3:15 NKJV). Wait, what about Adam? He was there; he ate of the tree too!

You see, God at the very moment man and woman fell was acknowledging the virgin birth, that the deliverer would be produced from the woman, by the very seed of God and not from the seed of a fallen man. He would produce this deliverer by using His created being, thereby correcting or restoring His first creation.

With the words *"I will put,"* God acknowledged that He is the One who would bring about the enmity between the serpent and the woman, that He was the one who would produce this offspring with the woman, and that this promised deliverer would come from His seed and that of the woman. He would defeat satan using the very mudcake satan first deceived, a woman! It is Mary who is the most important one here, and Joseph makes it a completely royal household!

And now, class, for our number 10 and our number 14 generation!

10. Jesus of Nazareth! *"Wonderful, Counselor, the Mighty God, Everlasting Father, the Prince of Peace; of the increase of His government and peace there will be no end!"* (Isa. 9:6).

We have a lot to be excited about, those of us who know Jesus, that is, so let's go on to the next chapter and see just who this Jesus is!

Chapter 15

The Second Adam

"When a person comes to Christ, God recreates again and says, 'Let there be Light.'" –Billy Graham

Sixty generations from Adam, the most significant mudcake of them all was about to be born.

The fulfillment of the promise in Genesis 3:15 was announced to a woman named Mary 60 generations from Eve. Not only was the birth of Jesus foretold to Mary, but the birth of the prophesied messenger, John the Baptist, was also foretold. John would precede Jesus to prepare the way for His ministry. Let's pick up the account in Luke chapter 1:

> *In the sixth month, God sent the angel Gabriel to Nazareth, a town in Galilee, to a virgin pledged to be married to a man named Joseph, a descendant of David. The virgin's name was Mary. The angel went to her and said, "Greetings, you who are highly favored! The Lord is with you." Mary was greatly troubled at his words and wondered what kind of greeting this might be. But the angel said to her, "Do not be afraid, Mary, you have*

*found favor with God. You will be with child and give birth to a son, and you are to give Him the name Jesus. He will be great and **will be called the Son of the Most High.** The Lord God will give Him the throne of His father David, and He will reign over the house of Jacob forever; **His kingdom will never end.**" "How will this be," Mary asked the angel, "since I am a virgin?" The angel answered, "The Holy Spirit will come upon you, and the power of the Most High will overshadow you. **So the holy one to be born will be called the Son of God.** Even Elizabeth your relative is going to have a child in her old age, and she who was said to be barren is in her sixth month. For nothing is impossible with God." "I am the Lord's servant," Mary answered. "May it be to me as you have said." Then the angel left her* (Luke 1:26-38).

The Birth of Jesus

Now for the fulfillment of the promised deliverer these generations had longed for:

In those days Caesar Augustus issued a decree that a census should be taken of the entire Roman world. (This was the first census that took place while Quirinius was governor of Syria.) And everyone went to his own town to register. So Joseph also went up from the town of Nazareth in Galilee to Judea, to Bethlehem the town of David, because he belonged to the house and line of David. He went there to register with Mary, who was pledged to be married to him and was expecting a child.

While they were there, the time came for the baby to be born, and she gave birth to her firstborn, a son. She wrapped Him in

cloths and placed Him in a manger, because there was no room
for them in the inn (Luke 2:1-7).

The Shepherds and the Angels

The very first mudcakes to be heralded with news of the Messiah were
humble shepherds:

*And there were shepherds living out in the fields nearby,
keeping watch over their flocks at night. An angel of the Lord
appeared to them, and the glory of the Lord shone around
them, and they were terrified. But the angel said to them, "Do
not be afraid. I bring you good news of great joy that will be
for all the people.* **Today in the town of David a Savior
has been born to you; He is Christ the Lord.** *This will
be a sign to you: You will find a baby wrapped in cloths and
lying in a manger."* **Suddenly a great company of the
heavenly host appeared with the angel, praising God
and saying, "Glory to God in the highest, and on earth
peace to men on whom His favor rests."** *When the angels
had left them and gone into heaven, the shepherds said to one
another, "Let's go to Bethlehem and see this thing that has
happened, which the Lord has told us about." So they hurried
off and found Mary and Joseph, and the baby, who was lying
in the manger. When they had seen Him, they spread the word
concerning what had been told them about this child, and all
who heard it were amazed at what the shepherds said to them.
But Mary treasured up all these things and pondered them
in her heart. The shepherds returned, glorifying and praising
God for all the things they had heard and seen, which were just
as they had been told* (Luke 2:8-20).

God must re-create; He must reestablish the dominion on Earth He had given His mudcakes in the Garden of Eden. He must restore that which was stolen from them through their disobedience in the first mudcake rebellion in Eden. Before He could restore the created world to its original intent, He must first restore the spirits of people to intimacy with the Spirit of the Living God, the Creator. Why?

Once the mudcakes are restored in spirit, in union with the Creator, then all of creation can be restored!

Just as He did with Adam, He must once again breathe the breath of His Spirit directly into the body of a man. Then, just as the mudcakes had lost their dominion and intimacy with God through *disobedience,* they would be afforded the opportunity to receive back their rightful standing before God through *obedience.*

God would not remake their corrupted physical bodies yet; therefore, this restored or rejoined spirit within the obedient mudcakes would be housed within a corrupted physical body until a later time when God would once again give them glorified bodies.

This restoration would require another *mudcake rebellion;* this time it would be not against God, but against evil, sin, and death. This rebellion would be accomplished by One who would choose obedience even if it meant death on a Cross. He would need a perfect spirit in the flesh of a man so that the flesh could be sacrificed just as the flesh of animals had been sacrificed for a temporary atonement. The sacrifice of animals only "covered" Israel's sins; it could not take them away. Animal sacrifice was a temporary fix until the ultimate sacrifice could be made. The flesh of this ultimate sacrifice would be sacrificed to atone for the sins of those who would choose to rebel in their own personal mudcake rebellions. Their rebellions would also be against sin and against satan, and they would receive the Spirit of the Creator as a result.

The *third mudcake rebellion* is a personal rebellion, one that each of us must decide to enter into—or not.

The Creator knew that He must destroy evil once and for all so that it could never enter the heavenly Kingdom. The unjust sacrifice of one without personal sin would pay the debt of personal sin for every mudcake who would ever choose to rebel against lucifer and enable them to return to a right relationship with the Creator. The spirits of these obedient ones would eternally be restored to the Creator, and their physical bodies would be restored to perfection when the Kingdom finally manifested on Earth. In the meantime, their spirits would be released to their Creator upon the physical death of their corrupted fleshly bodies, which would remain on Earth. Their spirits would rejoin their bodies when they are resurrected and re-created according to their original design of Eden in the *seen* Kingdom of Heaven.

No wonder the angels were singing! Over a period of thousands of Earth years, the angels had been watching and waiting for the deliverer promised to Eve. The Bible tells us that the angels rejoice when one person is saved; this celebration must have been incredible!

We always see these pictures at Christmas of the nice little choir of angels in the sky singing to the shepherds, but I contend that this celebration was probably more like when the Holy Spirit falls on the participants of a massive *"church-lady"* convention—dancing, singing, shouting. Can you get a picture of that in your mind? No wonder the shepherds took off for town! I don't think they said in King James English, *"Let us now go see this thing which has come to pass."* I think it was more like, *"Wow, man…this is awesome! We gotta go see this. C'mon, these angels are pumped! Let's go see what they are shouting about."*

The Bible tells us that God is no respecter of persons, which means that His love or redemption is not dependent on our status in this world. The first people to learn about the birth of the Christ were shepherds. Being a shepherd was the lowest level of work one could do in the society of that day, yet

God sent angels to tell the shepherds first! The shepherds hurried off to see this new life, foretold long ago.

A new life, or was it? Who was and is this Jesus?

This small child was the embodiment of the Holy Spirit of the Creator in the flesh of an infant who would be 100 percent man and 100 percent God. *This God-Man was the stamped image of the Almighty God in a person so that we could see God!* (See Hebrews 1:3.) Jesus by His own admission was God. He said while upon this Earth, *"Anyone who has seen Me has seen the Father"* (John 14:9). This coming to Earth of God in a man's body would be tantamount to me choosing to become an earthworm, crawling around in the garden with the other earthworms. He was God, and humanity was full of sin and wallowing in the dirt. I suppose I would be willing to do that—if I loved the earthworms as much as God loves His children.

My wife Andi once wrote, "Isn't it wonderful how God took on the humblest of human forms? He took the form of a human child, an infant with His birthing crib in the manger of an animal, in an animal shelter. He had to allow human parents to change His diaper and care for His most basic needs in order to meet our most important need—redemption!"

We cannot go back to the beginning, for it did not begin in the womb of Mary. In John 8:56-58, Jesus told the Jews that it was He who had talked to Moses from the bush (see Exod. 3:2-6; 13-14). He also prayed, asking God to *give Him the glory He had before the world was* (see John 17:5). The prophet Micah foretold His coming as one *"whose goings forth have been from of old, from everlasting"* (Mic. 5:2 KJV).

We cannot go back to His beginning; neither can we go forward far enough for His death. It is true that He did die, but it was only a momentary cessation of bodily activity for three days. He came back into His body, alive again, and He will remain that way for eternity. This will also be true for the spirits of those who accept freely His choice as God to take human form and to live and die as a man-sacrifice for the purpose of our redemption. He was a man whose Spirit was bounded by eternity on both sides of His earthly life in the flesh for 33 years. God voluntarily allowed Himself to be born, and He voluntarily allowed Himself to die in order to be a once-and-for-all sacrifice. Then He rose from that death to once and for all defeat sin and death and the purveyor of it, lucifer!

The apostle John in John chapter 1 also attests to His eternal pre-existence and calls Him the *Word*. The society of the day was greatly influenced by Greek philosophy, and knowledge was held in high regard. John calls Him the *Word* not only because was He the promised perfect sacrifice for redemption, but also because He was the very *Word* of God (see John 1:1).

There was no higher knowledge than the Word of God, the very Word that flung the Earth and the stars into space, lit up the sun, and created these mudcakes whom He now sought to redeem. That Creator now speaks a *Word* of redemption and restoration and embodies it in a mudcake body to be sacrificed to pay for all the sin of the world. Jesus amazed the scribes in the Temple at the age of 12 and as an adult teaching from the Hebrew because He had never been trained to do so. The reason He could do so was because *He was the Word of God!*

Jesus also further attested to His deity by allowing Himself to be worshiped nine times in the New Testament, despite His statement in Matthew 4:10 that *"no one should receive worship but God, not even angels."* (By the way, angel worship has grown in these days even by those professing to be Christians. Jesus said this ought not to be; He alone should be worshiped, prayed to, and regarded as deity. *No one else!)* Angels are ministering servants of the Most High God; they are repulsed by the worship of men and women. It goes against their servant nature.

It is important to note here that Jesus had a favorite name for Himself. Yes, we mostly refer to Him as the *Christ* (the anointed one) and the *Son of God*. God the Father even referred to Him as His *"Beloved Son"* at Jesus's baptism in the river Jordan by John the Baptist. Jesus, when speaking of Himself, always referred to Himself by another name.

Before we get to Jesus' favorite name for Himself, let me clear up something that has been difficult for many people to understand: the idea of the *Trinity* or *triune God.* Specifically, we are referring to the concept of *God the Father, God the Son, and God the Holy Spirit.* Doesn't that make three? How can they all be God when there is only one God?

Our misunderstanding of this comes from trying to fit God into a "mind box" as we talked about earlier in this book. You see, it is true that there is only one God, but there are three different aspects of His personality. I began to understand this as a kid when someone gave me a clover leaf. (I hear there are four-leaf clovers, but I have never seen one.) The ones I've seen only have three independent leaves connected to one stem. This gives us a picture of the Trinity; the three are one, but there are three different aspects of His Godhood. The first is as *God the Father,* a spiritual being who is the Creator of all things, the Almighty God who rules the universe. The second is as *God the Son*, the God-Man we have been talking about, the aspect of the triune God who became flesh, but possessed the Spirit of the Father God. The third is as the *Holy Spirit,* that aspect of God who is able to indwell something. The Holy Spirit was able to indwell the *Son*—and all who receive the redemption provided by the Son. This indwelling *Holy Spirit* restores the intimacy and connection with *God the Father.* He is our connector with Jesus the Son and with Father God.

Perhaps understanding this illustration will help you understand the *triune* personality of God, three separate and distinct persons in one God. Take me for an example. There is only one of me, but there are different aspects or roles in my life in accordance with my nature. I am a son, I am a brother, I am a husband, and I am a father. I am not four different individuals; it is simply me in four different roles that are consistent with my nature. Fulfilling those aspects of my life is part of my nature. It is *not* part of my nature to be a daughter, a sister, a wife, or a mother; that's against my nature. In God there are not only different roles (like I can have), but there are three distinct persons in one God, each with a unique role. In my illustration, however, there is only one person—me, with three different roles. This is a hard thing for us, with our finite minds, to understand.

Being an all-powerful God who desires to redeem, restore, and have an intimate relationship with His creation is part of God's nature, and He needs all three aspects of His nature to accomplish that. To be evil, deceitful, or unloving is *not* part of His nature. So, like the three leaves on a clover stalk, the leaf of the Father, the leaf of the Son, and the leaf of the Holy Spirit are three separate aspects or persons of the nature of God—the Creator (Father), the Redeemer (Son), and the Indweller (Holy Spirit).

God says to *you*, I can be your Father and your God *(Father);* I can understand what it is to be a person of flesh, and I can redeem you and blot out your sin *(Son);* and I can be with you wherever you go, guide you, and have an intimate relationship with you *(Holy Spirit)*.

In a nutshell, God not only made all flesh, He took it on Himself and became flesh, and then He puts His Spirit within all those who receive Him.

*Simply put, God wants so much to have a relationship with you, that He will put His Holy Spirit in you if you accept the Son's sacrifice of redemption. He goes where you go, and He **never** will leave! It is important that you understand who God is to **you!***

Now, back to that favorite name Jesus had for Himself. Even though Jesus acknowledged His deity as the Son of God, He mostly referred to Himself by another name, *the Son of Man*.

In order to understand this term, we must look back again to the Garden of Eden and to God's promise that Eve's offspring would *"crush"* the serpent's head. In expectation of this promise, she promptly named her son "Cain" or "the deliverer," but he turned out to be a murderer of her other son Abel instead.

Jesus recognized that He was the Son of the *seed* of the woman who would destroy satan's head. (Lucifer/satan recognized this as well, which is why he sought to destroy Jesus first.)

Jesus was not only referring to this promised deliverer of Genesis 3:15, but also to Daniel's prophecy in which he saw *"one like a **Son of Man,** coming with the clouds of heaven"* (Dan. 7:13). When Jesus responded to the High Priest in Matthew 26:62-66 and referred to Himself as the fulfillment of the prophecy of Daniel 7:13, the High Priest cried, "Blasphemy," rent his clothes, and sought Jesus's death. Every time Jesus referred to Himself as the *Son of Man,* He was attesting to the fact that He was the promised deliverer of Genesis 3:15.

This re-creation of the mudcakes through a new *Son of Man* is what started the process of taking dominion, of restoring the original creation spiritually first, and then physically in the not-too-distant future.

As the God-Man, Jesus was qualified to understand and to represent us. Let's take a look at a passage in the Book of Hebrews 2:1-18. It starts with a warning to pay attention, which many are not doing in this current day!

> *We must pay more careful attention, therefore, to what we have heard, so that we do not drift away. For if the message spoken by angels was binding, and every violation and disobedience received its just punishment, **how shall we escape if we ignore such a great salvation?** This salvation, which was first announced by the Lord, was confirmed to us by those who heard Him. God also testified to it by signs, wonders and various miracles, and gifts of the Holy Spirit distributed according to His will* (Hebrews 2:1-4).

Jesus Made Like His Brothers

Made like one of us, Jesus fully understands and sympathizes with our humanity:

> *It is not to angels that He has subjected the world to come, about which we are speaking. But there is a place where someone has testified: "What is man that You are mindful of him, the son of man that You care for him? You made him a little lower than the angels; You crowned him with glory and honor and put everything under his feet." In putting everything under him, God left nothing that is not subject to him. Yet at present we do not see everything subject to him. But we see Jesus, who was made a little lower than the angels, now crowned with glory and honor because He suffered death, **so that by the grace of God He might taste death for everyone.** In bringing many sons to glory, it was fitting that God, for whom and through whom everything exists, should make the author of their salvation perfect through suffering. **Both the one who makes men holy and those who are made holy are of the same family. So Jesus is not ashamed to call them brothers.** He says, "I will declare your name to My brothers; in the presence of the congregation I will sing Your praises." And again, "I will put My trust in Him."*
>
> *And again He says, "Here am I, and the children God has given Me."*
>
> **Since the children have flesh and blood, He too shared in their humanity so that by His death He might destroy him who holds the power of death—that is, the devil—** *and free those who all their lives were held in slavery by their fear of death.*

For surely it is not angels He helps, but Abraham's descendants.
**For this reason He had to be made like His brothers in
every way, in order that He might become a merciful
and faithful high priest in service to God, and that
He might make atonement for the sins of the people.
Because He Himself suffered when He was tempted,
He is able to help those who are being tempted**
(Hebrews 2:5-18).

Simply put, He is a majestic heavenly being, God Himself, who can sympathize with our weakness. The atonement He made for us allows us to come to God and be understood. Jesus stands between us, 100 percent God and 100 percent man, totally without sin, perfect!

Imagine the terror in the heart of lucifer when he saw this second Adam. He had not seen a mudcake without sin since the Garden of Eden. No wonder he sought to destroy this mudcake, and while it appeared that he would succeed at the Cross of Calvary, instead, he was playing right into God's plan. From the very moment Jesus was born, satan sought to destroy Him.

Because Jesus came in an unexpected form, He was rejected by most people of the day. Unfortunately, the same is true today; Jesus comes to us in a form that most of us do not want to accept, so we reject Him and look for a better way on our own. We pursue worldly wealth and desires, not wanting to surrender anything to the One who can give us all we could ever want and more.

Jesus spent only three of His 33 years on Earth teaching us about this coming Kingdom and inviting all to be part of it; then He went to Calvary to purchase a ticket for all to ride the train to this Kingdom. The ticket to ride is free, but we have to ask for and receive it. What do I mean by a "ticket"?

The Kingdom Train

Just before I wrote this chapter, I had a dream.

In the dream I was on a train track; there were platform walls on either side of me with no way off the tracks. I could see and hear a train coming incredibly fast, its golden light glistening and getting brighter and brighter as it rumbled toward me. There were others on the track as well. In my dream I began to run, my feet very heavy, while the train grew closer and closer at lightning speed. It was futile to try and run on my own, so I braced for the moment of impact.

There was a crack of lightning and thunder; at that moment, I suddenly found myself in the most comfortable train seat beside my wife Andi. She was very smiling and happy, enjoying the ride. The car was incredibly beautiful and laden with pure gold trim, gold signage, and diamonds. As I sat admiring it, a hand came down on my shoulder. I turned to see the conductor in the most incredible uniform, with real gold buttons and trim. His face was the kindest face I had ever seen. I responded to the hand on my shoulder by saying, "I thought you were going to run me over!" With a big smile on His face, He reached to the back of the seat in front of me and took a ticket from the ticket pocket; He punched it with a golden puncher, then handed it to me, smiling and gently shaking His head: "No, you have a ticket!" I looked at the ticket, and the name of the train was *"The Kingdom of God."* The destination on the ticket read simply *"The Kingdom."* I knew the conductor; I recognized His face, those eyes that looked deep within me and filled me with the warmth of love—I had seen it before!

As I woke up from this dream, I heard the verse, *"From the days of John the Baptist until now the **kingdom of heaven** suffers violence, and violent men take it by force"* (Matt. 11:12 NASB).

While I believe this dream had some personal application to me, it impressed me with the fact that the price has been paid. There is nothing I can do on my own; I cannot follow the tracks and run on my own because death is approaching. But it cannot hurt me because I have a ticket, and physical death is simply a transfer to eternal life.

Interestingly, my wife Andi, who has prophetic dreams, had a dream about a train that same year. She dreamt that she was at a train station, and Oral Roberts, the great evangelist of our time, was there, getting on the train. He was not elderly in the dream, but young and vibrant, and he turned and announced to her, "I am going to see Evelyn (his wife who had died)." She shared this dream with our friends Richard and Lindsay Roberts when we were together in August 2009. Oral was elderly, but not ill at the time. Oral passed away that year just before Christmas after he announced to Richard and Lindsay at Thanksgiving that he would be with Evelyn for Christmas. I also recall telling Richard earlier that year on the phone that I discerned that Oral would go home before the end of the year after He had remarked that he knew it would not be long before his dad's passing. How did we all know? How did Andi, Richard, Oral, and I know? We knew because we all have the same Holy Spirit within, and the Holy Spirit knew and was revealing it so that they could be prepared for the impact on their ministry.

Oral was getting on the train because he had received the ticket! Our ticket is the Holy Spirit who is combined with our spirits. Upon the death of our physical bodies, those who have this ticket are transferred to the very heart of God by the Holy Spirit. The Holy Spirit within us returns to the Creator and takes our spirits with Him because our spirits are one with the Holy Spirit. Those who do not have this ticket can only return to the one they chose to follow into eternal damnation.

I have a ticket because I know intimately the face of the One who gave me the ticket! I accepted His sacrifice, and because of Him, I am qualified to ride on *"The Kingdom of God."* We get on that train and escape eternal death when we accept the Son Jesus as Savior and Lord of our lives! The reason Andi was on board when I arrived was that she was saved before me! I believe that when Oral got on that train, he sat down beside Evelyn.

Do I believe that when we die and go to Heaven we are picked up by a train? No, I don't believe it happens that way. God, through His Holy Spirit, will use things familiar to us to convey a message to us. I know that the way we are transferred is so glorious, there is no description available to us here on Earth, and so great we cannot comprehend it. This moment will be as terrifying to those who have not received their free ticket as it will be glorious to those who have.

How about you? Do you have a ticket? Do you know this *second Adam,* this *Son of Man,* or are you trying to get there on your own? I tell you it won't work; you cannot get there on your own. The Kingdom of God is coming much too fast with great power, and you need a ticket. If you don't have a ticket, it will be pure hell when the Kingdom of God arrives. The good news is that the conductor has one for you, and it is all paid for. You must just receive it.

The conductor calls, *"All aboard!"* You can get your ticket if you do not have one already by going to "The Secret of Eternal Life" at the end of this book. Don't wait until you finish. Do it now; then come back and join us in the next chapter.

Chapter 16

The Seeds of a Revolution

———•◆•———

Lucifer immediately went to work in his attempt to destroy this sinless second Adam, this promised deliverer. If he could kill Jesus before He could take back the dominion lucifer stole from the first Adam in Eden, then God's plan would be foiled. Then surely God would destroy these mudcakes, and the devil would have dominion—yes, "he would be like God!"

It would all begin before Jesus was two years old. At Christmas we often see nativity scenes depicting the three wise men visiting the baby Jesus at the stable. This is incorrect; we are not told how many of these men made this trip. The number three has been assigned because these men brought three different gifts to the second Adam.

These men were wealthy kings from the east, most likely from the area of present-day Iran, who had seen a special star appear that, according to their understanding, would announce the birth of a special King who would be above all kings. This star appeared the night of Jesus Christ's birth.

> *When they had heard the king, they departed; and, lo, the star, which they saw in the east, went before them, till it came and* ***stood*** *over where the young child was* (Matthew 2:9 KJV).

Astronomers tell us that there was a star that went super nova or exploded at that time in history. When a star becomes a super nova, the explosion makes it so much brighter that it often seems as though the star has just appeared. Over time the explosion settles down, and the star can go back into obscurity. However, the most plausible explanation for the Bethlehem star is that a triple conjunction of the star *Regulus* and the planets *Jupiter* and *Venus* created one big, bright star. This star would have been in the proper place in the sky to lead the magi, and the retrograde movement of Jupiter caused by the rotation of the Earth would have made it appear to stand, as the Bible says, over Bethlehem. Do you want to guess in what constellation this conjunction would have occurred? It's just some more fingerprints of the Father working behind the scenes—for this event occurred in the constellation of *Virgo* or the Virgin, you know, like Mary! Then it moved to the constellation of *Leo* or the Lion, you know, like Jesus, the Lion of Judah! This event has been recreated in planetariums over the years.[1]

The point is that God created the heavens and the Earth and throughout history uses His creation for His purposes as He does here. As we talked in the beginning of this book, *everything that happens in the **seen** world is a physical manifestation of that which happens in the **unseen** world.*

Where did these wise men or kings get the idea about this star? These men were not Jewish and were from the land of the Medes and the Persians.

The great historian Herodotus tells us that they these wise men were *magi* or priests in the race of the Medes; most likely they were astrologers who knew the stars and the constellations.[2] They were well acquainted with Jewish prophecy because the Jews had been carried off by Babylon and ultimately became part of the kingdom of the Medes and Persians. Held in high regard among the Medes and Persians was the one considered to be the wisest of the wise by the Medes, the Jewish prophet Daniel. Daniel's influence was still being felt hundreds of years later. They knew Daniel had prophesied a coming King, a deliverer of His people, the Jews!

God connecting the dots again!

The magi traveled to Bethlehem over a period of time, not arriving at the stable, which I and other theologians believe had long been vacated by Joseph, Mary, and their baby. These magi first went to the palace in Jerusalem; surely Herod, the king of the Jews, would know where this prophesied King would be. In doing this, they played into lucifer's plan by tipping off a notorious, self-serving, evil king!

Herod frantically called in the scribes to advise where this prophesied King was to be born, and after telling the magi of the prophecy, Herod asked them to return with news of this child's whereabouts so that he too could worship Him! He concealed his wickedness under a mask of piety. Even though he had reigned 35 years and was an old man, he could not stand the idea of a rival, a successor to his throne. Satan used this jealousy to try to accomplish his wicked scheme. Just as God uses men and women as His agents on Earth, satan in the same way uses men and women as his agents to carry out his evil plans to destroy the mudcakes and all creation. He wants to keep the dominion he stole. If he cannot take God's place in Heaven, he surely will on Earth.

This child was no threat to Herod; he had already defeated himself with his wickedness. This child also later would profess that His Kingdom was not of this world. Herod was no king anyway; he was a puppet of the Roman government in their rule of the Jews. He was not of the kingly line of David ordained by God, but was appointed by the Romans.

The magi had followed the star to Bethlehem, and after their visit to Herod, they narrowed their search to find the Child King and present Him with gifts of gold, myrrh, and frankincense. These gifts were not only valuable and would help fund Jesus's earthly parents' protective flight from Herod to Egypt, but they were also symbolic of the mission of this second Adam.

Frankincense, a balsamic juice from Eastern trees, was highly valued by the Egyptians; it was used for fumigation and embalming, and could easily be sold at a great price. Myrrh was also valuable and used for these same purposes. Myrrh was a lovely smelling perfume. Both frankincense and myrrh were associated with Jesus's "sweet smelling sacrifice" (see Eph. 5:2) on the Cross. Gold was valuable for its purchase power, but it was also used in worship and was considered a fitting gift for a King!

Wait, there is even more to the significance of these gifts, more fingerprints of God here.

Gold is not native to the land of Israel and has had to be brought there from other nations. The bringing of gold from other nations to this eternal King who will reign from Jerusalem for all eternity is symbolic of the prophecy of this coming Kingdom recorded in Isaiah 60:5: *"…The wealth of the Gentiles* [non-Jews] *shall come to you"* (NKJV), indicating that the Gentiles would bring gold and incense to this mighty coming Kingdom. The magi were doing on a small scale to this small King what the people of the world will do on a large scale when this same mighty King comes back a second time to claim His full inheritance! God proclaims in the Book of Haggai the prophet, *"The silver is Mine, and the gold is Mine,' says the Lord of Hosts"* (Hag. 2:8 NKJV).

We just keep peeling this onion of God's Word here, layer by layer, as we unfold His plan to redeem creation in the Scriptures, and it just keeps getting more powerful and potent! The Bible is a work of intricately woven *confirmations*—not *contradictions*—given to many people over many years with such an accuracy that the more one studies it, the more clearly one sees that it is divinely inspired and contains the infallible Word of God! This is my question for those who claim that Scripture is full of contradictions: How long are you going to run down those tracks holding onto a philosophy rooted in ignorance of the Word of God instead of looking into it with an open mind?

The wise men found and worshiped the Child King, and then the Spirit of God divinely intervened through dreams to protect His plan. God historically has often used dreams to communicate with those who seek Him. We are told in Matthew 2:12 that the wise men were divinely warned in a dream not to return to Herod, but to take a different route to return to their country. When they left, an angel also appeared to Joseph in a dream warning him that Herod sought the child's death and that he was to take Mary and the baby and flee to Egypt. They would remain there until after Herod's death.

Herod became, as Matthew tells us, *"exceedingly angry,"* and in his anger ordered the death of all male children two years old and under (Matt. 2:16 NKJV). When people allow themselves to be agents of evil for satan, it is unbelievable the level of evil that can come from their hearts. Herod sought to destroy the King of Glory because of his own selfish desires and spread grief throughout the kingdom with the heinous order to kill innocent little boys. It is here we see a foreboding prophecy of the prophet Jeremiah fulfilled: *"A voice was heard in Ramah, lamentation and bitter weeping, Rachel weeping for her children, refusing to be comforted for her children, because they are no more"* (Jer. 31:15 NKJV).

Rachel was a wife of Jacob (Israel) and is figuratively referred to here since she was a notable mother of the nation of Israel. Imagine the grief of mothers and fathers as satan through Herod tried to destroy God's plan, terminating the lives of many precious little boys in the process. Herod's efforts to kill Jesus were in vain, however, as Jesus was safely in Egypt.

God would deal with Herod, satan's agent. We are told in the Book of Matthew that when Herod died, Joseph was again visited in a dream and told that Herod and his henchmen were dead. Imagine the fate of one like Herod who would stand before God after trying to kill the King of Glory, God's own Son! Yes, the same fate that would be dealt to him also awaits not only satan, but all those who reject this King and the sacrifice He made for them.

My friend, do not let this fate await you; receive this King and His free gift of salvation and eternal life now. *Remember that this life is a brief moment in eternity for the purpose of your redemption!*

Joseph obeyed the directive of the angel and brought Mary and Jesus back to Israel, fulfilling yet another prophecy, this time from the prophet Hosea. In Hosea 11:1, we read the prophecy, *"...Out of Egypt I called My son,"* referring to this event. Joseph, hearing that Archelaus, Herod's son, was now king, decided not to return to the Jerusalem area, but to go north into Galilee to the city of Nazareth. Here Jesus would grow up to be a man who at the age of 30 would fulfill yet another prophecy and begin His ministry there in Galilee (see Isa. 9:1).

We do not know much of Jesus's childhood life, with the exception of two events. Prior to the family's flight to Egypt, Jesus was consecrated in the Temple where both a prophet and a prophetess recognized this infant child as the promised deliverer. Simeon, described as a *just and devout man on whom the Holy Spirit rested* (see Luke 2:29), was told by the Spirit that he would not die until He saw the promised deliverer. He took the baby in his arms and, lifting his head to Heaven, prophesied:

> *Lord, now You are letting Your servant depart in peace, according to Your word; for my eyes have seen Your salvation which You have prepared before the face of all peoples, a light to bring revelation to the Gentiles, and the glory of Your people Israel* (Luke 2:29-32 NKJV).

We are told also in Luke 2:36-38, that a prophetess known as Anna, who for 84 years had continually *"night and day"* fasted and prayed at the Temple, also prophetically recognized Jesus and spoke of Him in regard to being the promised deliverer to the nation of Israel (see Luke 2:36-38).

We know little of Jesus's days growing up in Nazareth with Joseph and Mary. Joseph, a carpenter, would have taught his trade to Jesus, and it is likely that He spent His days working with Joseph. One of his youthful experiences would have been the annual Feast of Passover trip to Jerusalem. On one trip when He was 12, Jesus gave His parents quite an anxious moment. On their return trip, they discovered He was not in the group of people from

Nazareth that they were traveling with. The roads between the cities were dangerous in those days, full of murderers and robbers, so it was customary to travel in large groups for protection. Joseph and Mary finally found Jesus in Jerusalem astonishing the teachers and leaders in the Temple with His understanding of the Scriptures. Not surprising to us though, because as we know, He was the very *Word of God.*

Ironically, this very same group of people would reject His Word 20 years later.

At the age of 12, the biblical number of government, Jesus began to lay the groundwork for a "one-world government"—His Kingdom! He continued to lay the groundwork for the very same Kingdom to which He referred when standing before Pontius Pilate at His trial: *"My kingdom is not of this world"* (John 18:36 NKJV).

Then, at about the age of 30, He would choose 12 men to lay the groundwork to form this new spiritual one-world government.

Here again is that fingerprint of God in numbers!

As *12* men established *12* tribes of Israel, which as you remember was the earthly pre-type of this coming heavenly Kingdom, Jesus would also establish His eternal Kingdom, beginning again with *12* men known to us as *disciples.* He would equip them during His life on Earth to advance His Kingdom by feeding His sheep. He would teach them to start with what they had, and He would multiply it. Jesus fed 5000 people with a little boy's lunch of five loaves and two fish. (See John 6:1-14.) He took the boy's "two-piece fish-and-biscuits happy meal" and multiplied the food to feed them all. Afterward He had them collect the leftovers. The disciples found that they had *12* baskets left over, one for each of them. Jesus had told them to "feed His sheep"; symbolically He gave them the "bread of life," while physically giving them the bread. By so doing, He taught them that He would equip them with what might be spiritually multiplied to accomplish what He was ordaining them to do. He was teaching and ordaining them to advance His Kingdom. Their work and influence would spread throughout the whole world over the ages, forming a new *remnant* in God's plan to accomplish His purposes.

Yes, we have another remnant here! *This new remnant would come to be known as the* **Church.** They would share in God's promises to Israel and in Jesus Christ's inheritance from the Father God. They would rule with Christ in the *seen* Kingdom, a physical manifestation of the *unseen* heavenly Kingdom, *a return to Eden, a Kingdom ruled by God Himself!* This Kingdom would be a *"Kingdom without end,"* overthrowing all earthly kingdoms and destroying satan in the process. That time was coming, but first He must lay the groundwork for redemption of the mudcakes.

My purpose in this chapter is not to necessarily trace the steps of the life of Jesus to Calvary; the best place to read that is in the Gospels of Matthew, Mark, Luke, and John. Instead, I want to investigate what Jesus, the One who would establish this heavenly Kingdom, taught about this Kingdom while He was on Earth.

Jesus never taught about Heaven; He only talked about the Kingdom when He was on the Earth. In the Book of Matthew alone, Jesus refers to the Kingdom over 50 times. In the four Gospels of Matthew, Mark, Luke, and John, we find Him referring to the Kingdom over 120 times. *His purpose in coming to Earth was to proclaim the arrival of God's Kingdom on Earth and through His sacrifice and blood provide a* **"ticket"** *to all who would come.* (Remember my dream of the train?)

It is difficult to cover all the things Jesus taught about the Kingdom, so what I will do here is give you a sampling from the beginning of His ministry to the Cross. Let me just list in a brief commentary some things He taught regarding the Kingdom with the biblical references. We will primarily look at the Gospel of Matthew. Matthew was one of the 12 disciples, and he wrote this account. Here is a sampling of what Jesus taught about the Kingdom:

1. John the Baptist had announced the coming Kingdom by preaching that they should *"repent, for the kingdom of heaven has come near"* (Matt. 3:2). Jesus, after being tempted by satan in the wilderness for 40 days, began to echo the message that the Kingdom was near (see Matt. 4:17).

2. Jesus's ministry consisted of teaching and preaching the Gospel of the Kingdom and healing people, which was a physical manifestation of the spiritual recreation that was coming to people. It also attested to the power of the Creator who indwelt Jesus (see Luke 4:14).

3. Jesus taught that a hierarchy would be created in the Kingdom. Those who would do the will of God and follow His commands while on Earth will become great in the Kingdom. Those who do not keep His commands will become the least in the Kingdom, even to the point that they will be kept out of the eternal Kingdom (see Matt. 5:19-20).

4. Jesus taught that your righteousness must exceed the righteousness of even those considered the most righteous in society. You must be completely righteous to enter the Kingdom or there is no reward. It is a righteousness that men and women cannot attain on their own. Only the righteousness given freely by Jesus will open the door to the Kingdom (see Matt. 5:20).

5. Jesus taught that we are to pray, *"Thy Kingdom come, Thy will be done in earth, as it is in heaven"* (Matt. 6:10). We are to pray that God's will is established on Earth, the *seen* Kingdom, as it has been established in Heaven, the *unseen* Kingdom. We are to acknowledge that it is His Kingdom (see Matt. 6:13).

6. Jesus taught that if we seek the Kingdom and its righteousness provided by God, it will bring us into a completely fulfilled life (see Matt. 6:33).

7. Jesus taught that not all who claim to be Christian will enter the Kingdom. If you claim His name without doing His will and following

His commands, you will *not* enter the Kingdom. Plain and simple, there will be and are those who are "phony" Christians. They too will be barred from the Kingdom (see Matt. 7:21).

8. Jesus taught that many will come into the Kingdom from outside of Israel (Gentiles), and many who are inside of Israel will be thrown outside of the Kingdom (see Matt. 8:11-12).

9. Jesus sent out the 12 disciples and told them to preach that the Kingdom of Heaven is near. The basis of the message then, as it is now, was to appeal to the world to seek His salvation now! (See Matthew 10.)

10. Jesus taught that a person perfect in following Old Testament law (if it were possible) would be considered inferior to one covered in the righteousness of the Christ. No one could have lived a more spiritual life than John the Baptist, yet without the righteousness of Christ to cover him, he would be considered inferior. There is nothing we can do on our own, no matter how "good" we are, to attain salvation on our own. We must receive that free ticket of Christ's righteousness to get us there! (See Matthew 11:11.)

11. Jesus taught that the *"violent"* or forceful would take back the Kingdom. Only the spiritually forceful or violent would seek the Kingdom because it would be a rebellion against the status quo. Just as physical violence was used to try and stop the Kingdom from appearing, spiritual violence would be used to establish the Kingdom of Heaven on the Earth (see Matt. 11:12).

12. Jesus taught that the casting out of demons was a sign that the Kingdom of Heaven was here (see Matt. 12:28).

13. Jesus taught that the mysteries or the secret revelations of the Kingdom are only given to those who follow Jesus (see Matt.13:11).

14. Jesus taught that the Parable of the Tares gives us a picture of the Kingdom of God. The enemy sowed tares, or weeds, in God's perfect Garden, but the owner is coming back, and He will destroy the tares at the harvest or at the *end of the age*" (see Matt. 13:39).

15. Jesus fulfilled the prophecy in Psalm 78:2 by teaching in parables. He taught in these parables that the Kingdom of God is like:

- A sower (see Matt. 13:1-23)

- Weeds or tares (see Matt. 13:24-30; 36-43)

- A mustard seed (see Matt. 13:31-32)

- Yeast (see Matt. 13:33)

- A hidden treasure (see Matt. 13:44)

- A pearl (see Matt. 13:45)

- A net (see Matt. 13:47-50)

16. Jesus taught that those who receive the teachings of the Old Testament principles and the teaching of the Kingdom will be like a homeowner who is able to bring old and new treasures out of his storeroom (see Matt. 13:52).

17. Jesus taught that the Kingdom would be within them and that there were some who would not die before they would see the Kingdom come with power. He was referring to the infilling of the Holy Spirit of the believers on the day of Pentecost (see Matt. 16:28; Luke 17:21; Acts 2).

18. Jesus taught that we must enter the Kingdom with childlike faith and that the humble in spirit would become the greatest in the Kingdom of God (see Matt. 18:3-4).

19. Jesus taught that people focused on worldly, temporal things (most people today) will find it harder to enter into the Kingdom. The irony taught here is that spiritual wealth trumps worldly wealth and makes worldly wealth more eternally valuable (see Matt. 19:21-24).

20. Jesus taught that the Kingdom of Heaven is for those who actually do the will of God in their lives, not for those who say they do. Many say they believe in Christ, but their lives and philosophies do not reflect Christ (see Matt. 21:31).

21. Jesus taught that the Kingdom is not for those who are complacent about Jesus's second coming; the Kingdom is for those who are watchful, who know the signs of His coming, and are prepared when He arrives (see Matt. 25:1-13).

22. Jesus has entrusted His servants with the truths of the Kingdom while He is away; they are to be faithful with these truths and be about the business of advancing His Kingdom until He returns (see Matt. 25:14-30).

23. Jesus taught that when the *"Son of Man"* comes in *"glory,"* He will separate the *"sheep"* (those who do His will) from the *"goats"* (those who do not His will). He will tell the sheep to come and receive their inheritance of the Kingdom, which was *"prepared for them before the foundation of the world"!* He will then also curse the goats and cast them into the same place (hell) prepared for lucifer/satan and his demons (see Matt. 25:31-46).

This is just a quick summary of what Jesus taught. Each teaching is a study in and of itself, and I could write a chapter on each one. There is much to learn in the Word of God, yet the average person spends little or no time in preparing for something with such eternal significance. *Life is short; eternity is forever!* It is eternally important for you to look deeply into the things of God and understand what is in this Word that He left to guide you. The Bible truly is the instruction manual for this life. After this life, there is no second chance!

Jesus, in His ministry, reintroduced the Kingdom lost in Eden, established it through His sacrifice, and took back dominion of the Earth from lucifer. He then gave the right to exercise that dominion to all who would accept Him. These redeemed individuals, through the work of the Holy Spirit in them, would come into His full inheritance of the Kingdom of God.

Jesus' intention was to put the Holy Spirit of the Creator God back into us! Let me say that another way, for it is important that you understand. *Jesus came the first time to provide a way for us to receive the Holy Spirit of the Creator back into us, as it was with Adam before he rebelled. He is coming the second time to establish the Kingdom of Heaven physically on Earth for all those who by their own choice received the Spirit within them.*

Receiving the Holy Spirit does not happen automatically when people are born; they must accept Him into themselves by their own decision. In Jesus's words, they must be *born again* of the Spirit. That is why you hear of people who are *born again*. The term, coined by Jesus Himself in His meeting with Nicodemus in John 3, refers to those who have willingly accepted Jesus and have made Him Lord of their lives. When they do this, they receive the Holy Spirit of the Creator to indwell them as He did in Eden before the first mud-cake rebellion.

The Old Testament people did not receive the indwelling of the Holy Spirit; only the prophets could hear from God. This was because, in contrast, the Spirit literally *rested on them* (see Luke 2:25) or because they were visited by angels.

Do you see the importance here in God first reestablishing His Spirit within the mudcakes before mounting a physical military coup against satan and sin and reestablishing the perfect created order?

If Jesus had come as the military leader the Jews were looking for, He may have delivered the Jews and restored Israel to independence, but men and women would still not be restored to intimacy with God.

Before we get to the Cross, we need to understand what was in the Creator's mind as He sought to carry out His plan to redeem and restore creation.

God must first restore His intimacy with the mudcakes before He can restore the recreated order of the world! *Lucifer/satan had stolen the dominion originally given to man by God, and God must first restore their alliance with Him in order to take back that dominion from lucifer/satan.*

Man and woman first rebelled and lost intimacy with God, and the light of God's presence went out, showing them their nakedness. Then creation went into a decline and degradation. So before restoring creation, He must first restore that intimacy with the Creator! He must put the light of the Spirit back inside of them and then allow time for men and women to come to Him. (That's where we are in this scenario now.) Once all who will come to Him have come, He then can restore the created order of the Earth to its former glory, including the very bodies of the men and women who have come to Him, those who have received the free ticket to His Kingdom!

Then, together with these renewed-in-spirit and in-dominion mudcakes, Christ will attack the forces of satan and evil on this Earth. In this final rebellion, good will rebel against evil, and Christ will cast satan out of the physical realm forever, thereby eliminating evil from the world forever! Satan will never be able to tempt those in this eternal Kingdom, who of their own will rebelled against satan, sin, and evil while they were in this evil world and thereby took back their dominion from him!

There it all is in a nutshell—what Jesus was up to in planting the seeds of this rebellion in the hearts of 12 men, multiplying those seeds for nearly 2000 years, and sealing it by going to the Cross.

It has been hard for people in all ages to get their minds around this concept. Herod understood the Messiah's Kingdom to be a political kingdom that would rival his kingdom, which is why he sought to destroy Jesus. The Jewish leaders who crucified Jesus did not understand a "spiritual king"; they wanted someone who would free them from the Romans. Even the prophesied forerunner of Jesus, John the Baptist, became disillusioned when Jesus did not mount a resistance to overthrow the Romans and get him out of prison (see Matt. 11:1-6).

Even the disciples did not get it! Their minds were on political independence for their country rather than on personal eternal salvation and restoration to intimacy with God. They never understood this until after Jesus's resurrection and ascension. Just before Jesus ascended to Heaven from the Mount of Olives, the disciples asked, *"Lord, are You at this time going to restore the kingdom to Israel?"* (Acts 1:6). It was not until later when the Holy Spirit was given to them on the Day of Pentecost that they understood and launched the work of the new *remnant,* the Church of Jesus Christ. The Holy Spirit was sent on Pentecost (see Acts 2), and intimacy was restored. The Spirit of the Creator was once again within the mudcakes who believed.

Spiritual things are sometimes not discerned without the Holy Spirit indwelling and revealing the mysteries of God to you. That is why the Word of God shows us that God shares His secrets with His friends. (See Matthew 13:11; Luke 8:10; 1 Corinthians 4:1; and Daniel 2:28.) You are a friend of God if you have the Holy Spirit indwelling you, and the only way you can receive that Spirit is by personally accepting Jesus Christ's sacrifice on the Cross of Calvary. I did not make this up; it is in the onion (the Bible) we are peeling!

The Kingdom Jesus came to found was not a political kingdom. He came to set up His throne in *your* heart to reign within *your* life; He came to transform *your* life into all He has for *you* so that *you* might reign with Him in this world and in the Kingdom to come. He wants *you* to love Him as He loves *you,* adore Him as He adores *you,* be devoted to Him as He is devoted to *you,* and to change *you* to be a reflection of His love. When *you* submit yourself to a loving God, the result is the regeneration of *your* soul and the transformation of *your* character. *You* will grow into the beauty and comfort of a transformed life indwelt by the Spirit of the living God.

That is what He has done for me, my wife, Andi, my children, Mindy and Ben, and so many others. Some have been even willing to be beaten and die themselves for what He has done for them rather than denounce Him. I do not know how people go through the trials of this life and then face death without the Holy Spirit. I could never do it because the end is so empty.

You see, I know what it is like to have Him indwelling me, sharing His mysteries with me, having an intimate friendship with my Creator, just because He loves me! Once you have that, you cannot fathom what it is like to be without that. It's that awesome! In my near-death experience, I had a taste of what is ahead, and I want it! I realized that the best this world has to offer is nothing by comparison.

I also understand, as the Lord allowed me to experience a glimpse of hell in my near-death experience, what it is like to be at that point of death without the indwelling Spirit and redemption offered by the sacrificial "Lamb of God." It is sheer terror! It is eternal separation from everyone and from God; it's hell!

. Many people ask, **would a loving God condemn people to hell for all eternity?**

No, it is their own sin that condemns them. God provided the way of escape, Jesus Christ! It is their own choice that they are condemned to hell. If you do not choose Jesus, you choose hell by default. You must make a conscious and heartfelt decision to follow Christ. It does not just happen! You are not a believer just because your parents were; God has no grandchildren, only children. You are not a believer just because you go to church and have lots of qualifying papers stuffed in your Bible and a perfect attendance pin or because you were baptized as an infant; you must make a conscious decision! I made mine in July 1964 at Camp Sankanac in Spring City, Pennsylvania, in the Mohicans cabin just after evening devotions. Where did you make yours? If you do not know, why don't you make that moment right now? Again I encourage you to visit "The Secret of Eternal Life" portion in the back of this book!

I also do not understand why so many who profess Jesus Christ and the indwelling of His Spirit never seek to develop that intimacy with Him, but instead develop friendships with the temporal things of this life that pull us away from God! Jesus said that *"not everyone who says to Me, 'Lord, Lord' will enter the kingdom of heaven..."* (Matt. 7:21). If you claim His name without doing His will, you will not enter into His Kingdom! I see so many public figures and leaders today who declare that they are Christians, but support and do ungodly things. I pray for those who have tasted of the cup of God's goodness, but who do not desire to drink the whole thing! We will gain a better understanding of how this happens when we examine later how satan tries to prevent the Church from accomplishing the purpose for which God has called her.

If you are reading these words and claim to call Jesus your Savior, but spend most of your energy pursuing worldly, temporal pursuits, perhaps you should stop and reconsider your commitment. I urge you to make Jesus not only your Savior, but also your *Lord.* Do not be one who just wants fire insurance to escape hell; be one who surrenders all to the will of the One who died for you and accomplishes the eternal purpose for your life.

Pursue the One who relentlessly pursues you, the One who pursued you even to the Cross!

Chapter 17

The Second Mudcake Rebellion

---◆---

The Jews were looking for a military Messiah who would deliver them from their enemies and restore their kingdom; John the Baptist and the disciples of Jesus expected the same. However, the prophet Isaiah had foretold 700 years earlier that the world would not recognize the Messiah when He appeared on the Earth, and they didn't. They all believed He would deliver the nation of Israel and restore the nation to world power. He is going to do that, but not in the way that they thought!

The good news is that satan also thought Jesus was going to restore Israel! Why is that "good news"?

Satan expected Jesus to restore Israel, which he so successfully had destroyed, scattering the people; therefore, he also sought to destroy Jesus to maintain his stolen dominion. He failed to understand that on this first visit, Jesus would first restore intimacy with God and reestablish the dominion originally given to the mudcakes in Eden. These "spirit-filled" mudcakes would then take back His Kingdom, which would be established physically upon the Earth at Jesus's second visit or what is commonly referred to as His "second coming."

It was a two-step restoration plan:

1. Restore intimacy with God by providing them with the opportunity to once again possess the Spirit of the Creator God. Humans are useless and lost without the Spirit of God because they cannot have a relationship with a perfect, sinless God.

2. Restore the physical world to its originally created order, including the canopy of water that protected the Earth, casting out forever satan and his demons and removing the potential for evil eternally from this Kingdom of Heaven on Earth.

God would restore this intimacy by becoming a mudcake Himself, one who had no personal sin nature of His own. This *God-Man* would rebel against satan and the forces of sin and evil, take on the mudcakes' sin nature, and pay the death penalty for them. In doing so, He would plant seeds for a subsequent rebellion by the mudcakes against sin and evil. Their intimacy would be restored with God when they received the gift of this payment of their death penalty. They could now of their own free will choose to return to God and make Him Lord of their lives, but it would be an individual choice, a choice that all the mudcakes would not make.

You see, it was Adam and Eve's own free choice to rebel against God; therefore, it must be the free choice of a man or woman to rebel against sin and evil and return to intimacy with God.

Lucifer/satan did not understand this, nor did the mudcakes understand whom Christ came to save, but this all played into the hands of God's greater plan to redeem them.

Lucifer would seek to destroy this God-Mudcake and be victorious at the Cross of Calvary, but instead of the Cross becoming a symbol of lucifer's victory, it became a symbol of his defeat and the mudcakes' redemption.

Let's take a look at Isaiah's prophecy given approximately 700 years before Jesus's birth and see how it precisely described God's plan for redemption and deliverance, a script that all who sought to kill Jesus unknowingly followed with such precision. For 2000 years the Jews have tried to pass this passage off as a description of the plight of the Jews over the years. I am a man of Jewish descent, and I will call that exactly what it is—rationalization. Jesus is still not the type of Messiah they are expecting, so they rationalize Him away. There are many Jews today in the Messianic Jewish movement who have recognized who Jesus is, and prophecy tells us that one day all Jews will recognize Him and *"all Israel will be saved"* (Rom. 11:26). That day is still in the future at the time of this writing.

Here is the Messianic prophecy found in the Book of Isaiah:

> *See, My servant will act wisely; He will be raised and lifted up and highly exalted. Just as there were many who were appalled at Him—His appearance was so disfigured beyond that of any man and His form marred beyond human likeness— so will He sprinkle many nations, and kings will shut their mouths because of Him. For what they were not told, they will see, and what they have not heard, they will understand.*

> *Who has believed our message and to whom has the arm of the Lord been revealed?*

> *He grew up before Him like a tender shoot, and like a root out of dry ground. He had no beauty or majesty to attract us to Him, nothing in His appearance that we should desire Him.*

> *He was despised and rejected by men, a man of sorrows, and familiar with suffering. Like one from whom men hide their faces He was despised, and we esteemed Him not.*

> *Surely He took up our infirmities and carried our sorrows, yet we considered Him stricken by God, smitten by Him, and afflicted.*

But He was pierced for our transgressions, He was crushed for our iniquities; the punishment that brought us peace was upon Him, and by His wounds we are healed.

We all, like sheep, have gone astray, each of us has turned to His own way; and the Lord has laid on Him the iniquity of us all.

He was oppressed and afflicted, yet He did not open His mouth; He was led like a lamb to the slaughter, and as a sheep before her shearers is silent, so He did not open His mouth.

By oppression and judgment He was taken away. And who can speak of His descendants? For He was cut off from the land of the living; for the transgression of My people He was stricken.

He was assigned a grave with the wicked, and with the rich in His death, though He had done no violence, nor was any deceit in His mouth.

Yet it was the Lord's will to crush Him and cause Him to suffer, and though the Lord makes His life a guilt offering, He will see His offspring and prolong His days, and the will of the Lord will prosper in His hand.

After the suffering of His soul, He will see the light of life and be satisfied; by His knowledge My righteous servant will justify many, and He will bear their iniquities.

Therefore I will give Him a portion among the great, and He will divide the spoils with the strong, because He poured out His life unto death, and was numbered with the transgressors. For He bore the sin of many, and made intercession for the transgressors (Isaiah 52:13–53:12).

Let's look at Jesus' mission of the Cross in the light of this prophecy. Jesus came to Earth first to serve and to save, so God refers to Him as "My servant." The passage says that He will be *"raised and lifted up and highly exalted,"* referring to both before and after the Cross. Jesus was *raised and lifted up* on the Cross and then later exalted by God the Father.

After Jesus's "trial," which was no trial at all, Pilate ordered that He be beaten. First of all, it was not customary for a criminal to both be beaten and crucified by the Romans. Pilate hoped to appease the Jewish leaders by beating Him, but they wanted Him crucified as well. Jesus was taken out and beaten (see Matt. 27:26) with a whip that had glass, metal, bone, and stone embedded in it. As the whip would strike the flesh, wrapping completely around the body from head to toe, it would also tear out chunks of flesh as it was withdrawn. The standard order was for this to be done 40 times. If the one doing the whipping gave more, it was ordered that he be whipped as punishment. Therefore the one doing the whipping would deliver only 39 lashes just in case he miscounted. As I previously said, it is amazing how evil people can become in their ungodliness. Jesus was beaten in this manner so that *his appearance was so disfigured beyond that of any man and his form marred beyond human likeness* (see Isa. 52:14).

In the filming of *The Passion of The Christ,* produced and directed by Mel Gibson, I heard Jim Caviezel who played Jesus relate in a personal interview with Paul Crouch Jr. on TBN's *Praise the Lord* show how they wanted to depict this whipping so accurately that a real whip of this type was used. With a board strapped to his back for protection, Jim was actually tied to the post and whipped with this whip. However, at one point, the actor doing the whipping missed and one of the ends of the whip came around the board and caught Caviezel in the side. He describes a paralyzing pain and was so traumatized that he was taken to the hospital in such a state that Mel Gibson later confessed that he was concerned for Jim's life. Jesus endured 39 lashes for you, all the tails of the whip striking him, being pulled back tearing the flesh from His body—with no board strapped to Him to protect Him. Can you imagine how this would have disfigured Jesus's body? I am literally in tears right now!

As we move into Isaiah 53, we read, *"He grew up before him like a tender shoot, and like a root out of dry ground…"* (Isa. 53:2). Jesus was born in a time when it appeared all was lost. Israel was scattered, and its land was in captivity to the Romans; God's remnant was disabled, and evil was growing upon the face of the Earth. The Romans were ruthless captors and immoral to the highest degree. It truly was dry, cracked, and parched ground. Creation and the mudcakes were sinking to their lowest levels.

Then one night in a stable in Bethlehem a green *"tender shoot"* (Isa. 53:2) sprang up in the parched Earth, a hope for the future for a new *"Tree of Life"* in the garden of the world, and the one who would eventually destroy the "tares" that had been planted by the enemy. This shoot continued to grow, but remained in obscurity, not being noticed for 30 years. Instead of being received by those He was sent to, He was rejected, despised, and suffered much. Instead of this *tender shoot* from the *root of David* being looked to as the hope of Israel, He was totally ignored. "He is not what we want, so we will not only ignore Him, we will destroy Him!" they said.

Is that not what people do today, ignoring Him because He is not what they want?

People today want a savior who will allow them to do whatever they want, live however they want to live, give them what they want, and then at death pull them from the fires of hell. They want "fire insurance," not a *Lord!*

It does not work that way. Have you ignored Him?

Take this *tender shoot* of hope and salvation and plant it in the dry ground of your life. Let Him grow in intimacy with you, and you will be amazed at how you are transformed.

Isaiah 53 goes on to describe the Messiah who, on the Cross,

> *…took up our **infirmities** and carried our **sorrows,** yet we considered Him stricken by God, smitten by Him, and afflicted.*

But He was pierced for our **transgressions,** *He was crushed for our iniquities; the punishment that brought us* **peace** *was upon Him, and by His wounds we are healed* (Isaiah 53:4-5).

Jesus at the Cross *"took up our infirmities and carried our sorrows"* (Isa. 53:4). He also was *"pierced for our transgressions"* (Isa. 53:5). The words *infirmities* and *transgressions* tell us that there is the sin nature that we receive at birth, and there are the sins that we commit of our own volition.

The word *infirmities* refers to that curse of a sin nature without the Holy Spirit that was passed to us from Adam and Eve in the first mudcake rebellion; the word *transgressions* refers to those sins for which we are solely responsible. Our *"griefs"* (KJV) refers to the calamities and anxieties of life, and *"sorrows"* (KJV) refers to our emotional hurts and pains. The *"chastisement"* (KJV) or *"punishment that brought our peace"* (NIV) refers to our welfare or prosperity. The Hebrew word for peace, *shalom,* means "nothing missing, nothing broken," which includes our well-being and prosperity in this life. Finally the wounds that He received on our behalf were for our healing from sickness and disease, for *"by His wounds we are healed."*

Jesus took all these issues of our lives and He allowed them to be nailed with Him to the Cross!

What does this mean? The blood He shed delivered us from subjection to these issues of our lives.

How? What is all this talk about blood anyway?

Let's consider the seven (there's that number again) ways that Jesus bled during His sacrifice for you and see spiritually how Jesus's physical suffering and death were significant to all areas of our lives.

Here are the seven ways Jesus bled during this sacrifice:

1. Jesus sweated drops of blood in the Garden of Gethsemane (see Luke 22:44). It is a medical fact that during times of intense emotional fear and agony the capillaries below the surface of the skin will burst, and sweat will be as drops of blood. Jesus knew what He was facing and was under much duress. Jesus, therefore, understands our hurts, fears, and anxieties. He understands stress to the extreme, and in His death on the Cross He gave us the power to rise above our circumstances. Jesus gave us power (*dunamis* in the Greek) through the Holy Spirit to do that which seems impossible for us (see Acts 1:8). I have always wondered how those without Christ can handle the death of a family member or face disease and death without the Holy Spirit and knowledge of the Holy God! Jesus understands our trials and tribulations and is someone who *"sticks closer than a brother"* (Prov. 18:24). He is there in that time of need to help us rise up against seemingly impossible circumstances. He became a mediator between us and God, a mediator who understands what it is like to be flesh. He felt everything you have ever felt or will ever feel, and He understands and gives you a way to overcome your circumstances. Hebrews 4:14-16 assures us of this.

> *Therefore, since we have a great high priest who has gone through the heavens, Jesus the Son of God, let us hold firmly to the faith we profess.*
>
> *For we do not have a high priest who is unable to sympathize with our weaknesses, but we have one who has been tempted in every way, just as we are—yet was without sin. Let us then approach the throne of grace with confidence, so that we may receive mercy and find grace to help us in our time of need* (Hebrews 4:14-16).

2. Jesus was beaten with 39 lashes of the whip. Isaiah 53:5 says that *"by His stripes"* (KJV) or *"wounds"* (NIV) *"we are healed."* The stripes He bore on his back that grossly disfigured His body bought physical healing for the redeemed. Jesus bore our diseases and took them to the Cross; we can trust Him for physical healing in our bodies when we are sick. Ultimately, the redeemed mudcakes will receive a new body in glory.

3. Jesus received a crown of thorns. In Genesis 3:17-19 we read that when Adam and Eve rebelled in Eden, God cursed the ground with thorns and thistles and told Adam that he would struggle to make his living by the sweat of his brow. Thorns were a sign of the curse of poverty, and sweat was a sign of bondage. The Earth would begin to deteriorate, and by the time of Noah, even the canopy of water encircling the Earth would degrade in its orbit and rain down upon the Earth, flooding it. The sun's rays were now unfiltered, threatening the mudcakes with sickness and disease, famine, and poverty. The mudcakes would struggle from that day forward to have the things they needed.

The soldiers at Jesus's trial fashioned a crown of thorns and mockingly shoved it onto His head, sinking the thorns deep into His brow. However, what satan meant for evil and torture, God meant for our good. We see again that satan plays right into God's plan of redemption for His mudcakes. Second Corinthians 8:9 says, Jesus *"became poor, so that you through His poverty might become rich."* In other words, Jesus's death on the Cross also delivered those accepting His salvation from the curse of poverty—but how? When the crown of thorns was shoved onto Jesus's brow, the blood of His brow flowed onto the thorns. The curse of Genesis 3:17-19 was broken in the lives of the redeemed.

The Lord told me in my near-death experience that many of the redeemed today do not know this so they do not claim this redemptive work in their lives, a gift of Christ lying unopened on the table. One of the callings on my life is to teach and preach this message, and I have done so internationally, seeing the curse of poverty broken in the lives of so many of the redeemed. I love hearing the testimonies of so many who have been in those services and exercised that teaching in their lives, claiming this part of Christ's redemption.[1]

4. Jesus was pierced by nails in His hands. God gave His authority to do His will upon the Earth to Adam and Eve; they were to use this authority to subdue the Earth. However, in the first mudcake rebellion, they gave that authority to lucifer. Hands are a sign of authority. When Jesus's hands were nailed to the Cross and blood flowed from them, the redemptive work of the Cross also bought back our God-given authority. God then gave back to the redeemed the authority to use His name and carry out His will upon the Earth. Unfortunately, most redeemed mudcakes today do not understand that they have this "power of attorney" to bring the world in which we live under subjection to the Word of God.

5. Jesus was pierced by nails in His feet. Closely tied to the authority of the hands is the dominion of the feet. Feet are symbolic of dominion or subjection. When Jesus's feet bled from the nails, the dominion lost in Eden became the property of Jesus Christ. Hebrews 2:6-8 tells us that *all* things are brought into subjection to Jesus and are *"under His feet."* The dominion of this world was bought back from satan, who stole it from the mudcakes through deception; Jesus then returned dominion to the mudcakes again, but only to those who claim this purchase price as their own!

6. Jesus's blood and water flowed from His sword-pierced side (see John 19:31-34). Jesus's side was pierced by the sword of a Roman soldier as He hung on the Cross for you. Why would God allow this to be done? *Precious Jesus's heart was broken for you, my friend!* Through His redemptive act on the Cross, Jesus provided a way for your broken heart to be healed. Don't continue to live with your hurts. He gave us the ability to overcome our hurts, rejections, and losses of the past, present, and future, and then He restores joy and peace to our hearts. *You must only accept this redemptive act, calling it your own, and allowing Him to be Lord of your life.* Jesus forgave on the Cross all those who were killing Him, and I have seen that same ability to overcome hurts and pain manifested in the lives of many.

I recall weeping the first time I saw a film clip of Elisabeth Elliot, wife of the murdered missionary Jim Elliot, whose story was depicted in the movie *The End of the Spear.* In the clip, Elisabeth was friendly and smiling while cutting the hair of the man who killed her husband. This man had come to salvation as a result of the work of Elisabeth and the other wives of the slain missionaries. The tribe in Ecuador had come to Christ after slaying Jim Elliot and his co-laborers in this evangelistic effort. The man who killed Nate Saint, one of Elliot's co-laborers, today is considered like a grandfather in the family of Saint's son, who was a child when this man killed his father. *This illustrates the power of the Cross to heal your hurts! Oh please receive it—don't wait!*

7. Jesus was bruised for our iniquities. A bruise is not outward bleeding, but bleeding within the body. Jesus was not only whipped, but also bruised. Bruises are sometimes so deep they cannot be seen. During my days playing football, I remember having sore spots especially on my forearms from blows taken during the game. Sometimes they would manifest in black and blue spots and could be seen, but at other times I would be the only one who would know they were there. They were not visible, but tender to the touch. Sometimes our inward hurts are not visible to others, and *"nobody knows the troubles* [we've] *seen…"* as the old spiritual goes. Ah, but the rest of that line is *"…but Jesus."* Yes, the redeemer knows, and He provided a way to heal those inward hurts when He was on the Cross. His bruises also provided for healing of our iniquity, which indicates an inward sin nature inherited from Adam and Eve. If you accepted Jesus's purchase price of redemption for you, you are forgiven inside and outside.

This redemption does not mean I am perfect, but that I am forgiven. Jesus said that we would have trials in this world, but *"be of good cheer; I have overcome the world"* (John 16:33 KJV). You and I cannot be perfect in this fleshly body, only in the recreated body we would have received in Eden. That body awaits us in the Kingdom! Talk about a total body makeover—wow, you ain't seen nothing yet!

The Holy Spirit works with us and within us to regenerate our human spirits by becoming one with it, and one day the Holy Spirit will regenerate the whole body. Human life has an end, but divine life has only a beginning. God's Word says that *"It is appointed for men to die once, but after this the judgment"* (Heb. 9:27 NKJV).

When this body in which we live dies, all the sorrows of this life are buried in the ground with the body and remain there while the spirit is released. The spirits of those who are one with the Holy Spirit return to Christ, the one who gave them the Holy Spirit, just as the apostle Paul wrote, and as I experienced, *"absent from the body and ...present with the Lord"* (2 Cor. 5:8 NKJV). Those who do not have the Holy Spirit mixed with their human spirits go to a holding place to await judgment.

When Jesus was on the Cross, we are told by those present that He cried with a loud voice, *"It is finished,"* and then *"He bowed His head and gave up His Spirit"* (John 19:30). Jesus did not die from His wounds, but from a resultant heart attack from suffocation as crucifixion caused His lungs to collapse, depriving Him of oxygen.[2] The Spirit was pushed out of Him as He died, and He left behind the earthly body born from the body of his mother Mary, together with all the hurts, pains, and rejections of His life—but He left no personal sin or sin nature. We will talk about where His Spirit went in a minute. What is even more amazing is that He also left the sins, hurts, rejections, and losses of the whole world! The Bible says that He became sin for us (see 2 Cor. 5:21). What does that mean?

In 2009, my wife Andi came down the steps one morning upset by a dream she had just had. She did not want to tell me about it at first and said that the dream was demonic in nature; she was disturbed that she would even have such a dream. She said that she had rebuked the devil in the name of Jesus for the dream. She mustered the courage and told me of it, and I agreed; it was disturbing!

Our son Ben was in Tulsa, and later that day, Andi was speaking with him and telling him of the dream. Ben is gifted by the Holy Spirit in many ways, and it has become apparent that one of those spiritually discerning ways is in the interpretation of dreams. Andi related the dream, telling him she felt it was demonic because it upset her.

In this dream she was watching from a distance as a Christ-like figure was taken to a hill where He was pushed to the ground. A few minutes later, He was lifted up, and it was then that her vantage point was drawn in closer, as if zoomed in by a camera, until she could see His face. She saw caked and matted blood as well as fresh blood on a face that slowly turned and looked toward her. What she saw then was what disturbed her so much. The face that turned toward her was a face that was so demonic in its appearance that it startled her awake, reeling in fright at the hideous face and sending her down the steps in distress. She asked why someone with the Spirit of the living God within her would have a dream portraying her beloved Jesus in such a way.

Ben listened as his mother told him the dream and without a moment's hesitation blurted out the interpretation. "Mom, it was not a demonically in-spired dream to upset you! The Holy Spirit was showing you what God saw that day when He looked at Jesus on the Cross when He became sin for us and bore the sins of the world in His body. Bearing the sins of the world for all eternity past and future would make Jesus appear to be the absolute picture of evil. Mom, you saw what God saw! He had to turn away too!"

The interpretation struck our spirits with such a resounding confirma-tion that we now share it wherever we go together to speak. Let me explain.

When Jesus was hanging on the Cross, we are told that at one point Je-sus cried out with a loud, distressed voice, *"My God, My God, why have You forsaken Me?"* (Matt. 27:46). It was at that very moment that God turned His back on Jesus because, in His holiness, He could not look upon the evil that Jesus had become as the sins of the world were heaped upon Him. For the first time in God the Father's, God the Son's, and God the Holy Spirit's eter-nal pre-existence, the Son was totally separated from them. Jesus was left all alone in the hands of the prince and powers of darkness, lucifer! (See Acts 2:27-31.)

Can you imagine the despair Jesus felt as God the Father turned His very Son over to the powers of satan to heap the punishment of the world upon Him? In His eternal pre-existence, Jesus knew that this day was coming in God's plan of redemption, which is why He sweats great drops of blood in the Garden of Gethsemane, yet He *chose* to go to the Cross.

Why would Jesus ever do such a thing when He had the authority to call 10,000 angels to His aid to deliver Him? *Why?*

He went through with His choice because He loves you with such a great love that He laid down His life. When He walked upon the Earth, He said, *"Greater love has no one than this, to lay down one's life for one's friends"* (John 15:13). If you accept this sacrifice, you become His friend, *"a friend who sticks closer than a brother"* (Prov. 18:24).

Jesus was not a martyr! He was a sacrifice, a perfect, once-and–for-all sacrifice. He did not die a physical death for anything He did; He died for what we all did, and He took our place. He became sin for *us!* That is what a sacrifice is—giving up something in order to obtain something for someone else.

He gave up His life to get you back!

The Cross is the revelation of God's judgment on sin and the rebellion. The mudcakes' rebellion and sin needed to be judged. The punishment prescribed by God in the Garden of Eden was for the mudcakes to be turned back to dust and their spirits to be sent to the abyss of hell much as lucifer's spirit wandered in the abyss of the chaotic Earth after God cast him down to the Earth.

The death of a sinless man as a sacrifice does not prevent physical death; it only redeems our spirits from judgment. The bad news is that you still have to die in order to free your spirit; the determination as to where your spirit then goes depends on your decision before that day of your death. There is no second chance after death. I suggest you get it straightened out with God now since you do not know what day your life will cease.

Physical death is a moment of passage or transference of the spirits of men and women to their eternal destinations.

I learned this in my near-death experience, which was for me a life experience. It was a life experience because of my prior decision to receive Christ's sacrifice as my own physical and spiritual death and my willingness to live for Him and not for me. I found myself as Paul said, *"absent from the body and… present with the Lord"* (2 Cor. 5:8 NKJV). There was no light to embrace me, as the New Age people say; I was talking to the anesthesiologist one minute and with Jesus the next. I know beyond a shadow of doubt that those who see this light are actually being drawn to the former angel of light, lucifer. They are being taken to their destination, the same one prepared for him. Remember that lucifer was an angel of light prior to his fall. I have talked to some of these people who have seen this light and found that they did not know Jesus then. The experience has given some a false sense of security.

My experience made me more aware and in pursuit of my spiritual side—the part that is eternal. The Bible says that *"if any man be in Christ, he is a new creature: old things are passed away; behold, all things are become new"* (2 Cor. 5:17 KJV). This newness is because of the Holy Spirit creating a new or recreated spirit within the redeemed person. These new creations cannot live bound to Earth, but aspire to realize their spiritual side. While still in the flesh, they become more and more interested in that spiritual side. If they do not become more interested in the spiritual side, it is very possible that the new spirit was never taken in the first place or that the flesh has become distracted with worldly pursuits. Yes, even a redeemed mudcake can still sin because sin still has a grasp on the physical, but the spirit is free and redeemed. When the spirit is released from the earthly body at death, it will never sin again!

I was not the same man when I woke up in the Intensive Care Unit, as I said earlier in this book. Instead, a different man returned with a burning passion. My passion was not to experience the hell I had just witnessed, but to experience the glorious life Jesus has prepared for those accepting His redemption. I am distressed to see so many in this world toying with their lives and missing the big picture. I see even Christians in the pursuit of worldly pleasures and goals to the point that spiritual understanding is set aside. I have seen the face of Jesus reel in grief over the things believers allow to pass before their eyes as "entertainment." Such things as illicit sex, violence, witchcraft, drugs, and alcohol are tolerated and enjoyed as entertainment by those claiming this redemption.

All these things prevent them from achieving their greater purpose by quenching the work of the Holy Spirit in their lives.

The Lord showed me how this works. When you are entertained by the counterfeit supernatural, by witchcraft, violence, illicit sex, or other forms of evil, it temporarily satisfies the longing for the supernatural power of the Holy Spirit. Then you become dulled to His leading in your life. It's not just entertainment, my friends; it is a tool of lucifer to distract and dull you to the leading of the Spirit of God and cause you to be ineffective in Kingdom work.

We either don't know, don't care, or forget that this life is a brief moment in eternity for the purpose of our redemption and the advancement of His Kingdom. As the Bible asks, *"How shall we escape if we ignore such a great salvation?..."* (Heb. 2:3). We need to understand the essence of the Cross and its power to recreate us into the perfect mudcakes God intended for us to be, before the foundation of the world.

Did you know that before the foundation of the world was laid you were in God's mind? Even more, did you know that on the Cross, you were in Christ's mind? Did you know He did it for you?

The Cross—the center of time, the center of eternity past and eternity future.

It is the answer to the mysteries of both the past and the future. It is the destruction of free moral disobedience against the will of God. It is the single act that results in the restoration of all creation.

It is a second,
spiritual "Big Bang"
that shook the universe in the center of time!

Chapter 18

The New Remnant

———— ·•· ————

Sin and eternal death now were defeated, and a new creation was under way. This new creative process was designed to first re-create the spiritual side of the mudcakes and then to re-create the Earth. The recreation of the physical Earth would occur when satan and the forces of evil were completely eliminated so that evil could never corrupt the Earth again. The Earth would need to be purged of all the evil, sorrows, hurts, and pains that lie buried in it with all the mudcakes who had returned to the dirt throughout the ages.

Upon Jesus's death on the Cross, He went to the abyss, or to hell, as we refer to it. If you think His torment on the Cross was great, it was just a fraction of what He endured during the next hours of Earth time after His death (see Acts 2:27-31). The God-Man went into the pit of evil itself, a place where everything was contrary to the nature of God. Lucifer screamed with glee as the very Son of God entered hell. Surely now God would destroy the mudcakes for what they had done to His Son, and His plan would be defeated. Lucifer thought he had God right where he wanted Him, but the opposite was true. The redemptive act had now been accomplished, not only right under lucifer's nose, but with his help as well.

The Lord told me very clearly and plainly one day, *"Evil always oversteps itself, reveals itself!"*

Such was the case here; Lucifer's evil plan went too far, overstepped, and defeated itself. Now it was just a matter of time before God's victory through Jesus would be accomplished.

Let's take a moment to clear up a few things. The word *hell* is often translated in English from different Hebrew and Greek words in the Bible. When we think of hell, we have a certain concept in our minds from stories and movies we have seen, most of which are a perversion of the truth. Our idea of hell as a lake of fire is correct, and the actual Greek word translated for hell is *gehenna.*[1] *Gehenna,* or "the lake of fire," is actually the place reserved for lucifer and the angels who fell with him. God did not intend hell for the mudcakes, but because of their rebellion in Eden, it is now also reserved for all the unredeemed mudcakes. They, together with lucifer and the demons, will be tormented there forever. Here is piece of information that may be a new concept to you—*no one is there yet!*

No, satan does not live in hell. Where is he? The Bible tells us that he *"walks about like a roaring lion, seeking whom he may devour"* (1 Peter 5:8 NKJV). You see, no one is sent to the eternal place of judgment known as hell until the great judgment of Christ at the establishment of the eternal Kingdom. Then, satan, his demons, and all the mudcakes who have chosen to follow satan's way will be sent there forever, eternally separated from God and everyone else. Just so you know, the default decision should you die without deciding to follow Christ is to join satan in hell at the judgment. This life is the only time you have to make that decision; there is no second chance.

So where is everyone who has already died? Where are Adolf Hitler, Joseph Stalin? Where are all the deceased "church ladies"? Where is Aunt Sally?

Let us first talk about where those who died in their sin, without accepting Jesus as Lord, went. Another word translated in English as "hell" is the

Greek word *hades*[2] or the Hebrew word *sheol*.[3] This is a different level of hell, which serves as a temporary prison where the spirits of the unrighteous will remain throughout history until the judgment day of Christ known as the *"Great White Throne Judgment" where at that time we see that the sea, death and hell delivers up those that were "in them"* (see Rev. 20:11-13). Their fate is already determined by how they lived upon the Earth; they are just waiting sentencing on the Day of Judgment.

You may ask, what about those who died before Christ died on the Cross? Well, they can have redemption too. If in their lives, they had a heart toward God, were obedient to God, and looked forward to the day of the promised *deliverer*, they would not go to hades, but to a pleasant and joyful compartment within hades known as *Paradise* (see Luke 23:43). It was also referred to in the Bible as *Abraham's Bosom* (see Luke 16:22). *Paradise* was a place of comfort where those with an obedient heart (see Acts 13:22), God-loving mudcakes, were held until they were made righteous by Jesus Christ through His sacrifice. These individuals died looking forward to their deliverer and to the day of their redemption and atonement provided at Calvary. They looked forward to Calvary for their redemption just as we today look back to Calvary for ours.

The Scriptures also seem to indicate that there is a third part of hades known as *tartarus* in the Greek. This seems to be a place where certain fallen angels are being held until the final great judgment day (see 2 Pet. 2:4).[4]

So what did Jesus do when He died? Where did He go? According to First Peter 3:18-20, Jesus descended into hades, where He *"preached"* to the captives. Preaching is proclaiming; it was not as if Jesus was giving them another opportunity to choose righteousness; instead, He was proclaiming to them His victory over sin and eternal death and holding the keys to unlock the doors of hell. He had the power over hell and could decide who would go there and who would not. *Jesus went to the pit of hell because that is where we are ultimately destined to go without redemption.*

Then, after Jesus went to hades and proclaimed His authority and dominion over sin, death, and hell, He did something really awesome!

He went to *Paradise* and took those made righteous by His sacrificial death and ascended to Heaven with them. Paradise was closed down that day because ever since that time, those who die covered in Jesus Christ's righteousness immediately go to Heaven to be with Him. Ephesians 4:7-10 refers to Jesus's release of the captives in *Paradise:*

> *But to each one of us grace has been given as Christ apportioned it. This is why it says: "When He ascended on high, He led captives in His train and gave gifts to men." (What does "he ascended" mean except that he also descended to the lower, earthly regions? He who descended is the very one who ascended higher than all the heavens, in order to fill the whole universe)* (Ephesians 4:7-10).

So Jesus was crucified and died. He then descended into that prison of eternal separation from God. In that prison, one's unforgiven or unatoned-for sin is the lock on the gate that holds one there. *Without redemption, the unrighteous person is separated from God for all eternity with no hope.*

This is where satan made his fatal mistake.

He failed to recognize that the lock on that prison was a mudcake's own personal, unforgiven sin. Being sinless, Jesus could not be locked in, and so He escaped, not only breaking the bars of that gate, but also taking the keys to unlock hell for whomever He desires!

He desires to unlock them for you!

Jesus then took those keys to the Father, delivering them in trade for an eviction notice, which He will serve on satan when He returns to set up His Kingdom! At that time, satan will be cast into hell for good, his own sin locking him in forever.

On His way to Heaven with the freed captives of *Paradise* trailing behind, Jesus picked up His body in the garden tomb. That morning the garden tomb was lit up with a force of the Almighty God's re-creative power. The bruised and battered body of the *Lord* Jesus had to be literally re-created into the glorious body. He later appeared to the disciples in this glorified body.

Jesus had been in the tomb three days of Earth time just as Jonah had been in the belly of a great fish for three days before being delivered onto dry land. The number three has been a fingerprint of God throughout the ages as well; it is interesting to note that theologians have been able to calculate the date of Jesus's crucifixion, based on known dates, to be April 3, A.D. 33, when Jesus was also 33 years old![5]

Jesus' spirit re-entered His body, and a re-created body rose up from the grave. He was unbound from the grave clothes, but before He left the tomb, He also left a message for all who would find that empty grave. He neatly folded the napkin and left it laying in the tomb—why?

According to ancient tradition, servants knew when their master was done with his meal if he left the napkin unfolded and wadded up on the table. If for some reason, the master left the table with the intention to return, he would neatly fold the napkin on the table. The servants would see the napkin and not clear the table because they knew their master would be back.

By folding the napkin, Jesus left a message to all who would find the empty tomb—*"I'll be back!"*

And He did come back! Jesus not only appeared to the disciples, who had gathered together, doubting, mournful, and disillusioned, but He also continued to appear to people for 40 days until His ascension to Heaven where He was seated at the right hand of the Father God. Jesus continually promises His "friends" that He will be back to establish His Kingdom on Earth!

After 40 days (the number 40 again) of appearing to the disciples and hundreds of other people and teaching them about the Kingdom, Jesus made a promise to His disciples. He promised to send the Holy Spirit to them, who would teach and guide them (see Acts 1:4). He commissioned them to carry on His work and take it to the nations. This group of 12 men, who became known as the *apostles* after Christ's ascension, would be the governing group in the start of a new, spiritual remnant—the Church. The Church would become the spiritual or *unseen* nation that parallels the physical or *seen* nation of Israel. Both the Church and Israel would be used to carry out the Creator's plan to establish the *seen* Kingdom of Heaven on Earth over the next 2000 years.

The Church does not replace the nation of Israel, as some have taught in the past. If you study the roots of this doctrine of *replacement theology*, you will find that it was adopted centuries ago when anti-semitism crept into the Church. Israel is and always will remain God's *timepiece* in working out His plan to establish the *seen* Kingdom upon the Earth. The Church spiritually has been *"grafted in"* to all the promises made to the nation of Israel (see Rom. 11:17-24). The Bible tells us that eventually all of Israel will be saved, and the people of the nation of Israel and the people of the Church will be one in Christ (see Rom. 11:26). Jesus Christ will rule the eternal Kingdom, the spiritual Israel from the New Jerusalem, for all eternity.

The Church is given the task to spiritually advance the Kingdom of Christ until it manifests in the establishment of a *seen* Kingdom upon the Earth by Jesus Christ when He returns. The Church is to do this by spreading the Gospel of His sacrifice, which provided redemption to all mudcakes in all nations.

After hearing their assignment, the disciples watched as Jesus ascended from the Mount of Olives, the same place to which He promises to return when He comes again. As He was lifted up and taken from their sight, two angels were sent to them as messengers. The message that they conveyed to them from Jesus Christ was, *"I'll be back!"*

Chapter 19

The Secret Kingdom

———•———

Jesus told His disciples in Matthew 11:12 that *"from the days of John the Baptist until now, the kingdom of heaven suffers violence, and violent men take it by force"* (NASB). He also told them that they should not look for a physical, earthly Kingdom, for *"the kingdom of God is within you"* (Luke 17:21 NKJV). Standing before Pilate, Jesus told him, *"My kingdom is not of this world..."* (John 18:36). What did Jesus mean when He said the Kingdom of God is "within you"?

Prior to Jesus's ascension to Heaven from the Mount of Olives in Jerusalem, He gave the disciples some significant instructions after commissioning them to take His message to the nations. In Acts 1 we read these words of Jesus:

> *Do not leave Jerusalem, but **wait for the gift** My Father promised, which you have heard Me speak about. For John baptized with water, **but in a few days you will be baptized with the Holy Spirit** (Acts 1:4-5).*

Here it is! *The moment is coming for the reestablishment of the spiritual connection with the Creator lost in Eden with the spirits of those choosing to follow Jesus.* Jesus tells the 12 foundational pillars of this *new remnant* to wait in

Jerusalem for the gift of the Holy Spirit. Then in verse 8, He tells them that when the Holy Spirit comes upon them, they will receive *"power"* to accomplish what He has commissioned them to do. They will once again spiritually be connected to the power and mind of God.

This word *power* is an interesting word when we study the Greek word from which the English word is translated. In Greek and Hebrew there are multiple words for which the English language has only one word with different meanings. English words are often general while Greek and Hebrew words have more specific meanings. Such is the case here, for this word translated "power," which in the Greek is *dunamis,* means "God-like power" or "miraculous power."[1] Yes, it means "the power to do the miraculous"! That is what Jesus meant when He told them before His death that they would do greater things than He did. (See John 14:12.) Jesus was making an awesome promise here that was fulfilled in Acts 2.

By the end of this incredible day, the Church grew from 120 people (see Acts 1:15) to 3000 people (see Acts 2:41)—what a revival service they must have had! Let's look at what happened.

The disciples went to Jerusalem as instructed and remained there until the *Day of Pentecost.* In the Jewish tradition, Pentecost occurred 50 days after the Passover and was a holy day in which the Israelites were to remember their bondage and consecrate themselves again to the Lord. It would also later become the day on which the Jews would celebrate the giving of the Law to Moses at Mount Sinai and the birth of their national existence as the remnant nation of Israel.

The *Day of Pentecost* would also come to be celebrated as the day of the birth of the next remnant called out and used by God in accomplishing His plan. It is on this day that the next remnant, the Church, was officially established by the giving and rejoining of the Holy Spirit to the believers as Jesus had promised. The first day of Pentecost after the ascension of Jesus Christ into Heaven is considered to signal the beginning of the Church Age. This

Church Age was to continue for approximately 2000 years for the purpose of the advancement of the Kingdom through preaching the Gospel of salvation to all who would hear.

The 12 disciples came together to celebrate the *Day of Pentecost* as recorded in Acts 2. From this day forward the Lord gave the Holy Spirit to all who would receive His free gift of salvation through His sacrificial death. It was also a strategic time, for there would be Jews from all over the world who would be in Jerusalem for the celebration of this *Day of Pentecost*. This would be a day when the Church would grow from 120 to 3000 by the end of the day.

Yes, 3000 people accepted Jesus Christ's death on the Cross in their place, redeeming them from eternal spiritual death. They would trade eternal death in hell for eternal life in the promised Kingdom following their physical death. After Peter, one of the 12, gave a sermon, they received and were filled with the Holy Spirit in a powerful event.

Let's take a look at Acts 2 as Luke gives an account of what happened when Peter preached and Jesus gave this *God-like* or *dunamis* power to believers and enjoined His Spirit with theirs for the first time since Eden!

> *When the day of Pentecost came, they were all together in one place. Suddenly a sound like the blowing of a violent wind came from heaven and filled the whole house where they were sitting. They saw what seemed to be tongues of fire that separated and came to rest on each of them.* **All of them were filled with the Holy Spirit and began to speak in other tongues as the Spirit enabled them.**
>
> *Now there were staying in Jerusalem God-fearing Jews from every nation under heaven. When they heard this sound, a crowd came together in bewilderment, because* **each one heard them speaking in his own language.** *Utterly amazed, they*

asked: "Are not all these men who are speaking Galileans? Then how is it that each of us hears them in his own native language? Parthians, Medes and Elamites; residents of Mesopotamia, Judea and Cappadocia, Pontus and Asia, Phrygia and Pamphylia, Egypt and the parts of Libya near Cyrene; visitors from Rome (both Jews and converts to Judaism); Cretans and Arabs—we hear them declaring the wonders of God in our own tongues!" Amazed and perplexed, they asked one another, "What does this mean?"

Some, however, made fun of them *and said, "They have had too much wine"* (Acts 2:1-13).

Peter then stood with the other apostles and spoke to the crowd:

..."Fellow Jews and all of you who live in Jerusalem, let me explain this to you; listen carefully to what I say. These men are not drunk, as you suppose. It's only nine in the morning! No, **this is what was spoken by the prophet Joel:**

"In the last days, God says, I will pour out My Spirit on all people. *Your* **sons and daughters will prophesy,** *your* **young men will see visions,** *your* **old men will dream dreams.**

"Even on My servants, both men and women, I will pour out My Spirit in those days, and they will prophesy. **I will show wonders in the heaven above and signs on the earth below,** *blood and fire and billows of smoke.*

"The sun will be turned to darkness and the moon to blood before the coming of the great and glorious day of the Lord.

"'And everyone who calls on the name of the Lord will be saved.'

"Men of Israel, listen to this: Jesus of Nazareth was a man accredited by God to you by miracles, wonders and signs, which God did among you through Him, as you yourselves know. This man was handed over to you by God's set purpose and foreknowledge; and **you, with the help of wicked men, put Him to death by nailing Him to the cross.** But God raised Him from the dead, freeing Him from the agony of death, because **it was impossible for death to keep its hold on Him.**

"David said about Him: 'I saw the Lord always before Me. Because He is at My right hand, I will not be shaken. Therefore My heart is glad and My tongue rejoices; My body also will live in hope, because You will not abandon Me to the grave, **nor will You let Your Holy One see decay.** You have made known to Me the paths of life; You will fill Me with joy in Your presence.'

"Brothers, I can tell you confidently that the patriarch David died and was buried, and his tomb is here to this day. But he was a prophet and knew that God had promised him on oath that he would place one of his descendants on his throne. Seeing what was ahead, he spoke of the resurrection of the Christ, that He was not abandoned to the grave, nor did His body see decay. **God has raised this Jesus to life, and we are all witnesses of the fact. Exalted to the right hand of God, He has received from the Father the promised Holy Spirit and has poured out what you now see and hear.** For David did not ascend to heaven, and yet he said,

"'The Lord said to My Lord: "Sit at My right hand until I make Your enemies a footstool for Your feet."'

"Therefore let all Israel be assured of this: **God has made this Jesus, whom you crucified, both Lord and Christ."**

When the people heard this, they were cut to the heart and said to Peter and the other apostles, "Brothers, what shall we do?"

Peter replied, **"Repent and be baptized, every one of you, in the name of Jesus Christ for the forgiveness of your sins. And you will receive the gift of the Holy Spirit. The promise is for you and your children and for all who are far off—for all whom the Lord our God will call."**

With many other words he warned them; and he pleaded with them, "Save yourselves from this corrupt generation." Those who accepted his message were baptized, and **about three thousand were added to their number that day** *(Acts 2:14-41).*

Luke records that these believers became unified in an uncommon fellowship:

They devoted themselves to the apostles' teaching and to the fellowship, *to the breaking of bread and to prayer. Everyone was filled with awe,* **and many wonders and miraculous signs were done by the apostles.**

All the believers were together and had everything in common. Selling their possessions and goods, they gave to anyone as he had need.

Every day they continued to meet together in the temple courts. They broke bread in their homes and ate together with glad and sincere hearts, praising God and enjoying the favor of all the people. **And the Lord added to their number daily those who were being saved** *(Acts 2:42-47).*

This passage connects the dots of all we have discussed so far in this book right up to the present. Yes, we are still in the *Church Age*, and the

Kingdom has forcefully advanced as Jesus said it would; now, at this present time we see that it has penetrated into the whole world. The *Church Age*, as we understand it through prophecy, would continue for about 2000 years before a change begins to occur to set up the next age. We are at that time of transition now. We will talk more about this in a later chapter of this book, but what we have discussed in these last two chapters is important to you. It determines your future and whether you are part of that Kingdom or not.

God's plan to redeem the mudcakes was established; now the next phase of His plan to advance and establish the Kingdom and redeem all creation is under way. God began to use the Church to carry out His plan to establish His Kingdom, initiating a 2000-year-long process to penetrate into the whole world starting with Jerusalem. Israel is not replaced, but now becomes a timepiece for following prophecies regarding the coming Kingdom.

From the moment of the Church's inception, lucifer tried to do exactly what he has been trying to do with Israel from its roots—and that is to destroy it! These Holy Spirit-filled believers are such a threat to him that he desires to destroy the Church and cause it to fail in its mission. Lucifer's pride, despite his failures, still makes him refuse to believe that he has lost. *If he can destroy Israel completely, and then destroy the Church as well, the redemptive sacrifice by Jesus on the Cross will be meaningless. In his mind, if he cannot have dominion on the Earth, then Jesus will not either.*

The Church would have to learn to exercise their newfound authority and dominion in waging war with lucifer and the powers of darkness. Lucifer from this day on would seek not only to destroy Israel, but also the Spirit-filled mudcakes known as *Christians*. Israel's enemy from the day of Ishmael, now known as the Arabs, would also include these Christians as their target for destruction. Even today we see that the Arab (Muslim) world verbally proclaims its intention to destroy Israel as well as the Christians whom they claim are "infidels." Because the United States has supported Israel, due to its Judeo-Christian influence, it has been referred to by the Muslim world as "the great satan." Nations like Great Britain, Canada, Australia, and others are also marked due to their support of the Israeli state. That support is waning in these last days.

Let no misunderstanding exist here. The God of Abraham, Isaac, Jacob, and the Church, the one who sent Jesus to die on the Cross for you, is not the god of the Muslims known as Allah. Mohammed taught, as the Muslims do today, that Jesus was not the Son of God, but they do embrace His teachings as a good teacher. They acknowledge the virgin birth and revere Him as a prophet.

Mohammed declared that God had no need of a son. Yet, if Jesus's teachings were divinely inspired as the Muslims say, then what about Jesus's claim to be the *"Son of God"* and one with the Father God? Here is a gross contradiction of Islam. Lucifer is the great counterfeiter, and in an effort to distract mudcakes from the truth, he has created counterfeit religions. With that said, who do you think Allah is?

God is loving, tolerant, and long-suffering, but the god of the Koran is demanding and angry. The concept that God loves them is a foreign concept to the Muslims, so we must understand that we do not all serve one God, as the humanists and the politicians purport. Allah is the opposite of God.

Perhaps you are one of those people who believe all religions lead to Heaven. While that is a nice, comfortable, politically correct concept, it is doctrinal heresy and makes Jesus Christ the greatest liar of them all. Why? Jesus said in John 14, *"I am the way and the truth and the life. **No one comes to the Father except through Me"*** (John 14:6).

We need to stop trying to please everyone—because our eternal destinies and their eternal destinies are at stake. If you say in your defense at the Great White Throne judgment, "God, I was tolerant of people, respected their religious beliefs, and was politically correct in all my views;

therefore, I am righteous in my own eyes and believe I should be admitted to Your eternal Kingdom," *God will only be interested in one thing: do you know Jesus?*

If you have not accepted Jesus as Lord of your life, Jesus will speak up as He said He would in Matthew 7:

> *Not everyone who says to Me, "Lord, Lord," will enter the kingdom of heaven, but only he who does the will of My Father who is in heaven. Many will say to Me on that day, "Lord, Lord, did we not prophesy in Your name, and in Your name drive out demons and perform many miracles?" Then I will tell them plainly, "I never knew you. Away from Me, you evildoers"* (Matthew 7:21-23).

Did you know that there is a verse that is repeated twice in the Bible word-for-word? Here it is; draw your own conclusion: *"There is a way that seems right to a man, but in the end it leads to death"* (Prov. 14:12; 16:25).

I too have repeated things in this book sometimes in different ways. Do you know why? I repeat things I want to be sure you understand. Apparently, God wants you to understand that it does not matter what your opinion is, for if it is different from His, it ends in eternal death!

It does not matter what you or other people "think," "believe," "feel," or "debate"; it only matters in the end what God says!

Proverbs 19:2 says, *"Desire without knowledge is not good—how much more will hasty feet miss the **way**!"* Jesus said, *"I am the **way** and the truth and the life. No one comes to the Father except through Me"* (John 14:6). The Bible also says, *"Where there is no revelation, the people cast off restraint"* (Prov. 29:18). Many people today have a lot of zeal for politically correct issues, but if they do not understand their need for a redeemer, in the end, their zeal is as worthless as *"filthy rags"* (Isa. 64:6).

I would hope, by this point in the book, you have had ample knowledge and revelation to see the signature of God on this plan to redeem His mud-cakes and, in particular, to redeem you.

You are part of the reason lucifer wanted to neutralize the mission of the Church and destroy it. His mission of 2000 years ago is the same today: neutralize and destroy Israel and the Church.

And his strategy has not changed:

1. Distract and neutralize

2. Discourage

3. Destroy

It would not be easy for those who would be involved in yet another mud-cake rebellion.

Yes! A third mudcake rebellion!

This third mudcake rebellion is once again against sin, death, and the forces of evil, and it too is a personal rebellion.

Jesus's death on the Cross was a personal choice; it was His own personal rebellion against sin, death, and evil. Just like Jesus's rebellion, this third rebellion is also a personal choice for those who choose to join Jesus. The Church's numbers grew daily until it infiltrated the whole world. It grew as a result of the personal rebellion of one mudcake at a time making a personal choice to follow Jesus. This rebellion of mudcakes against evil, sin, and death manifests what we are calling here the third mudcake rebellion!

It is a rebellion, one person at a time, that advances a secret Kingdom—secret in the sense that it is growing quickly and steadily and will one day rule the world!

The fight continues day after day until the Kingdom manifests as a *seen* Kingdom on the Earth. I rebelled years ago and have had to keep fighting and rebelling as the enemy tries over and over again to distract and discourage me. Yes, He has even tried to destroy me. He did so when I had my near-death experience. I survived by the grace and intervention of God, and my survival has only made it more difficult for lucifer to achieve his cause.

Every day when my feet hit the floor in the morning, I want to cause lucifer as much trouble as I can and advance the Kingdom of Jesus Christ. The Holy Spirit is even giving Andi and me prophetic dreams in the night just as the prophet Joel said would happen. These dreams help us and others launch a counterattack against the works of lucifer.

By giving His redeemed mudcakes dreams, God can use you when your feet are not even on the floor! I am willing to receive direction and guidance in that way; I want lucifer to scream again when my feet hit the floor in the morning, "Oh no, he's up again!"

Just as God appointed Adam and Eve as stewards in Eden with all authority to be His agents to subdue the whole Earth, Jesus now reappoints and gives His authority to His redeemed. They become His agents to use His authority and dominion to take back the Kingdom and to bring Jesus and us as well into His full inheritance—the eternal Kingdom! (See Matthew 10:1; Luke 9:1.) His inheritance is ours too, since the Word of God tells us we are *"co-heirs with Christ"* (Rom. 8:17).

Throughout the almost 2000 years since Jesus's death, resurrection, and ascension, the Church has struggled as it advanced the Kingdom. The *"Bride of Christ"* (see Rev. 22:17) has been persecuted, infiltrated with corruption, and even killed for the cause of Christ. From its birth during the Roman Empire, the Church became the target of this demonically controlled empire. Believers became known as *Christians,* which literally means "little Christs" or "followers of Christ." They were persecuted by the Romans and even made into human torches to light the Roman roads. They were used for sport in their coliseums and fed to the lions for entertainment, yet the Church in Rome continued to spread throughout the Roman Empire. Throughout the ages to follow, Christians were persecuted wherever they went. Even in America today they are called intolerant and accused of spreading hate because they oppose things contrary to the Word and will of the Creator. Christians are not supposed to be politically correct; God is anything but politically correct.

All of this is a fulfillment of the words of Jesus when He said that if the world hated Him, it would hate His disciples also (see John 15:18). Just as the Jews of Jesus's day did not want to hear about the truth and repent, our society today yells, "Don't force your religion on me!"

First of all, I want you to understand that being a Christian or "follower of Christ" is not a religion. The word translated *religion* means "return to bondage." Jesus did not come to start a religion; He came to release us from the bondage of religion. He said that the truth we understand will set us free! (See John 8:32.) No, He came to establish a relationship between the Creator and the mudcakes He loves so much.

Christianity is not my religion; it is my relationship!

Redemption for the mudcakes means relationship reestablished! Mudcake, has your relationship with God been reestablished through Jesus Christ?

The secret Kingdom is still being expanded one person at a time as more and more mudcakes are joining the revolution started by Jesus Himself. Those who sign on to this revolution have found themselves in battle against the principalities and powers of darkness (see Eph. 6:12). We do not have time here to retrace the history of the Church and the battles it has fought through the 2000 years since its establishment on the *Day of Pentecost*. It is important, however, for us to take a look at where the Church is headed.

*The Church's responsibility today is to use its authority and its **dunamis power** to advance the Gospel and take back the Kingdom.*

You may ask, *"How can that be?"* If the Church has so much miraculous power, then why has it in many ways become culturally irrelevant to our society? Why do the wicked rule in this world?

While there are bright spots from time to time—even in nations like the United States founded on Christian principles—the Church seems to be largely ineffective in changing the societies in which we live. What is the problem?

Unfortunately, too much of the world's character has gotten into the Church.

However, a change is coming; we are going to see how that will happen. First I want us to take a look at how the Church has become culturally irrelevant in our society and how the enemy has been successful in distracting, discouraging, and neutralizing the Church from accomplishing all Christ intended it to.

Chapter 20

Warfare and Weapons

———•———

In my book, *The Coming Financial Revolution*, I included a chapter called, "The Ultimate Identity Theft." I included the chapter because Andi and I discovered as we traveled in ministry that the Church did not really know who they were or the power they possessed to accomplish the impossible. As this book has been read by people around the world, I have been amazed at the number of comments we have received on the book and how it specifically affected the lives of the people who read it. What was more amazing to me was how many people commented on this chapter, "The Ultimate Identity Theft."

In that chapter, I asked the question, *"If lucifer thought he could steal God's identity, do you think he might try to steal yours?"*

We then discussed all the ways satan tries to steal your identity and all the things God says in His Word about you. It was astounding for us to discover how many "redeemed mudcakes" do not have the power of the Holy Spirit operating in their lives simply because they do not know who they are in Christ and the power that was given to the *Church* on the *Day of Pentecost*.

In the last chapter we talked about lucifer's plan to destroy the Church. That plan is to *distract a*nd *neutralize* the Church, to *discourage* and ultimately *destroy* it and its mission. He has worked hard to discourage the redeemed mudcakes from using their *dunamis* power.

According to the Scriptures, the potential power of one Spirit-filled mudcake is greater than any army or government in the world. The power of a child of God is beyond our imaginations. Jesus did great things; He even raised the dead, and He said that His mudcakes would do greater things than He did! (See John 14:12.)

So where are those to whom Jesus referred? Why have we not seen the power? When we have seen power, it has been spotty and elusive. Where is the miraculous Church like we saw in the Book of Acts?

Let me give you some reasons why the Church does not yet consistently manifest these greater works. *I am not saying that this is not happening now; I am saying that it is "spotty" and not happening at the level God wants them to manifest it!*

I believe that as we approach the Kingdom and move into the time of transition from the Church Age to the Kingdom Age, we will see an increase in the miraculous. We will learn the strategy of the enemy, and many within the Church will close the door on these distractions and the things that neutralize our power.

Here are some of the major reasons that *dunamis* power is not manifesting in the lives of many Christians:

1. There is little or no understanding of the Word of God (the Bible).

The thing that the Church today does most with their Bible is carry it. They carry it to church; they carry it home; they carry it to special meetings, but they spend little time studying it and applying its truths to their lives. This lack of understanding of the Word causes most of the other reasons for powerlessness we will discuss. Since you have read this far, perhaps you have seen that the Bible is not boring; the more you get into it, the more the Holy Spirit reveals to you. My favorite thing to do is study the Word, and I have a lot of other life skills I am good at and enjoy. Remember that onion, like my wife Andi teaches; the more you get into it, the more potent it becomes.

The apostle Paul told Timothy, a young pastor in the early Church, that it was important for him to know the Word so that he could guard the faith (see 2 Tim. 1:13-14). I hear so many Christians today espousing viewpoints that are not in line with the Scriptures. They have been so influenced by the secular progressives on TV; the information sounds good to them, so they embrace that viewpoint. The problem is that it does not line up with Scripture and is, therefore, outside of God's will. Because of their lack of understanding, they speak and act outside of the will of God, and this diminishes their power.

I have taught for years the differences between *knowledge, understanding,* and *wisdom.* Let me explain.

Knowledge is the facts we know; it's the information we have.

Understanding clarifies what the information we have means.

Wisdom is the ability to apply the facts we know and that we understand within the will of God. Simply put, it is to know God's will and apply it!

Believers without the Holy Spirit and knowledge of the Word of God can gain knowledge and even understanding, but they are unable to apply it to the will of God because they do not know the Word of God, nor do they have the revelation of the Holy Spirit working within them. Therefore, they come up with conclusions that are not in line with the Word of God. *Christians who do not know the Word or how to tap into the Holy Spirit's revelation and guidance will often follow worldly wisdom because they do not understand the difference.*

Therefore, when you act outside the will of God, no matter how good it sounds, it will diminish your power because it weakens your connection with the Holy Spirit.

2. There is little or no real understanding of who we are and of the power of Holy Spirit within us.

As a result of our not knowing the Word of God, we do not understand what God thinks of us and what it means to be a *"new creation."* The Word of God tells us that we are different from the world, citizens of another Kingdom. In fact, First Peter tells us that we are a *"peculiar people,"* a *"chosen generation, a royal priesthood"* (1 Pet. 2:9 KJV).

In *The Coming Financial Revolution*, I gave a list of 25 things that God says about mudcakes who are redeemed. Let me recount them here:

God says we are

- *"New creatures."* Old things have passed away (2 Cor. 5:17 KJV).

- *"Ambassadors for Christ."* We are given authority to represent Him (2 Cor. 5:20 KJV).

- *"The righteousness of God."* Because Christ covers our unrighteousness (2 Cor. 5:21 KJV).

- *"Saints of God."* Numerous scriptural references refer to us as "saints," which means "one set apart as God's possession." You belong to God, and you will *"judge the world"* (see 1 Cor. 6:2).

- *"More than conquerors."* Pretty powerful words, don't you think? (Rom. 8:37).

- *"Children of God."* Who's your Daddy? (John 1:12; Phil. 2:15).

- *"Holy and blameless."* Because we have accepted Christ's sacrifice and made Him Lord of our lives (Eph. 1:4).

- *"Bride."* Is there anyone more important to the groom at the wedding feast of the Lamb than the Bride? (Rev. 21:2).

- *"Joint-heirs with Christ."* There are numerous places where we are referred to as "heirs." We get what Christ gets from the Father! (Rom. 8:17 KJV).

- *"Partakers of His promise."* You're invited to the big party! (Eph. 3:6 KJV).

- *"God's workmanship."* Remember, God don't make no junk! (Eph. 2:10). You're His fashion statement! (Ps. 33:15 KJV).

- *"Citizens of Heaven."* Is there any greater citizenship? We are citizens with all the rights and privileges therewith! (Phil. 3:20).

- *"Ones who will do greater works."* Jesus said this about us! (John 14:12).

- *"Body of Christ."* It also says we are "members in particular." We have an individual purpose in a glorious Body (Rom. 12:5).

- *"Fellow workers and ministers of God."* We have a monumental task to accomplish in a sliver of time (2 Cor. 6:1-4).

- *"Salt and light."* Salt gives things flavor, and light illuminates and shows the way. We are the salt of the Earth and the light of the revelation of Christ to the world (Matt. 5:13-14).

- *"Children of light."* Have you let the enemy steal your batteries? (Eph. 5:8).

- *"Shining stars."* Have you always wanted to be a "star"? Forget American Idol! (Phil. 2:15).

- *"Temple of the Holy Spirit."* Because the Spirit of God is in you, when others encounter you, they also encounter the Spirit of the living God! (1 Cor. 3:16).

- *"Apple of His eye."* God says that anyone who messes with us touches the apple of His eye. You don't mess with God's kids, or you will have Him to deal with! So when the devil messes with you…tell your Daddy! (Zech. 2:8).

- *"Chosen generation."* The Greek word here means "favorite," and it means "elect." God voted for you! He picked you out special! (1 Pet. 2:9 KJV).

- *"Royal priesthood."* I love this one! We are royalty because we are members of the King's family. That makes us princes and princesses! Just call me…Prince Buck! In our house live Prince Buck and Princess Andrea! (Try it with your name.) Not only "royal," but also a "priest" in a fraternal order of priests. This is really exciting because according to *Fausset's Bible Dictionary,* there are four characteristics of the priest. He was (1) chosen of God; (2) the property of God; (3) holy to God; (4) *he offered gifts to God, and took back gifts from God.*[1] How neat is that? (See First Peter 2:9 KJV.)

- *"God's household."* You are an important part of God's family; you live in His house. You are family! *Family* literally means "father's house" (Eph. 2:19).

- *"Those made alive with Christ."* Just as God raised Christ from the dead, He also raised us together with Christ to a new life (Eph. 2:5).

- *"Those for whom Christ died."* Is there any greater than this? *You were worth dying for!* Jesus said that there is no greater love than for a man to lay down His life for His friends…then He went and did it! (See John 15:13.) If you were the only sinner in this world, He would have died just for you (Rom. 5:8).

Now you see why the devil wants to stop you—he sees your potential! You are a threat to all he has planned!

When we come to Jesus Christ and ask Him to be Lord of our lives, God anoints us, sets His seal of ownership on us, and gives us the Holy Spirit as a deposit on His promises, guaranteeing them in our lives. We need to collect on this guarantee and pursue the promises of God in our lives. I am talking about Second Corinthians 1:20-22 here. Listen to what the Word of God says about us:

> *For no matter how many promises God has made, they are "Yes" in Christ. And so through Him the "Amen" is spoken by us to the glory of God. Now it is God who makes both us and you stand firm in Christ.* **He anointed us, set His seal of ownership on us, and put His Spirit in our hearts as a deposit, guaranteeing what is to come** (2 Corinthians 1:20-22).[2]

In that book I also noted that satan tries to steal our power by stealing our identity. He has a strategy he uses; he will attempt to steal our identity in the following ways:

- *Satan gets us to tell ourselves lies about ourselves.* You never experience the power and success God has for you because you believe the lies the enemy has you tell yourself.

- *Satan sends others to tell us lies about ourselves.* Comments and statements from parents, teachers, peers, coaches, relatives, employers, and even our spouses can cause you not to see yourself as God sees you—for you believe his lies spoken through others.

- *Satan causes us to seek other identities.* We look for the approval of men and women, so we pursue titles, awards, and recognition, or we identify with certain groups to feel good about ourselves. When we do this, we are tapping into worldly power and not the *dunamis* power of the Holy Spirit.[3]

Satan is known as the *"accuser of our brethren"* (Rev. 12:10 KJV), and I have simplified his strategy when it comes to his attempts to affect how we feel about ourselves. Putting it simply,

He tells you what is wrong with you (you believe you);

He tells others what is wrong with you (you believe them);

He tells you what is wrong with others (you tell them, and they believe you);

He tells God what is wrong with you (God doesn't believe him).

Yes, not understanding who you are will steal or drain your *dunamis!*

3. There is a lack of understanding of the work of the Holy Spirit within the Church.

Jesus said in John 16:7 that it was better for Him to go away to Heaven so that the Holy Spirit could come. Why would it be better to have the Holy Spirit than to have Jesus walking with us in the flesh? The answer is that He knew He could have greater intimacy with us through His indwelling Holy Spirit than He could walking in our midst. His power would be multiplied to each believer. Jesus understood the power within us, but we do not understand its power to reveal mysteries, overcome all the power of the enemy, do greater things than Jesus did, and use His authority and dominion to take back the Kingdom.

Before the Holy Spirit came at Pentecost, the Spirit dwelt in the Holy of Holies in the Temple of Israel and in the Tabernacle before that. The Spirit of God only *"rested"* upon the prophets; He did not indwell them. However after Jesus's death, resurrection, and ascension, the promised Holy Spirit was given, and the Church became the dwelling place of God. I am not talking of a church building here; I am talking about the spiritual union of the human spirit and the Holy Spirit.

This is why the apostle Paul said in First Corinthians 6:19, *"Do you not know that your body is a temple of the Holy Spirit, who is in you, whom you have received from God? You are not your own; you were bought at a price."*

Paul was addressing the fact that the Corinthians were behaving like unredeemed mudcakes, involved in sexual immorality and subjecting the Holy Spirit within them to that behavior. Because of their behavior, the Holy Spirit would not be able to work in their lives with *power*, instead, He would be *quenched*. First Thessalonians 5:19 tells us that we can *"quench"* (KJV) or *"put out the Spirit's fire"* (NIV) by our behavior.

Hmm…so that is where the power is going!

The challenge presented to the Church, those within whom the Holy Spirit dwells, is to know when we are listening to the Spirit and when our minds and emotions are dictating our behavior.

In my experience with Him, the Lord showed me clearly why we as human beings have so much trouble with our emotions. In fact, if we act guided by our emotions, it almost always leads to the wrong decision, yet we are created as emotionally-driven people. Why? Was this a flaw in His creation that makes us not always respond in the best way?

No, there was a "disconnect" when the light of God's presence within the mudcakes went out in the Garden of Eden at the first rebellion. Let's take a look at what happened using our understanding of computers to aid us.

The Lord showed me that the emotional system of the original mudcakes was like *the operating system* of a computer. The emotions were what sensed the presence and the leading of the Holy Spirit *(software or programming)* and transferred the information from the Spirit of the Creator to the mind of the mudcake. Then the mind *(processor)* of the mudcake would have the body *(hardware)* respond according the will of God. The mind of the mudcake simply processed the communication between the spiritual and the physical side of the mudcake and vice versa.

The mind was never to give orders on its own, only process the commands of the Creator's Spirit. The mind, therefore, was what satan *(the hacker)* targeted for a specially designed *virus,* which we shall call the *"pride virus."*

Satan's appearance as a serpent when he tempted Adam and Eve to eat of the *Tree of the Knowledge of Good and Evil* appealed to their minds. The serpent prior to the curse of God in Genesis 3:14 was a beautiful and appealing creature, and he appealed to the rational ability of the mind—the ability of the mind to think on its own. (Tempting is like trying to download a virus into the computer.) He took advantage of the mind, with its ability to transfer information to the emotions, and he "hacked" into it. Their minds stirred the emotions, received back an erroneous directive from the emotions, and sent a message to the body. The body responded as it was designed to do, but in a way that was not in accordance with God's will when this virus blocked the original hardware's programming, which was *"Don't eat of the tree."* Therefore, the hardware or the body responded incorrectly, and they ate of the tree.

Instead of seeking direction about their actions as they did for everything else from the Spirit, once the *virus* was downloaded, they took the directive of the serpent, something people do too often today—even in the Church.

Because of their disobedience, their light went out as the Spirit of the Creator God left them, exposing their nakedness. The Holy Spirit's connection to the minds of the mudcakes through the emotions was at that moment also disconnected. Since the emotional operating system was disconnected and could not discern directives and guidance from the Holy Spirit, the mudcakes now turned to the only connection they had from which to receive information and directives—the mind! From this moment on, the mudcakes would be in a battle between the mind and the emotions. The mind would send information it received from stimulus of the hardware or body to the emotions for directions; the emotions could not connect to the programming of the Holy Spirit because it was not there, so it would return a confused directive to the mind, and the body would respond according to the directive.

In the unredeemed mudcake, the mind sends and receives information to and from the mind to the emotions with the emotions frustrating, angering, distressing, and tempting the mudcake in many ways. The mind then responds to the emotions and manifests the directive of the emotions in a physical response of the mudcake—sometimes right, sometimes not so right! I think we can all relate to this issue in our lives!

The mind becomes the battlefield instead of a processor for the mudcake!

The challenge for the Spirit-filled believer is much like a person who has had a stroke and lost the ability to speak. The potential is there to speak, but he or she with great difficulty must *relearn* to speak; in time, it gets better and better. Some people recover completely, and others accomplish varying degrees of recovery.

So it is with Spirit-filled mudcakes; they must relearn to connect their minds through the emotions to the Holy Spirit to receive guidance and directions. The mudcakes must now be able to discern when their minds are receiving a directive from their emotions stimulated by their own minds or a directive or information from the Holy Spirit.

The best tool we have to make this discernment is a working knowledge and understanding of the Word of God and an understanding of the nature and will of God!

That means peeling that onion—I mean, studying the Word of God!

Learning this process of reconnecting your mind and actions through your emotions to the Holy Spirit is what I believe theologians call *sanctification*. This is also what is referred to by the apostle Paul as the *"renewing of your mind"* (Rom. 12:2) or as *having your mind set on what the Spirit desires* (see Rom. 8:5-6).

I continue to teach what I call the *three Rs of the mind*. We need to complete the process of our sanctification by *"renewing"* and *"resetting"* our minds so that we can have a *"resurrected"* mind, which the Word of God calls *"the mind of Christ"* (1 Cor. 2:16). This is learning how to reconnect the mind to the directives of the Holy Spirit and navigating the sea of emotions as we do so. We need to be able to understand the Holy Spirit's thoughts and not follow our own.

Now you understand why you have so many problems with your emotions and do not always behave the way you really want to. *When you are "misbehaving," you are simply following the directives of your emotions through the mind and not the Holy Spirit.*

Let me address an area that causes disunity within the Body of Christ and steals *dunamis* from us.

It is human nature to criticize what we sometimes do not understand. I know; I have done it! Many believers cast aside and criticize what they call "emotional" praise and worship services where the redeemed mudcakes respond with numerous emotional responses such as crying, laughing, jumping, and running, as well as others. Let's take a look at this issue in the light of our preceding discussion.

In such a service, the knowledge and understanding of the Word in the redeemed mudcake mind stirs the emotions. They are stirred by love for Jesus, awe and reverence, praise, and prayers for circumstances in their lives. If the emotions are stirred for any other reason, it will produce false results! During this time, the discernment and guidance of the Holy Spirit begins to connect as the mudcake focuses on the Spirit with the mind through the emotions. This connecting process may manifest in numerous ways. I have even connected with the Holy Spirit during the writing of this book. Sitting at my computer, I have wept in joy and in anguish, laughed, shouted, sat in silence before the Lord, got up and walked around as I was so moved by a revelation, or just simply stopped writing to praise His holy name! Why?

You see, as the Spirit begins to send responses to my mind, my emotions are stirred to transfer this information; in that stirring of my mind through the emotions, my mind sends signals to my physical body (hardware) to express as best as it can actions that reflect what is going on during my communion with the Spirit. However, the onlooker who who does not have this understanding or has not reestablished this connection will say, "It's just emotions!"

Well, yeah it is!

My operating system is working, and that is all that is visible to the critical onlooker; you cannot see what is being communicated to my mind and to my spirit. I am hearing the Spirit of God speak to me, and the critical onlooker is seeing the flashing and beeping of the lights of the hardware! And to be frank, some mudcakes flash and beep more than others!

Now, understand this concept: People manifest physically the communing of the Holy Spirit in different ways. Personally, my most common response is total silence before the Lord, listening for Him to speak to me, reveal to me, and even love on me. When I do that, I am soaking in the hot tub of the Holy Spirit, feeling His presence and His awesome warm love bubbling around me! *Ahhh...* To you I appear to be peacefully standing with my eyes closed and maybe my hands raised.

However, the guy next to me may physically feel overwhelmed by the same presence, and he starts shouting and then dancing! We are both experiencing the same thing, but our hardware receiving the signals from our minds interprets them in a way most like our own nature.

Now you ask, "Are some of the dancing, singing, shouting mudcakes not in communion with the Holy Spirit?" Yes, some are not, for there are some who have not learned to connect with the Holy Spirit, but are simply sending emotional messages back and forth from the mind to the emotions and getting themselves all stirred up.

How do you know which it is? If the behavior is disruptive or inappropriate to the moment, then it is most certainly emotional and must be dealt with by the one charged with maintaining the order in the worship. We need to understand that even in our churches there are mudcakes in varying stages of recovery. In any given group of worshipers, some are communing, some are practicing, some are learning, some are mimicking, and some may be inappropriate. The inappropriate ones are usually so because they are getting their instructions from a counterfeit or demonic spirit! Yes, demons come to church; they get there on the people!

The true test of whether the mudcake is really connecting or not to the Holy Spirit is determined by whether they received direction, guidance, or healing from their time of worship before the throne of God. They must ask the following question: Did I give and receive love to the Lord, or do I feel the same way when I go home as I did before I came?

I have been in services where shouts of praise are going up, but I found myself disturbed by the actions of one or more in the service. I know the *feeling* that comes up inside me; it is one where the Holy Spirit is telling me that the response is not of Him. I will usually describe these moments by saying that "my spirit did a backflip," which describes my reaction in my spirit.

Usually this happens at a time when a physical manifestation appears out of order such as shouting or crying out loud when a spirit of silence has come over everyone. It actually could be a counterfeit demonic spirit trying to "distract or neutralize" the situation, or it could be someone who is just overcome with emotions. This would be someone who has learned to stir the emotions, but not to hear the Holy Spirit in the stirring.

We need to understand our emotions in the light of their originally created purpose and understand the will of God and the Word of God in order to interpret our emotions properly. The mind must interpret directives and feelings according to the guidelines of the Word.

I recall hearing one time about a church leader who announced that the Spirit was guiding him to a certain woman as his life mate and that he knew she was sent to him by God.

How nice!

Not really! He was already married with a family. If he left his current wife and family, he would need to divorce the first wife, leave his family, and marry the woman he was already involved with. The Word of God says that God hates divorce, and He also hates adultery. The directive of the Spirit here as the man claimed was contrary to the nature, will, and Word of God, so the source of that directive was his own mind and emotions with demonic influence yelling, "Go for it!" He had not tested it with the Word, probably because he did not want to; instead, he cooked up a recipe for disaster in his life. This example is more obvious than most, but it illustrates the need for us to know the Word and will of God in order to understand the leadings our minds get through our emotions to be sure they are from the Holy Spirit.

Lucifer robs us of *dunamis* because we do not understand how the Holy Spirit works within us.

4. There is a lack of Holy Spirit power due to the lack of unity in the Church.

The strategy of the enemy here is pretty straightforward. The apostle Peter warned us that *"your adversary the devil, as a roaring lion, walketh about, seeking whom he may devour"* (1 Pet. 5:8 KJV). Jesus likened His children to sheep and Himself to a good shepherd. The strategy of lions and wolves when it comes to sheep is the same. If you separate a sheep from the others, it makes that sheep easy prey.

This is another way the enemy neutralizes the Church by breaking up their unity. Paul warned in Ephesians 4:1-3 that one of the ways that we are to live and walk worthy of the calling on our lives is to promote unity, yet in the Church we find believers criticizing and gossiping about each other. Gossip is very destructive to the *"bond of peace"* Paul talks about (Eph. 4:3); this lack of unity is part of what diminishes the miraculous power of the Church.

Denominational differences have contributed greatly to the disunity of the Body of Christ, and this has disempowered it in many ways. While most denominations agree on the doctrine of salvation through the atonement of the blood of Jesus as a sacrifice for sins, the Church allows itself to be divided over those lesser doctrines that will not affect your salvation. Lucifer distracts the Church with arguments over these lesser doctrines and diminishes the power of the Church through disunity.

Today we have numerous churches in a city preaching salvation through the Cross of Jesus Christ, yet they stay to themselves and rarely organize anything together to impact the city for Christ. One of the most frustrating things that a believer can do today is to try to organize something to impact their city, seeking the participation of all the churches in that city. Godly wisdom is being proclaimed in the sanctuaries, but not on the streets as the Book of Proverbs says it should be (see Prov. 1:20). As the Church, we fail to impact our cities by being unified and "infecting" them for Christ; therefore, we become culturally irrelevant in society. The power of the Holy Spirit is diminished due to a lack of unity.

5. There is a lack of understanding of the strategies of satan to counterfeit the power of the Holy Spirit.

The Lord in my experience has made me keenly aware of satan's attempts to neutralize and even steal our ability to manifest supernatural power through the Holy Spirit by causing us to seek the counterfeit supernatural. Satan is the great counterfeiter; he tries to distract those who are not firmly grounded in the Word with philosophies, understandings, religions, and desires that lead to eternal death rather than life in Christ.

Every person is born with an innate desire for the supernatural because we were originally created to have fellowship with a supernatural being. Each person was also born with a desire to "control" because we were originally created not to be controlled by another, but to take dominion over all creation under the direction of the Spirit of the Creator within us.

This natural desire for supernatural power is the reason why people are so attracted to the supernatural. In books, movies, television shows, and throughout the media today, people are attracted to the depiction of humans manifesting supernatural power. People are drawn to witchcraft as a form of supernatural power to control circumstances and people as well.

In society today, the depiction of witchcraft and the macabre has become ever more popular and gets into our homes by stealth under the disguise of "entertainment." We even allow our children to be entertained by it instead of teaching them about the power of God and the Holy Spirit. We become more intrigued with the lesser power of the underworld than we are with the super power of the One who flung the stars into space with one word!

The depiction of witchcraft also caters to our desire to control; children fantasize what it would be like to deal with their adversaries in such a manner. It teaches manipulation and intimidation of others in order to control or to "get your own way." Manipulation and intimidation is a form of witchcraft. Studies show that women most often use manipulation, while men use intimidation, in an effort to control. I have read studies that show that the practice of witchcraft or Wicca has grown in recent years, and the number of young people getting involved with it has increased substantially. It should be no surprise to us since one of the most popular book and movie series at the present time depicts children employing the powers of witchcraft. Many of us sit idly by, smiling and enjoying ourselves because it is a "cute story."

Let me tell you, there is nothing cute about witchcraft! I have been face-to-face with real witches who were there to stop what I was doing, and there is nothing cute about them! A witch is a demonically inspired person tapping into the lesser supernatural powers of demons. Until you look into the eyes of a real witch tapped into this lesser supernatural power, you have not seen witchcraft in reality. I remember seeing the eyes of a witch who was there to stop what we were doing; they were red with white catlike pupils.

That is not cute!

Was I afraid? Nope! Were the witches successful? Nope! Why? They were not successful because their power was no match for empowered believers who knew how to tap into the Holy Spirit!

I recall visiting a village in Africa where I was told that there was a time when they could not walk where we were walking because of an infestation of snakes. People were regularly getting bit, even finding snakes in their beds. This infestation of snakes came as a result of witches placing a curse on the village in an attempt to control the people. We did not see a snake the whole time we were there. "Where did they go?" I asked.

I was told that an "army" of Christians in the village began praying and took authority and dominion over the land, over the witches, and over the snakes. As they continued praying and tapping into the supernatural power of the Holy Spirit, the snakes began to die all over the village. "There were dead snakes everywhere!" I was told. Soon this "army" confronted the witches and drove them out of the town, even casting demons out of some of them.

Wow, such a powerful story! Even better, I was about to meet the general of this army! I was moved to tears as this powerful general of the Holy Spirit walked toward us with a couple of other members of the army. I looked at this mighty person with a greater respect and awe than I would have looked at a reigning king or president of a great country.

The general of this army was wearing a pretty, colorful skirt and blouse with a pocketbook over her arm, smiling the sweetest smile as she and the two women with her greeted us! Everyone in the village called her "Mama."

This army of God was a group of Spirit-filled women who had learned to tap into their *dunamis* power over darkness and "infect" and "affect" their community for the Kingdom. The last I heard, there are still no snakes there! It appears Mama and her soldiers are still on guard.

These are the kind of stories we should be "entertaining" our children with!

Why do we not see this kind of power often today, especially in the Western world? Part of the reason has to do with the thinking of the Western world, which is based on Greek "logical" thinking. Logic leaves no room for the supernatural, so Western thinking tries to find a way to explain everything through the use of the mind. The mind tests everything, and if it cannot figure it out, it simply concludes that it is not real or that we just don't have all the information yet! Eastern and Middle Eastern thinking allows room for the supernatural. In many third-world cultures, they have been taught to *expect* the miraculous.

The emerging generation of the Church has allowed this desire to become infected with the counterfeit supernatural, just as the world has done. The enemy has launched a counterattack to attract this generation primarily through the media to sorcery and forms of entertainment that depict witchcraft and the demonic. This infection within the Church is further manifested in increased use of drugs and alcohol by young people. Instead of seeking comfort or highs that the Holy Spirit can provide, they seek it in drugs and alcohol. Yes, many young people in the Church today, there on Sunday singing with the praise and worship teams, are using drugs and drinking alcohol. I know this information firsthand! Alcohol is also called "spirits"; do you know why— because it attracts counterfeit spirits, neutralizing our youth from seeking comfort from the Holy Spirit. They cultivate a "buzz" that makes them feel mellow and accepted by peers instead of cultivating the ability to tap into His mighty power, a power that will kill a whole village full of snakes if they learned how to use it!

C.S. Lewis once said, "For spiritual nature like bodily nature will be served, deny it food [Word of God] and it will gobble poison."[4] Thus, Christian mudcakes come under deception because the spirit of the world and the Spirit of God are in opposition to each other. *Whatever spirit we focus on will become primary in our lives.*

Jesus taught us that we are not in the world because He has called us out of the world. Of course, we are physically in the world until our physical death, but Jesus was referring to being *spiritually* one with the world and following the deceptions of lucifer and his demons.

When we engage or are entertained by the supernatural, it will rob us of the **dunamis** *power that the Holy Spirit desires for each one of us, for one will repel the other. The one we retain is the one we embrace.* If we desire the *dunamis* power of the Holy Spirit in its fullness, we must wholly embrace it without compromise. We must not dabble in the counterfeit supernatural, even in the name of "entertainment."

6. There is a lack of commitment to the Kingdom; willingness to compromise diminishes the power of the Spirit.

One of the biggest thieves of the power of the Church is compromise. Satan even tried to tempt Jesus away from the Cross with the "easy way." When Jesus was in the wilderness for 40 days, satan offered Him all the kingdoms of this world if Jesus would just bow down to him. Satan at that time still had what he offered Jesus because Jesus had not yet redeemed the world and won it back on the Cross of Calvary. If Jesus had taken the "easy way," He would not have had to go to the Cross, our redemption would not have been won, and Jesus Himself would have become subservient to satan and the powers of darkness.

We see so much compromise within the Church today; it is no wonder that the power of the Holy Spirit manifested through believers is diminished. Christians and unredeemed mudcakes are entertaining themselves with the same things. I see young people who have grown up in the Church encouraging each other to get that margarita after a tough day at work or just because it is "Thirsty Thursday." Christians spend hours in front of the television and no time in the Word. At best, many of them pick up their "15 minute devotional," read it in 5 minutes, and then are off for the day to *"wrestle against principalities and powers of darkness"* with a barely charged spiritual battery flashing a low power warning light. Only a small percentage of the Church watches or even has Christian television, but they can tell you the latest on

American Idol or some other program. The desire for the spiritual is over-shadowed by the temporal.

The Church today, like Adam and Eve, partakes of forbidden fruit, trying to cover its actions, hiding from the presence and power of God, and substituting counterfeits, rituals, and traditions for the truths of the Word of God!

Many in the Church today live a life of convenience while espousing a secular worldview "tainted" with the teachings of the Word of God instead of projecting a biblical worldview occasionally "tainted" by secular thinking.

Which worldview do you have?

The success of satan's strategy rests on this fact: **Everyone wants a Savior, but not everyone wants a Lord. Everyone wants to escape the fires of hell, but not everyone wants to change their lifestyle.**

Commitment takes work; compromise is the "easy way."

7. The lack of an expectation for the miraculous has created an atmosphere of unbelief.

I mentioned briefly before that Western thinking and philosophies actually do not provide for an expectation for the miraculous. Even when a miraculous event such as a physical healing occurs, we seek to explain it away. Most of Western thought is based upon Greek thinking, which employs logic. We have trouble believing it if it is just not "logical." For this reason, I believe the demonic activity in this country is more subtle than it is in other countries where the people are more aware of supernatural activity. Most evangelists and missionaries who travel to other countries see a different mentality when it comes to the miraculous. We all agree that the people in these countries have *not* been taught this concept: *"If you cannot explain it or find a rational reason for it, then it is not real!"* They believe in the supernatural and expect it as part of their lives. Remember, our minds in their originally created state were only intended to process the supernatural, not to understand it.

This type of thinking is even prevalent in the Church. I grew up in it and was very aware of the dichotomy between what we said we believed, what we read in the Bible, and what we actually expected would happen. I remember discussing this with one of my pastors when I was young. He was a "closet believer" in the miraculous power within and told me that he believed the church was afraid of the supernatural gifts of the Holy Spirit. Over time he was going to teach the church more and more; he felt he needed to ease them into it. Well, let me tell you, the first time he hinted at the power to have the Holy Spirit work in their lives, the people got him right out of there. I heard them say, *"He has some funny ideas!"* I guess they were saying, *"We'll have none of God getting out of His box in this church; we'll have none of that miraculous stuff in here. Why, that's of the devil!"*

Yes, many in the Church today will attribute supernatural manifestations to the devil! Jesus even rebuked the people of His day for attributing the power He manifested to the devil. How ironic—we sooner believe that the devil does supernatural things than that God does! It can be an uncomfortable thing to step out believing that we can do the supernatural, so we retreat, proclaiming that the power was only for the days of the Book of Acts. How convenient! That is simply an excuse for not exercising our faith and developing our ability to tap into the power of the Holy Spirit.

8. Negative talk will cause us to walk in diminished power.

The Bible is full of exhortations to watch what we say. Why? The Bible says there is power in our words and that *"out of the same mouth proceed blessing and cursing…"* (James 3:10 NKJV). People say such derogatory things about themselves and about others. In the financial teaching that I have done, I cannot tell you how many people will say to me, *"Well, my grandparents were poor, and Momma and Daddy struggled to get by. I am sure I will never have much money."* Do you hear both the lie of the enemy they are repeating and the curse they are putting on themselves? God wants us to speak blessings over our lives, not curse them! God wants us to say,

"I can do all things through Christ who strengthens me" (Phil. 4:13 NKJV). I researched that word *all,* and do you know what it means? It's not rocket science here. It means *all;* yes, all things, no exceptions! The word *strengthens* in that verse is translated from the Greek word *endunamoo.*[5] Do you see our word *dunamis* (God-like, miraculous power) in this word? Well, this word we translated in English as "strengthens" means to "empower" with *dunamis,* God-like power!

All around us we hear negative talk. When I had my surgeries, the doctors told me all the things that could go wrong. I remember a surgeon telling me all the dangers of bleeding to death in the procedure he was about to do on an artery in my neck. I asked him how many times he had done it. He told me probably 1000 times. I then asked him how many times a person bled to death in those 1000 times. He said "none"! In today's society, we dwell upon the negative. The medical world, with its many successes, notoriously dwells upon the negative. I recognize that this is largely due to lawyers who seize on the negative in order to add to their personal bank accounts—so the medical community protects itself from them by cursing what it does—just in case!

I listen to the talking heads on television, and they say such negative things about people and situations. I do not like to hear people say, "That would devastate me," or "Now this little girl's life is ruined." While the situation may be tragic, there are many examples of Christ delivering a person completely from a tragic situation. Don't speak a curse over someone just because you have sympathy for what happened to them!

We talk and teach against the miraculous; we speak cursing out of our mouths, and we are surrounded by negative, cursing speech from others in our daily lives. All of this has created an *atmosphere of unbelief* in the world in which we live, and this poisoned air has gotten into the lungs of the Church as well.

We have been together in this book for a substantial amount of time now, and I want to share with you some things that the Lord has shared with me.

I have learned to tap more and more into this *dunamis* power since the day they took me off that operating room table, and I became more keenly aware of the spiritual world that is all around me and of which my spirit is part.

Now if you recall, I told you earlier that since the near-death experience I had in 1995, I have not been the same man. I have had a passion to develop an intimacy in my relationship with the Lord. I told myself that this idea of being able to tap into the Holy Spirit was either a lie, or I was going to get it! And I was either going to logically explain away my experience as due to trauma or morphine, or I was going to embrace it as being real!

As time has passed, I have spent untold number of hours in the Word of God and in prayer, usually at least two hours a day. During these times, I would sense God's presence so strong at times that I knew He had something to communicate to and through me.

I have found myself in increasing measure experiencing what I call "waking dreams," where God reveals a truth about His Word or the times in which we live; sometimes He gives me a word of exhortation or guidance for others regarding situations in their lives.

These experiences are happening more and more throughout the Body of Christ and are of the type prophesied in the Book of Joel. In that prophecy, we are told that in the *"last days"* dreams and visions would become part of the activity of the Holy Spirit within the Church. I was very skeptical of this type of thing until I encountered the glory of the Lord in that "near-death experience" and that glory began to manifest in dreams and visions in my own life. I was the most surprised person of all when the Lord began to reveal things to me I could not know any other way and then watched them manifest so accurately.

When one encounters the glory of the Lord, there is something inside that dies and something inside that just comes alive with power! This is what I have experienced.

The Lord often speaks to me as I said in what I call "waking dreams," and they have proved to be very prophetic in nature. He also speaks to me in times of prayer, especially when Andi is leading. I know that the Lord has something to say when a phrase starts repeating in my mind. This is why if you read any of these prophetic words that have been written down by my hand, the first phrase is often repeated twice before the writing continues. When I am aware of a repeated phrase, I grab a pen and paper and write, sometimes a lengthy dissertation. Actually much in this book was written this way, with revelation coming to me as fast as I can write. When I'm finished, it is written in excellence and often varies in style. Some of these written words have been passed around within the Church at large and recognized not only as exhortations, but as prophetic "templates" for events that have occurred after I spoke them in the Church.

My wife one time called me "the reluctant prophet" because my skeptical nature and training in my early Christian life made me test, test again, and just for good measure, test again. You know, God is so patient with a skeptic, and that is what I was!

I recall speaking in a large church, and in the middle of the message I was preaching, I suddenly realized I had just moved over into the prophetic ministry, words coming out of my mouth without forethought! I listened to them myself as I prophesied:

This church is about to experience an unexpected and substantial increase in growth and prosperity. There will be a growth in minis-try, people, and property, and you must be ready for it, embrace it, and support it. It's coming, and I tell you it's about to happen!

Later that day when I thought about what I said before all those people, I confess I listened a bit to the enemy when he said, "What were you thinking? Why did you do that? Do you know what you said?"

I put my concerns into the Lord's hand and forgot about it. Fortunately the people I ministered to did not forget, and later they reminded me of the word I gave when they called to tell us what had happened after our time there.

The week following our ministry there, the church was approached by another large church in the city asking that the ministries merge and that their ministry and property come under the authority and ownership of the church at which I had given the prophecy. As if that was not enough, within a few months, another church about an hour away asked if their ministry could become a satellite ministry of their church. About 100 acres of prime land came with the merger as well. I guess the Spirit of the Living God was using me to speak to His people.

I tell you all this so that you would understand some things I am going to share with you as we move to the end of this book. In fact, as I have said, many of the things in this book have come to me in this manner, even as I was typing. I did not research this information; I have given it to you as I have received it.

Let's get back to this *atmosphere of unbelief* for a moment. Where did I get such an idea?

You see, my family has a need for miracles. We know we have the faith, but they have not occurred as of the time of this writing. We also saw other situations needing a miracle in the lives of other believers, and they were not experiencing the miraculous yet, although they were walking in belief. I was very burdened by all of this and asked the Lord why we were not seeing them happen despite the promises of Scripture. What was wrong?

I know many of you reading these pages are asking the same question yourselves. Well, stay tuned; God is revealing and preparing to do something, and He wants you to be part of it!

While I was seeking a Word from Him, I began to notice a phrase kept coming up inside of me that meant nothing to me. The phrase was being repeated over and over inside of me: *"A charged atmosphere, a charged atmosphere."*

Recognizing that the Spirit wished to reveal something, I grabbed a notebook and pen. This is exactly what I wrote within a few minutes from start to finish as the Holy Spirit spoke through me:

A Charged Atmosphere, A Charged Atmosphere…

Behold it is I, yes; it is I, the One who laid the foundations of the world and re-created it upon its destruction by the evil one. Yes, it is I, the God of Abraham, Isaac, Jacob, and Joseph. Yes, it is I– your God. Your Father…I love you!

I must create again, for the atmosphere, the spiritual atmosphere has become charged with a poison which threatens My people, My precious children, and the ones who name My name. It causes some to not fulfill My purpose for them, and it causes some to die before their appointed time. These are those of whom I spoke when I told them they would do greater things than I when I put my Holy Spirit within them. They walk not in the miracles, prosperity, and abundant life I call them to because of the poison, the poison; they breathe it, they breathe it, it is all around them! Therefore the signs and wonders which were to follow them are limited, a fraction of My desire for them.

I must re-create again, I must remove this poison from the atmosphere that controls their minds and limits their power. I must filter it out. The poison they breathe is all around them, for the atmosphere, the spiritual atmosphere is charged with unbelief, and just as in Nazareth unbelief limited My power, unbelief limits theirs.

It is all around them; that unbelief is spoken so profusely that even My people have joined in. They look at the circumstances, the infirmity, the hurt, and they do not look to Me, so from out of their mouth they speak unbelief, placing limitations on Me.

They place their limitations on Me, for they are My mouth; they are My arm; they are My agents representing My power upon the Earth.

I must re-create belief; I must filter out unbelief. I will re-create it through My agents, My people who in the days ahead will breathe in the poison of unbelief and filter it through their heart and speak out belief. The world will say they are in denial, but I say they are in belief. In time, unbelief will diminish, and belief will fill the atmosphere, and miracles will increase and be noted among the people of the world. The level of belief will increase even within the medical community, who will even see the dead rise at their word.

I tell you it is coming; it is coming, a time of faith applied, a time of miracles. I say to you, you cannot pray the prayer of faith and look at the one needing it; you must look to the One who can give it. Do not put your shortcomings on Me, but put My power on you.

Breathe deep the gathering gloom, My child, and breathe out miracles, breathe out the abundant life, breathe out My name, breathe out belief! For you will do greater works than I![6]

Do you remember that part about our emotions being the operating system to connect the mind and body to the Holy Spirit?

The date of this writing is important to my family because it reflects an emotional time in our lives when our son Ben, who was on kidney dialysis, had just had a transplant fail at a hospital with a 99 percent success rate. I will not get into all the details of the situation now, but just to let you know, this was a particularly emotional time.

There was another time early one morning that a particularly accurate and poignant revelation was given through me, one that has been referred to by many as a "template" for an event that occurred soon thereafter. I received it early in the morning after the night my mother died!

What were my emotions doing at this time? They were reaching out to the Holy Spirit, and the revelations flowed down through my emotions to my mind and my hand wrote—what God had to say to His people!

Our minds need to rein in our emotions, direct them toward the Holy Spirit, and tap into that *dunamis* power! Then we will receive comfort, revelation, direction, and *"all power"!* We develop the mind of Christ as we learn to *renew* and *reset* our minds. We cannot do it unless we seek intimacy. I never would have developed a relationship and married my wife Andi if every time I had an opportunity to take her out on a date or spend time with her, I decided to watch television, go skydiving, or play ball, the other things I liked to spend time doing. I had to take time away from other things I enjoyed doing in order to get to know her and develop an intimate relationship with her.

You may laugh, but that is what we do with the Holy Spirit. Then when the circumstances of life come down on us, we ask, "Where is He?"

We should ask, "Where was I?"

We can only develop an intimate relationship with the Holy Spirit and walk in His power if we study and learn the Word of God, gain understanding of who we are and who He is, walk in unity, refuse to compromise or seek the counterfeit, and breathe out belief into the atmosphere of unbelief which surrounds us. *Those who learn to do this will become part of a group that will emerge in these last days before the return of King Jesus to claim His Kingdom.*

The Holy Spirit wants you to be part of an emerging, end-times remnant coming out from the Church at large.

Chapter 21

Flaming Torches

A radical change will take place as we approach this one-world Kingdom established by Jesus Christ. We are, no doubt, in the last days before some major prophetic events occur; in the next chapter we will see exactly why theologians today are convinced that the Kingdom of God is at hand.

We need to look at the activity of the Church as we approach this event and the fulfillment of the remaining end-time prophecies. As we look at these, we will notice that Israel is very much a part of the movement toward the Kingdom and actually serves as our "timepiece" to discern the times of the seasons.

The Church's mission is being kicked up a few notches as we approach the Kingdom. The Church has been effective in being salt and light and advancing the Gospel of Jesus for generations; *however, the powerless part of the Church is diminishing and will continue to diminish as the powerful part of the Church arises.*

We have seen that, from the days of Adam and Eve, every time the Creator God gets ready to do something big and transition to the next phase of His plan, He calls out a remnant from the people to take us to the next strategic level. Let's recall our list of remnants so far:

303

1. Adam and Eve

2. Descendants of Seth

3. Noah and his family

4. Descendants of Shem

5. Descendants of Abraham

6. Nation of Israel or the descendants of Jacob

7. Tribe of Judah (the Jews)

8. Jesus Christ the Messiah

9. The spiritual descendants of Jesus or the Church

And for our next remnant:

10. The "Overcomers"

Do you notice how many generations of remnants there are? Interesting! If you remember, the tenth generation has always done something significant, hasn't it? Also, if you recall, the number eight is the number of "new beginnings"; take a look at who was number eight! So who and what are these people in God's tenth remnant?

God says that He is the same yesterday, today, and forever. He will do exactly the same thing once again to take back the Kingdom of our Lord and establish it upon the Earth.

Let me restate and elaborate on it a bit.

The Church's mission is entering a new phase; this change is radical, and we are on the cusp of this occurring. *Those not discerning enough to see it and become part of it will not survive a powerless faith. There is a remnant emerging that will operate with the* **dunamis** *power of the Holy Spirit and establish the Kingdom.* Jesus called them *"overcomers."*

The Church is the mother of a great last-day ministry of the *overcomers* who will transition the world from the Church Age into the Kingdom Age!

The Christians of Rome were covered in pitch and set afire to light the streets in a demonically inspired attempt to stamp out the Gospel. Their sacrifice instead lit the way for the advancement of the Gospel throughout the whole world. In the same way, a remnant of Christians today, the *overcomers,* will allow themselves to become "flaming torches" to light the way to the establishment of the eternal Kingdom.

Let me share with you another prophetic word. I received this word on a flight to Tulsa, Oklahoma, at 33,000 feet. I initially resisted the repeated phrase within me: *"Flaming Torches, Flaming Torches, just as in Rome, Christians will once again be used as flaming torches."* I began to pray against the persecution of believers, which I believed the Lord was about to tell me was going to occur again, as it had in Rome.

However, when I had written out the completed word, the Lord spoke to me again and said, **"Flaming torches will arise wherever this word is released by you—preach My Word."**

I was ministering that weekend in a church in Tulsa, Oklahoma, and released the word for the first time with impact.

The Holy Spirit also revealed to me that the Lord will bless the ministries with flaming torches wherever this word is released, and we have seen that occur wherever it has been released. I believe that this word was in response to my prayers asking the Lord to reveal why we do not see the miracles of the church of Acts today and why miracles tarry for those truly expecting them. I believe that this word builds on the word given in January 2007, "A Charged Atmosphere," which I shared with you in the last chapter.

As you read this word I call "Flaming Torches," I believe you will see the things we talked about in the last chapter as well as in this chapter. Somewhere between Detroit and Tulsa at 33,000 feet over the heartland of the

United States, the Lord shared with me the following revelation written down in about 15 minutes:

> Flaming Torches, Flaming Torches, just as in Rome, Christians will once again be used as flaming torches…

> Yes, it is I, and I say to you the mission of the Church is expanding; it is at the point of increase for the end of the Church Age is coming. My Church has been effective in being salt and light and advancing the Gospel, which will continue, but a remnant will emerge who will transition the Church Age into the Kingdom Age. A radical change is coming and will take place as we approach the Kingdom, and the remnant of the Church will come forth in power, and their work will bring about My Kingdom.

> I say to you, much of the Church is falling away, caught in compromise, disunity, a lack of understanding of My Word and the power of the Holy Spirit within them. They do not know the enemy and submit to his strategies and are overtaken by the poison within the "atmosphere of unbelief" [reference to word received January 6, 2007, "A Charged Atmosphere"]. Yes, a change is coming, and those who are not discerning enough to see it, to become part of it, will not survive in a powerless faith much longer—they will either be swept one way or another.

> Laodicea, Laodicea, I wish that all would come to power, heated with the power of the Spirit, but those whom I do not spew out of My mouth will emerge as overcomers with power and take back My Kingdom. It is they who will sit on the throne with me [reference to Revelation 3:14-22]. The powerless part of the Church will diminish, and the powerful will arise. I say to them, *dunamis,* receive the *dunamis,* the power of the Almighty…walk no longer in unbelief and change the atmosphere to a Kingdom atmosphere where belief dominates and the miraculous is expected.

The Church, My Church, My Bride, like Eve is partaking of the forbidden fruits, trying to cover its actions, hiding from the presence and power of God and substituting rituals and traditions for the truths they represent. My faith is not an intellectual faith, but a faith of understanding and of power. It is not to be debated, just to be obeyed. Knowledge and understanding without power is fruitless. Call up, call up the power within you, oh dwelling place of the Most High!

The world seeks the supernatural, seeks that power, that presence of power lost in Eden, and satan bewitches them with the counterfeit, the counterfeit power. He attracts them to witchcraft, sorcery, alcohol, the elixir of the evil spirits, the occult, that counterfeit power which mimics the heavenly power. Books, movies, television display the counterfeit, and even My children, My Church indulges, for they do not know who they are, nor the power within them, and they foster the atmosphere of unbelief. The world looks at them and laughs. I spew that out of My mouth, for it is distasteful to Me, for it steals their power, their intimacy with Me.

This emerging generation will embrace witchcraft, the occult, or live vicariously through books and movies, and much of the Church will join them, but a remnant will break off and experience true power; the others will be swept away in a powerless faith. The need for the supernatural will cause a rising remnant to grab hold of true power, the *dunamis* the Church already possesses.

The last blockade of the enemy to stop the supernatural power of the Church is being chipped away, allowing sporadic miracles to leak through into the atmosphere of unbelief, increasing faith, and as the wall crumbles, miracles will increase in leaking through until the wall falls and the Lord suddenly appears in His Temples, releasing a flood of the miraculous, increasing faith, and ushering in the Kingdom.

Flaming torches will light the greatest show on Earth, for the emerging remnant is called to reveal the greatest power on Earth. Just as the physical flaming torches of Rome called attention to the Gospel and advanced it, so the spiritual flaming torches will call attention to My power within those torches, and My Kingdom will be advanced and established. Becoming a flaming torch is painful, and many of the powerful will be ignited through adversity, infirmity, persecution, hardship, and peril, but I say to you, they will emerge, they will emerge—blazing with the glory and power of the Almighty.[1]

I suggest you go back and read it again! You should also read again "A Charged Atmosphere," which is in the last chapter.

Before we go on, let me address the skeptics, the "God doesn't do that today" people. I know you are out there, 'cause I used to be one of you! I was one of those conservative, God-loving people who looked at anything supernatural, prophetic, or visionary with a very hairy eyeball! However, I also saw the dichotomy between what I believed and accepted and what I read in the Word of God. I often asked the Lord about it.

Then one day I had a near-death experience. God did not cause it, but He used an effort on the part of the enemy to destroy me. Why He chose me I do not know, but He did—maybe because I was a skeptic who was open to the truth.

I asked the Lord why He chose me one day, and then I opened my Bible right to the passage where God spoke in the Old Testament through Balaam's donkey! (See Numbers 22:21-31.) The message was loud and clear; God can use anyone or anything; they just have to be open and willing to become God's tool! I guess I was in good company.

My dear skeptic friend, what would you do if you had a near-death experience such as I described? What would you do if afterward you sought the Lord about whether it was a real experience or not, and during that seeking

He told you some things you did not know, and then you saw them come to pass? Then what if you sought Him some more; He revealed more to you, and those things too came to pass? What would you do?

Yeah, I know what you would do—you would preach it with a passion and a power like you never had before, and you would want more and more intimacy with the Creator and seek His power! My advice to you dear skeptic— seek intimacy with Him with a passion and be open to His leading. You'll see, I promise you; you'll see! Don't let your mind get in the way; it was only intended to be a processor of the Holy Spirit's directives. I want you to experience the *dunamis*, and I don't want you to get swept away in a powerless faith! Instead, I want to see you swept up into a powerful faith! I want you to become an *overcomer!*

So who are these overcomers transitioning us from the Church Age to the Kingdom Age, these spiritual flaming torches lighting the way with signs and wonders into the eternal Kingdom?

In the Book of Revelation we find Jesus speaking to seven different churches operating in the world in the last days. He refers to them by the names of seven early churches that were an example then of the type of churches we see operating in the world today. Jesus talks to them about who they are and the things that are pleasing and displeasing to Him, but He always references a group which will break out from them in power. He calls them *overcomers,* and He gives to these overcoming mudcakes a promise!

Let me summarize the churches and what they represent among the churches operating in the world today, including what the Lord found pleasing and displeasing in each one, as well as the rewards promised to the overcomers. (See Revelation 2–3.)

1. Church of Ephesus

Pleasing: Their hard work, rejection of false teachers, and unwearied perseverance.

Displeasing: They have lost the freshness and newness of their love for Christ as a bride may lose her freshness for her husband after years of marriage. He wants them to rekindle the freshness of their love by remembering the heights from which they fell and the depths from which He had redeemed them. The Groom is encouraged by the fact that even though they have lost the excitement of their relationship, still they hate evil, but Jesus wants them to experience complete intimacy with Him. This is a church like we see today, working hard to advance the Gospel, but not experiencing true intimacy and power.

Promise: Those who *overcome* by experiencing the freshness of intimacy with the Holy Spirit will have the right to eat of the new *Tree of Life* in the eternal Kingdom.

2. Church of Smyrna:

Pleasing: Despite their physical lack and the afflictions they have endured, they have become spiritually rich; this is a persecuted church much as we see in China and other oppressive countries. He warns them of further persecutions, death, and imprisonment for what they believe, but He knows they will remain faithful and receive the Crown of Life in the eternal Kingdom

Displeasing: Jesus is not displeased at all!

Promise: The *overcomers* will not be hurt at all by the *"second death,"* which is the spiritual death of the soul and eternal separation from the Creator. Physical death will bring eternal life in the presence of Christ, and there will be no second death at the judgment as there will be for those who have rejected Jesus Christ as Lord.

3. Church of Pergamum:

Pleasing: Jesus commends them for their steadfastness in the light of the trials and difficulties they have faced, especially since this church is planted in a place where there is much demonic activity; in fact, Jesus references their steadfastness in a place *"where satan's throne is"* even after a faithful witness in the city was put to death. Here is some quick information on Pergamum to illuminate it further for you. The altar of Zeus was in Pergamum, and sacrifices, including human sacrifices, were offered there day and night without ceasing. Jesus references a man named Antipas who was roasted on this altar. Despite the great demonic presence in this city, the church remained steadfast. (A bit of trivia here: this altar at Pergamum was moved to Germany by Adolf Hitler.)

Displeasing: Jesus reproves them for allowing people of corrupt principles, doctrine, and practices to fellowship and have communion with them. Though they remained steadfast, they were guilty of compromise. This church does not have sound biblical teaching, and there is a serious lack of knowledge and understanding of the Word. These people may be redeemed, but there is no power or understanding, so they tolerate false doctrine and carnal people among them.

Promise: Jesus promises the overcomers some of the *"hidden manna"* or the comforts and blessings of the Holy Spirit, which is not available to the rest of the world. He also promises *"a white stone with a new name written on it."* This alludes to a custom of giving a white stone to one who was acquitted of guilt, and the *"new name"* refers to a spiritual adoption where one is given the name of Christ.[2]

4. Church of Thyatira:

Pleasing: Jesus commends them for their love, service, faith, and perseverance. He also makes note of their growing fruitfulness.

Displeasing: Jesus reproves them for allowing people who practice and tempt others into sexual immorality in their church.

Promise: Jesus promises the overcomers in this church great authority and dominion over nations. He also promises them the *"morning star."* The morning star is none other than Christ Himself, and Jesus promises His presence continually with them.

5. Church of Sardis:

Pleasing: Jesus finds nothing pleasing about this church; it is totally dead.

Displeasing: This church appeared to men to be well with a great reputation, but it was full of hypocrisy, and faith was dead and dying. There was a form of godliness, but not the power. Sardis would reference the social churches of today where the Gospel is not preached and where the ungodly or the immoral could be leaders because there is not understanding or truth in their teaching.

Promise: Jesus promises the *overcomers* that they will be dressed in white, a symbol of purity in righteousness. Jesus says that their names will never be blotted out of the book of life and that He will acknowledge their names before the Father God.

6. Church of Philadelphia:

Pleasing: The church had an excellent spirit; they had love and kindness for one another. They have kept His Word and not denied His name. Jesus is very pleased with this church! This church has got it—they have an understanding of the truth and operate in power.

Displeasing: Jesus does not find one fault!

Promise: Lots of stuff! Jesus is very pleased and says that He will keep them from the hour of trial (the Tribulation) that will come upon the whole Earth. He will make them a *pillar* or a monument of grace in the Temple of God, and He will always be with them. He will give them a new name, a name of adoption, and Jesus will make them an heir to the City of God that will come down from Heaven.

Wow—I think I want to go to this church, don't you?

7. Church of Laodicea

(Note: This church is referenced in the word, "Flaming Torches.")

Pleasing: Nothing is pleasing to the Lord; this church is considered to be the worst of the churches!

Displeasing: Jesus declares that they are *lukewarm* or indifferent; they leave a bad taste in His mouth. They think highly of themselves and are rich in material possessions, but their souls are impoverished. They do not hear Him although He is knocking at their door and calling to them; they pursue their agenda and not that of the Kingdom.

Promise: The *overcomers* in this church will be given the right to sit with Jesus Christ on His throne.

Now study these churches and ask yourself, what kind of church do I attend? Now, you all can't say "Philadelphia"! Philadelphia was a church that exhibited love and kindness for each other. There was no infighting, no power struggles among the people, and sound biblical doctrine was being taught. The people sought intimacy with God and wanted more and more of His *dunamis* power. Yes, there are some churches like that today, though in reality not all of the people attending this type of church can be described this way.

Let me warn you of a trick of satan! Don't ever look at people in a church to understand Jesus; look to Jesus! The church is not a sanctuary of perfect saints; it is a hospital for sinners! You will see the spiritually dead and dying in the church as well as people at various stages of recovery. The redeemed mudcakes are not perfect; they are just forgiven and made perfect in the eyes of the Father because of Jesus's sacrifice. They only take on true perfection at physical death when they join Jesus Christ in glory.

Perhaps you attend a church that preaches sound doctrine, but there are a lot of problems and disagreements among the sheep. Perhaps there also is a real lack of power, and the miraculous is rarely or never demonstrated.

Perhaps there is a lack of follow through, and things are not done with excellence.

Perhaps you are in a church where nothing "spiritual" seems to happen; the Bible is barely taught at all, and you go away just as empty as you came. Perhaps it just seems like a lot of ritual and tradition that do not do much for you.

The good news is that whatever church you attend, if you attend at all, you can be part of this remnant of *overcomers*. You can come out of the church seeking intimacy with Jesus Christ and begin to tap into the power of the Holy Spirit in your life.

In these last days, Jesus will call a remnant out of every type of church there is; they will join with a larger remnant, and this group will begin to manifest in an ever-increasing manner the *dunamis* power of the Holy Spirit. These people will most likely come out of the churches Jesus is displeased with and will begin to attend Philadelphia or Smyrna-like churches while the others are swept away in a powerless faith.

I speak in a lot of churches all over the world, and while I have yet to find a "perfect" church, I see each of these types operating. Andi and I have made some observations.

The churches seeking the power of the Holy Spirit and teaching sound doctrine are increasing; some are increasing exponentially. This is the fastest-growing segment of the Church today. At the same time, we see other churches declining in membership with a serious lack of enthusiasm on the part of people to help in any way. They show up on Sunday if at all, and that is all they ever do. The rest of the week they do what the world does and at best grab their one-minute *"devotional"*—if they have time! There is much infighting, and things are done with a serious lack of excellence. Membership of the church is declining as well. People are either not going to church, or they are leaving and joining other churches where the *overcomers* are headed.

The churches that do not uphold or preach the Word of God with authority are where the socially minded go, not the spiritually minded. Many of these churches are pastored by individuals who may not even know Jesus themselves. I do not get invitations to speak at these churches because I preach the Word of God, and the Bible often contradicts their beliefs. They do not want someone who preaches the Word of God with power. They think the Word is outdated!

Occasionally, there is a church that Jesus is displeased with that starts seeking to be an *overcomer* church, usually due to the leadership's desire to be an *overcomer.* I have seen churches transformed into *overcomer* churches. This transformation will happen if the people do not throw the leader out before it happens. Sometimes the church just splits, and the half desiring to be an *overcomer* church emerges. Now, sometimes churches split because two groups want to have their own way, not because they want to be *overcomers.* Then you just have two churches with which Jesus is displeased.

Perhaps you go to a church because that is how you were raised, and you have always gone there. That's not a good reason to go to church. If you are not growing spiritually and experiencing the power and glory of the risen Jesus Christ, if you do not find yourself anxiously awaiting the message from the Word of God, if it does not change you, and if your faith in Christ is not your primary interest in life, then you are in the wrong church. If you in your heart want to be an *overcomer,* then you need to find a church where the *overcomers* are going.

From our experience, I see *overcomers* obviously collecting in the Smyrna and Philadelphia types of churches. In third-world countries and in areas where the Church is being persecuted, the Smyrna church predominates. In other areas, we see the Philadelphia church. These are the churches where the Spirit is going to fall on the people, and the *overcomers* will emerge.

Most *overcomers* today are not experiencing the full power, but they are actively seeking the power of the Holy Spirit and a deeper intimacy with Him.

Lucifer's wall of lies and the counterfeit is now holding back the miraculous power of the Holy Spirit within the Church in its full manifestation. This wall is crumbling, and increasingly we will see miracles leak through until a time when there will be a final surge as prophesied by the prophet Joel and by Jesus Himself. As the wall crumbles, the *atmosphere of unbelief* will be filtered through the hearts of the *overcomers*. As they breathe out belief in the power of the Spirit, the atmosphere will change to one of belief in the miraculous power of the Holy Spirit operating within the *overcomers*. The world will be impacted for Jesus Christ by the remnant of *overcomers* for a season before the Kingdom is finally, eternally established.

We are called to reveal the greatest power on Earth! Do you want it? If you are still with us at this point in the book, then my guess is that you do. If you do, then put yourself in the way of the power of the Spirit; let Him manifest through you despite your fears. When satan's wall crumbles and the miraculous begins to flood into the Church, the atmosphere of unbelief will be cleansed, and the *overcomers* will become "flaming torches" once again, lighting the way into the Kingdom!

That fire starts with a burning passion to know the Word and will of God, as well as the work of the Holy Spirit. Perhaps adversity, infirmity, calamity, or just an emptiness will take you there, and that is how many will come to be ignited with the passion and fire of the Holy Spirit.

Are you an *overcomer*? If not, there is still time to join us!

Chapter 22

Angels, Demons, Science, and the Supernatural

━━━◆━━━

*For the invisible things of Him from the creation of the world
are clearly seen, being understood by the things that are made,
even His eternal power and Godhead; so that they are without excuse*
(Romans 1:20 KJV).

Do you remember the statement I have made throughout this book? *Everything that happens in the physical world is a manifestation of something that is occurring in the spiritual realm.* Conversely, we are learning that physical actions as well can affect things in the spiritual realm. Science in recent times has become aware of this. Let's explore this a bit before we go on and see how the plan of God unfolds in these endtimes. It is important to our understanding of end-time events that we understand these two realms of existence and how they intertwine.

This all sounded to me for years like a lot of *"gobblely-gook"* until my experience in 1995 when I moved in and out of the spiritual world. Since that time, I have increasingly learned to tap into the Holy Spirit by reconnecting my spiritual link with the Holy Spirit that was originally lost in Eden. I have learned that the spiritual world operates side by side with the physical world. Since my experience, I have become more aware of my spiritual side, perhaps because I experienced life for a brief moment in Earth time as a totally "spiritual being" when I briefly checked out of the physical side of life. I know and "feel" things that I cannot express with words; there is no way, so I don't—I can't!

We operate in the physical world, but God the Father, Jesus, the Holy Spirit, the angels, and those mudcakes who have died before us operate in the spiritual world. That's where they are! A time is coming when Jesus and those who died before us will return to the physical world. Unfortunately, lucifer and one-third of the angels who fell with him also operate in the spiritual world, and this presents a unique challenge to us. Which is which?

We know this much; we can't see them!

Or can we? We always imagine the spiritual world as being somewhere else—in the Earth or up in Heaven—but in actuality, it is all around us, as well as in those places. Throughout the Bible we find instances where God opened the spiritual eyes of people who saw spiritual activity operating around them; the revelation gave them an understanding of what was causing their circumstances and how to deal with it. We have stories of missionaries who saw the manifestation of angels and demons as they found themselves in various situations.

How can things be invisible—and why do some become visible and then invisible again? Why can't we see the spiritual world?

Let me try to give you a brief explanation from my experiences and also from modern-day technology.

Often when I am receiving spiritual discernment or when I feel the Lord desiring to speak a word to me, I sense a "quickening" or "speeding up" in my spirit similar to the feeling I recall experiencing as I traveled in my near-death experience. It can mimic dizziness, and early on, I would fight it off, thinking I was getting dizzy. It is at that moment after the "speeding up" that I begin to receive information from and through the spirit. Since my emotions are the bridge from the spiritual to my mind, I shut off the transmitter of my mind and just leave the receiver on. Then the Holy Spirit, using the pathway of my emotions, begins transmitting information to my mind—sometimes turning on my mind to transmit that information either to my mouth or to my hand to write. In the case of dreams, He saves it on a flash drive for me to access when I awaken. I often feel what God feels, which is why sometimes I weep, laugh, or exhibit some other physical manifestation.

Sometimes I even see things in the spirit as I look with my eyes. At those times, if you were standing with me looking at the same spot, you would probably not see what I might tell you I see. The reason is that the imprint of the image on my mind is not coming from the neurological signals of my eyes as yours are, but is being imprinted on my mind by the Holy Spirit "downloading" information through my emotional system. When the Lord is done downloading to me, I conversely sense a "slowing" in my spirit.

I can have a similar experience while going about my daily routine. I might enter a place where I sense a demonic or angelic presence. Once when I was in someone's home, I sensed evil, and when I moved to a place where it was strongest, I saw DVDs and books of so-called entertainment depicting the occult. I have had many experiences like that. People don't believe me sometimes, and they definitely do not like to hear about it, but the Lord told me one time a number of years ago that "technology would become my friend." What the Lord was saying to me was that technology and science would begin to find evidence of the supernatural. I did not understand what that meant at the time, but it appears that perhaps that time is coming or has come. I know now that much of what I "knew" as a result of the near-death experience is now being backed up by evidence from science.

Now what is this speeding or slowing I sense? I asked the Lord, and after He gave me the explanation, I discovered that science is finding evidence to support this concept as they study what today is referred to as *quantum physics.*

Now we do not want to get too deep into this, but the research is going on. In fact, "paranormal investigators" use electronically sensitive instruments to detect what they call "signatures" of ghosts, and, yes, they are detecting something in the supernatural. However, they have little understanding of the spiritual world because they have little understanding of the Word of God or the things that we have discussed so far in this book.

Let me tell you what these "ghosts" really are. These ghosts really are demons operating in this world. They are not the spirits of deceased persons. They might resemble someone who has passed on, but these appearances are what we call "familiar spirits," demons taking on the image of something "familiar" to us in an effort to deceive and control us! (See First Samuel 28:7.) The "imaginary friends" of children are often manifestations of this type of thing. Young children are often spiritually more sensitive.

Why?

Young children have not yet learned to not believe in the miraculous, and we indulge their love for the supernatural with stories and fantasies. The enemy seizes on this in an effort to deceive them or lead them astray. This is why we should not let them be entertained with stories of witchcraft or the occult. This only makes them susceptible to the deception of the demonic counterfeit influences in the world.

Let me illustrate this with a personal experience that occurred in our family. In 1981, when our daughter Mindy was two, we moved into a big, old, beautiful house in upstate New York. The home built in 1814 had been a restaurant in the area for many years before being turned back into a home. The house had a rich history, and we were intrigued by it. We found out through the local historian that it was one of the oldest homes in the area built by a wealthy land owner. Presidential cabinet meetings had even been held there by President Millard Fillmore, who had grown up not too far from where the house was located. Even more importantly, it had been a strategic location of the Underground Railroad on one of the major routes used by the slaves to flee from the slavery of the south. The slaves would follow a nearby river by night and come to the house before daybreak where they could rest, be fed, and hide from their pursuers. At nightfall, they would be given directions to the next location; they would travel to their next destination until most of them ended up in Canada about 100 miles north of where the house was located.

We enjoyed showing our guests the secret room that you could gain access to by removing a couple of wall boards in the walk-in closet in the bedroom where Andi and I slept.

Our time in this house was best described as one with many difficulties and trials, personal mistakes, health issues, and battles. What we did not know was that the battles were as a result of spiritual activity in the house and its effect on us. We had numerous experiences in the house that were of a supernatural nature. We lived there a total of nine years.

Five years after we moved in (Mindy was now seven years old), we were blessed with our son Ben. We moved him into a crib *next to the walk-in closet* in our bedroom on the other side of the wall of the secret room.

Ben was a little character whom we called "Chuckles" because we would hear him laughing in the room all by himself when he was supposed to be napping. He had such a big belly laugh and such a vivid imagination, or so we thought at the time.

As he grew and began to talk, he began at first to tell us how something went "round and round" in the room. "Where?" we would ask. He would point to the ceiling, "Up dere, the light go round and round." We would smile, shake our heads, pick him up with a hug, and take him downstairs. Cute we thought, and it was!

As his speech improved, he would talk about "Goddy." Goddy, we thought, was an "imaginary friend." Ben would tell of the antics of Goddy in his room and by his crib. During this time of our lives, we had been having prayer meetings in our home, often with a couple with whom we had established a prayer partnership about the time Ben was born. Dan and Joanne are our prayer partners today, 24 years later, and we still meet and pray together. We have been there for each other through many difficult times.

Dan and Joanne were also very spiritually discerning; one day they told us that they believed the Lord was telling them that we were to move out of the house and to begin packing. We all had become discerning of some of the unusual circumstances of our lives and the spiritual activity around us. Once, I had turned to go upstairs and was startled as I saw someone dart into our bedroom at the top of the stairs. I was so sure I saw someone that I grabbed a baseball bat and went upstairs to investigate—nothing. No one was there, but I know I had seen it!

Not long after that, the Holy Spirit gave me another warning. We had recently become friends with a couple, and he was the local station commander for the New York State Police. He and I were going somewhere together, and he made his first visit to our home to pick me up. When he stepped inside the front door, I asked if he had any trouble finding us. He laughed out loud and informed me he had been there many times in the past when he was in the patrol car. He then went on to explain that people who had lived there years before had two sons. "They were really evil and were into everything, some really crazy and bizarre stuff; we were always here looking for them! Mom and Dad weren't much better either!" He told me.

Mr. Skeptic (me) was becoming more and more aware of the spiritual, but God was not done with me yet! I still needed a few more lessons! The big lesson in my life was still six years away!

Dan and Joanne told us that they both discerned through the Holy Spirit that an angel had been posted by the front door for our protection and to ensure that we would move to the place the Lord had for us. I received it and prayed about it, but still I was somewhat skeptical about the whole thing. I didn't see any angel at the door! At our request, they both independently, and without discussion with each other, wrote down a description of the angel they had seen through the Spirit. They both described him as *wearing a broad-brimmed hat!* It was a hat like Clark Kent (aka Superman) wore. I still did not quite buy the whole thing and took it with a grain of salt.

One day, I had come home and parked the car out in front of the house; my little buddy Ben was with me in his car seat. I lifted him out of his seat, and as I was shutting the car door, Ben twisted in my arms, and looking toward the front door of the house, pointed, and asked, "Dad, who's dat man?" I looked around; I did not see anyone.

"What man, Ben?" I asked.

Ben responded, "Dat man...by da door...wif da hat!"

Out of the mouth of babes! *Now what are you going to say, Mr. Skeptic?* I asked myself. We then walked up the steps and through the front door, past the spot where Dan and Joanne discerned that this angel was supposed to be standing as little Ben was pointing and smiling...at no one! Andi was watching us from the house the whole time.

I muttered under my breath in amazement toward the place Ben was looking as we passed by, "Clark Kent, I presume?"

That day Andi and I decided to start packing, with not a clue where we were going.

Ben today is an adult and working in Christian television as a producer, editor, and webmaster. Ask him about Goddy, and he will describe the being in detail and tell you that Goddy would visit him when he was alone in the room. He remembers his experience in detail to this day. For years, Ben has described it to us as a short being with grey skin wearing a jester's costume like revelers wear in the Mardi Gras in New Orleans. He called this visitor "Goddy" because it would come to the side of the crib, peer through the bars, and say, "goddy, goddy, goddy" in a mocking way. In Ben's mind, it was mocking God! He is insistent now as an adult that Goddy was not his imagination; it really happened. Perhaps I too had caught a glimpse of Goddy that day I went after it with the baseball bat.

Goddy knew how to get Ben's attention; it entertained him with the supernatural! Lucifer uses the same tactics to attract people's attention to the counterfeit today, and we call it entertainment!

When Ben was born, an older man known for his spiritual wisdom and discernment spoke a word over him that has been repeated by others through the years. The word was that he has special gifting in spiritual matters and would be very spiritually discerning with an unusual and powerful calling on his life. We have seen this from the very beginning of his life.

Now, do you want some more "chills"? I am not done with the story of Goddy. Let me, as Paul Harvey would say, give you the rest of the story!

Fast-forward with me 20 years after we moved out of that house and left Goddy behind. Ben, living in Tulsa after his graduation from college, began to discuss these experiences with us, especially in reference to spiritual warfare we were doing regarding a chronic medical need in his life.

Goddy—a "familiar spirit" in a jester costume like those worn in the Mardis Gras—was "haunting" a house in upstate New York. What is the connection? It made no sense in the light of the fact that Ben as a child had no exposure to the Mardi Gras or to jesters, so where did he get such an idea? It was only years later when he learned of this that he made the connection between the memories of Goddy and the Mardi Gras. The interesting thing is that Goddy's appearance as Ben described it was much like UFO grey beings or "Greys," except that this one was in a jester's costume.

Ben shared with the leadership of the church in Tulsa where he attends about his childhood experiences with Goddy. These leaders are originally from Louisiana. They shared their knowledge with him that the slaves in Louisiana were heavily involved in voodoo and other forms of witchcraft.

When he shared that with us, I began to research the Underground Railroad led by a black woman named Harriet Tubman. There was much information available to me on this since we live in the heart of where the Underground Railroad was headquartered. Tubman's home is nearby, and she is buried within minutes of where I write these words.

It was not a real railroad, but a system of prescribed routes for the slaves from the south to freedom. Along these routes was a network of "safe homes"; slaves could knock on the door early in the morning before the sun came up and be hidden in a secret room, fed, and kept safe throughout the day. Our home, as I said, was one of these homes in the early 1800s and through the Civil War era. The narrow river that passes by the house was one of the rivers followed by the slaves to their destination.

It was then that I made the chilling discovery more than 20 years after Ben saw Goddy. I traced the route that passed by our home back to the south and to my amazement found that it was the route used by the slaves from Louisiana! No doubt, slaves from Louisiana who practiced voodoo and witch-craft had at multiple times been in that closeted secret room on the other side of the wall next to Ben's crib! The early owners of the house, when they opened their doors of safety for these slaves, were also unknowingly opening the doors to the demons that these slaves had invited into their lives. Perhaps they practiced their curses against their pursuers and their enemies while in that secret room off our closet.

This illustration serves as a backdrop as we take an intriguing look at how the spiritual and the physical worlds operate simultaneously, and occasionally, as in the case of Goddy, overlap.

I was a licensed skydiver in my younger years, and the whole sport was based on things I could not see like gravity and the forces of thrust and lift. When I was in freefall, hooking up in formations with other jumpers or hanging in my parachute, I rode, navigated on, and used air. I could not see any of those things, but they were there! I never stood at the door of the airplane and refused to jump because I could not see the air, knowing full well I needed it to arrive safely on the ground! Air—it sustains us, but we cannot see it. Air is the most obvious of the invisible, but there has been much over the centuries that has not been so obvious, at least until the world of microscopes. When I was in school in the '60s and '70s, I was taught that the smallest thing was an atom and the electrons and neutrons that orbited it.

Quantum physics is the study of things so small we cannot see them. Scientists have discovered something even smaller than an atom, which they call a *quark*. A quark is a subatomic particle; it does amazing things that defy the laws of physics.

Jesus said in Luke 17:6 that we could move mountains if we had as much faith as a mustard seed, the smallest seed that you can still see with your eyes. Jesus was saying that small things can manifest great things in this world. Jesus also taught that matter responds to faith and to words. Jesus demonstrated this when He spoke to a fig tree and cursed it for appearing to be something it was not; it then withered and died. He turned water into wine, and He spoke to the wind and the waves, and they listened. Our words, according to Jesus, can influence matter, and now quantum physics is finding scientific evidence to agree with His teachings.

Did you know that these subatomic particles orbiting the nucleus of an atom exist in a wavelike state until someone looks at them? When they are looked at, they look like particles or dots.

How do they know they are being looked at?

These particles also behave differently to each observer. They also respond in different ways to words, depending on whether the scientist is speaking positively or negatively to the particles. The question here is, "Do they respond according to what the observing scientist believes?" All matter is made up of these particles, which are invisible, and they respond not only to words, but to attitudes as well. We can affect matter with our words and with our attitudes. Jesus taught it, the Bible teaches it, and now quantum physics is finding evidence of it as they are just barely getting started in these studies.

The Word of God says, *"Out of the same mouth proceed blessing and cursing..."* (James 3:10 NKJV); Hebrews 11:3 also states that *"...the things which are seen were not made of things which are visible"* (NKJV). Quantum physics is only in the beginning of finding evidence that physical things are being made out of invisible things! And you thought the Bible was outdated! Science is just beginning to catch up with words written thousands of years ago. We need to be careful with our words, for we can bring upon ourselves or someone else whatever we speak, not only according to the Bible, but also quantum physics.

How can a thing not be? It makes no sense until you bring it down to an atomic level. What may not be possible in the world in which we live appears to be possible in the subatomic world.

Here is a shocking correlation about the subatomic world. The quantum physicist has discovered that these "invisible particles" do something amazing. They call it "tunneling," which means that this subatomic world is not bounded by "barriers." In other words, particles have the ability to move through things they should not be able to move through.[1]

No, wait! Let me explain it in words with an illustration I know you will be able to understand. In the subatomic or invisible world, particles can "walk through walls" like Jesus did after His resurrection when He appeared to the disciples!

Quantum physicists have discovered a realm without physical boundaries that is part of the makeup of all physical things! What was that verse from that old Bible again? Oh, yes, *"the visible was made from the invisible"* (Heb. 11:3).

Simply stated, subatomic particles are not there until we look at them through a powerful microscope; then they appear! If we could see microscopically, we would see all things at this subatomic level moving very fast. The interesting thing about these subatomic particles is that they are moving at an incredible speed, but they will stop so you can see them when you look at them! Interesting, huh?

Two verses pop to mind as I consider these things. Hebrews 11:1 says, *"Faith is the substance of things hoped for, the evidence of things not seen"* (KJV). Hope exists in your heart and mind and is spoken out of your mouth! Here's my paraphrase of this verse in the light of quantum physics: *As you hope and speak, those things not seen will become a reality in your life!*

The apostle Paul in First Corinthians 1:27-29 says:

*God chose the foolish things of the world to shame the wise; God chose the weak things of the world to shame the strong. He chose the lowly things of this world and the despised things—**and the things that are not**—to nullify the things that are, so that no one may boast before Him.*

When the atheist scientist stands before God at the Great White Throne judgment and says that he or she did not believe based on scientific evidence, I think God is simply going to reply, *"A good scientist does not reach a conclusion if he does not have all the evidence. You simply did not have all the evidence!"* I told you earlier that I knew the nurse who took care of a very well-known atheist scientist as he lay on his death bed. She said that as he lay dying, he would cry out for God. She kept telling him that Jesus would come to him, but his stubbornness and pride caused him to be more willing to enter an eternity of darkness than to accept the light of the One who died for him. How tragic!

The apostle Paul knew this type of person well because he had been one of them, until one day on a road to the city of Damascus when he encountered the risen Lord Jesus Christ. On that day, he encountered and accepted the truth. He referred to people like this renowned scientist in Second Timothy 3:7 as *"ever learning, and never able to come to the knowledge of the truth"* (KJV).

The Word of God tells us that in the endtimes learning or *"knowledge shall be increased"* (Dan. 12:4 KJV), and we have seen that technology has advanced so quickly it is hard to keep up with it. Today we are finding evidence of a universe that exists in antimatter, which leads a scientist to talk about a *parallel universe* and even multiple ones! A parallel universe definitely exists, the universe of the *unseen;* now the *seen* universe is finding evidence of its gateways!

I remember studying the phenomena known as *black holes* at Houghton College with Dr. S. Hugh Paine, whom I referenced before as a godly man, scientist, professor, and friend, as well as one of the fathers of the *Gap Theory* we discussed earlier. I can still see him in my mind describing in class the black holes in space. Black holes are areas where nothing is visible, but there is so much energy coming from that spot, it literally draws all matter toward itself. Astronomers tell us that the laws of physics seem to change drastically at the surface of a black hole. Dr. Paine suggested that perhaps when matter got to this hole it was sucked into a parallel universe. I suggested that they might be gateways into the dimension of the spiritual, invisible, or *unseen* universe. He smiled and agreed, but warned that I would be laughed out of a room full of astronomers if I suggested such a thing as an invisible realm. "They don't believe in anything they can't see!" he said. That was before quantum physics, the study of the *invisible!* There these scientists go again, trying to match wits with an Almighty Creator they don't believe exists anyway because they can't see Him! Doesn't make sense, does it? As I often say, *we can be so intelligent in our own eyes, we become stupid!* Atheist scientists are *"stupid smart people."*

I would rather be thrown out of a room full of astronomers in this world than thrown out into *"utter darkness"* from the throne room of God at the judgment to come!

The evidence is increasing just as Jesus said. He said there would be signs and wonders that would increase in the last days. Science is now wondering about and researching an invisible realm!

Here is my understanding of all this put very simply: *The material or the* **seen** *world is the spiritual or* **unseen** *world in slow motion!*

Romans 1:20 says,

For the invisible things of Him from the creation of the world are clearly seen, being understood by the things that are made, even His eternal power and Godhead; so that they are without excuse.

In science, we have learned that when things reach a certain speed, the eye of the mudcake cannot see them! We can see a pot of water boil, but we cannot see the molecules speeding up, which makes the water heat to the boiling point—and that process is slow by comparison to some other things.

The atomic particles that make up an *invisible* spiritual being or thing are simply moving so fast they cannot be seen, nor are they bounded by the physical properties and forces that *seen* matter is made up of. Things in the physical world, however, do parallel things in the spiritual world and vice versa.

When a person has a prophetic dream or a vision, the mind receives an imprint of something through the bridge of the emotions as seen through the eyes of the Holy Spirit. When a person sees something with the naked eye in the spiritual as Ben saw "Goddy" and the "Clark Kent look-alike angel," he or she is simply seeing a spiritual being: the atomic structure slows down enough for us to catch a glimpse of it.

Yes, spiritual beings have the ability to slow their atomic structure in order to be seen in the physical world, and we have records of this occurring in the Bible. In Genesis, we are told that Lot was visited by angels in Sodom and Gomorrah. Angels also appeared to the shepherds, to the Virgin Mary, and at the tomb. After His resurrection, Jesus walked through walls, but then Thomas and the other disciples could touch Him. How did these spiritual beings become visible and even touchable? They are not bounded by matter and can speed or slow their atomic structure to move from place to place— and do it "in the flash of an eye."

However, a physical being like the mudcake is also a spiritual being. Why can we not speed up our atomic structure and become invisible? This ability could be especially invaluable if we did something stupid in front of a crowd!

The reason we cannot is because our spirits are bound *within* our physical bodies. Our spirits are still inside of the mudcake "shell" God made for them. We cannot speed up our atomic structure as long as our spirits are in there. That only occurs when the mudcake shell dies. Then the spirit is released immediately into the spiritual world, and the spirit's destination is determined by the decisions it made while still a mudcake!

When our loved ones die, we still have their mudcake shell, but they're gone! Perhaps instead of saying that they "died," we should say they speeded up! In my experience, as I looked at my body lying on the operating table, I had the same feeling toward it as you would toward a box you received something special in. You collect the item contained therein, and the next day you put the box in the trash. You were happy to have the box when you needed it, but now that you have what was really precious and important from inside the box, it has served its purpose! *Your body is the box your spirit came in!*

So we cannot see the spiritual world because its atomic structure is moving so fast we cannot discern it. When a spiritual being slows its atomic structure, as it can, it can become anything from a "ghost" to a physical being. In the glorified body Jesus received after the resurrection, He was able to speed or slow the atomic structure. The redeemed mudcakes will receive the same type of body in the Kingdom! Sounds like fun to me!

Let us not forget the fact that satan and the angels who fell with him are also spiritual beings, and they influence our lives and societies with an agenda of destruction from satan. They attempt to *distract, discourage, and destroy* us and what God has called us to do. They provide us with the counterfeit supernatural, mere child's play in comparison to the power of the Creator God. Yes, they can smash plates, open and close doors and windows, and move things around, but they cannot fling the sun, earth, moon, and stars into place with a single word or blow the breath of life into a mixture of dirt and water and make a human being!

We have seen in the Scriptures that these demons have at times slowed their atomic structure in order to copulate with mudcake women and produce evil races. We know a race of giants existed after the Flood too. Goliath is believed to be one of the Nephilim. Nimrod was considered to be one as well. This is how the "mythological" beings of Apollo, Osiris, and Gilgamesh came to be. All these beings were the same person; Nimrod was one of the Nephilim who led the world in building a tower to Heaven because he had conquered the world. Now he wanted to conquer Heaven, manifesting his master lucifer's desire to "be like God." And God went down to confuse their language because, He said, united these people could accomplish anything! Remember that the Nephilim were the offspring of mudcake women and the *fallen ones*, which are also sometimes referred to as "the watchers."

Well, what about UFOs? Are there Nephilim today? Can we see angels and demons?

Just like Goddy overlapped the spiritual and the physical realms, the activity of the demons and occasionally angels will overlap, and at those times we may catch a glimpse.

Over the years, photography has given us some interesting "blemishes" called *orbs*. Now our Western, "ain't no such thing as spirits" thinking tries to explain this away as dust particles reflecting back on the image. The interesting thing is that they cannot prove it or duplicate it, and it is only a theory to explain the phenomenon. They also only seem to appear where angelic or demonic activity is encouraged and is at work.

In 2008, Ben attended the NAB, or National Association of Broadcasters, convention held every year in Las Vegas. Ben loved the architecture and found the city very interesting, but the thing that he noticed the most on the strip was the degradation. It was so obvious wherever he turned his head. He discerned evil all around him. During his activities, he snapped pictures all over the city with his digital camera, which he had used extensively in the past.

When he returned home, he was enjoying looking at the pictures when he made a startling discovery. In certain places where he took pictures, there were *orbs* in the pictures. The pictures he took in the lobby of the Luxor Hotel were most striking; there were so many! He did not see them with his eyes, but the fast speed of his digital camera did! Interestingly, the lobby is decorated with Egyptian artifact replicas and images that are believed to be inspired by the fallen ones from whom the Egyptians were believed to get their advanced technology. The ancient Egyptians were very active with the demonic world. The appearance of *orbs* in photographs is common especially in places like bars and nightclubs where people do a lot of things they regret later. They appear in places where there is much or has been much ungodliness, and they also appear in areas where angelic activity may also be taking place, which makes us suspect that the camera's quick shutter speed may be catching spiritual activity while it is happening.

Photography analysts have postulated many explanations, but nothing conclusive, and they cannot duplicate it. Based on my own experience, the explanation is simple. The camera, with its fast capture of the image, is catching the "atomically slower" demonic or angelic activity at the location.

Interestingly, I was not aware of *orbs* until Ben told me of the photographs and explained it. When I looked at the pictures, I recognized them as something I had seen before. When traveling in a third-world country, I was praying as I walked about a particularly ungodly part of the city. I went into a business that was very dark inside, and the presence of evil gripped me while I was in there. I saw with my "spiritual eyes" these *orbs* inside. I tried to blink them away, and I passed them off as something I got in my eyes, until I saw Ben's photographs. I don't know for sure what was going on in that "business," but I know it wasn't good.

Recently, a professing Christian was sharing some photographs of a party he was at. The pictures of the party were full of orbs. The partygoers were holding up their drinks and smiling—with orbs all around. My eyes filled with tears! People unknowingly embrace the counterfeit supernatural when they can have it all, just because they do not understand the spiritual *unseen* world. We should be aware not to unknowingly enter places where we might be influenced by a contingency of the angels who fell with lucifer, but rather take authority over them.

What about angels? Yes, we may see them too! I recall a story Billy Graham told about some missionaries. They were preaching in the jungles to a primitive tribe that was anything but friendly. Word came to them that there were plans to attack and kill them in the night. They found themselves with nowhere to run, and believing that they should stay, they all went in to their tents and prayed for the protection of the Almighty. As they peered out into the darkness of the night, they were aware that they were surrounded with armed men preparing to attack them. As the night wore on, the attackers lingered, but eventually left without attacking.

In the morning they were visited by the leaders of the tribe, who were now very cooperative. The missionaries finally told the people that they were aware of their plan and asked why they did not attack. They were told it was because of the guards surrounding their tents—the guards with the flaming swords!

Wow! I guess we might say that some angels "slowed down" for a visit to show off their *swords of the Spirit!*

I believe that the light that went "round and round" on the ceiling of Ben's bedroom was Ben's guardian angel! There are a host of stories within the Body of Christ, just like the one I just told! We should be telling our children about these instead of buying them Harry Potter books that promote the counterfeit supernatural!

Now, what about UFOs—are they real?

Yep!

Are they from another planet?

Nope!

UFOs have been sighted all over the world. Many have proven to be fabricated hoaxes, but some highly credible people like airline and military pilots as well as astronauts have seen them in the air; and police and other individuals have seen them from and on the ground. Some of these UFOs have escaped the chase of the fastest of our jets as if they were standing still!

Simply put, UFOs are overlaps of spiritual activity into the physical realm where they are seen with naked eyes. Even the prophet Ezekiel is thought by some to perhaps have seen a UFO (see Ezek. 1:16; 10:10).

Lucifer and his forces use this type of activity to try to take advantage of our fascination with UFOs to *distract* and *deceive* us into believing that there are extraterrestrials and that perhaps they once visited people. This idea is advanced when considering ancient Egyptian, Mayan, and Phoenician cultures. Evidence of technological advancements beyond their time has also been found. Who then were these extraterrestrials? Simply put, they were demons who interacted and perhaps even copulated with mudcakes.

This fascination has led some New Age people to form beliefs about the revisiting of these extraterrestrials. I have news for them—they never left!

They can't because they were cast down to the Earth, but they can operate in the heavens as well. Lucifer has also had these New Age people develop a teaching known as *the cleansing* around these extraterrestrials to explain the "calling away" of the Church, which we will explore more a little further along in this book. They are teaching that these aliens will return and take away all of the "unenlightened ones!" Jesus would call these "unenlightened ones" His Bride! In the next chapter we will see that the so-called "enlightened ones" left behind after the calling away might better be referred to as "the ones who will be lit up!"

And finally, in our discussion of this "invisible world," we ask, "What about the pre-Flood Nephilim—will they be back?"

It appears that this activity between women and the fallen ones that occurred before the days of Noah also occurred after the Flood, as we have previously stated, with the Philistines and produced Nephilim such as the giant Goliath who was killed by David. We have also mentioned Nimrod as a Nephilim—as well as the mythological gods who may have had their roots in people of antiquity who were possibly Nephilim.

It intrigues me that all the tabloids of today seem to carry a themed story from time to time of a woman giving birth to an alien's child. In reports of alien abductions, people describe being subjected to examinations and experiments often sexual in nature. While many of these stories are fabrications, given the history of the world, one might wonder if the same thing is not happening, or at least being attempted, during this present age.

In antiquity, the Nephilim were very physically powerful because warfare was one-on-one and was based on physical strength; the physically strong "bully" ruled the world. Today, things are different; the ability to bully is based on intelligence and technology. We have seen some incredibly evil people in the last century rise to power through intelligence, charisma, and technology.

Is it possible that the Nephilim today could resemble people more like Adolf Hitler, Joseph Stalin, and the like—people who are so evil, they will stop at nothing in the pursuit of their evil agenda, even to the point of their own de-struction? I think so! The leader of a powerful country today does not need to be a physically strong person in order to wield the power of a nation. Perhaps this is how the enemy works to infect humankind! The *antichrist* or the one to whom the Bible refers as the *beast* will, in my opinion, be a Nephilim, one with the spirit of lucifer himself.

There have recently been a number of writings on this subject of the Nephilim, if you wish to explore it further. The fact remains that they have corrupted the genetics of the mudcakes in the past and may continue to at-tempt to do so as we move forward into the future. The Nephilim's corrupted DNA is still present in the world today. The Lord showed me that viruses that affect humankind are manifestations of this corruption. Viruses are de-scribed by medical science as stray DNA. A virus gains entrance into the body, multiplies, and sends corrupted signals to the body, making it sick; some viruses are more destructive than others. According to the revelations I received, I understood that this "stray DNA" is present in the world due to the presence of Nephilim and their corruption of genetics throughout the ages. Viruses are, so to speak, remnants of the Nephilim of the past still ac-tive in the world.

The point is that the evil spiritual world is increasing its activity to dis-tract the world from the message of the Cross and to corrupt and destroy the lives of the unredeemed mudcakes; at the same time, it's working to dis-tract the Church from its mission and undermine its work. This distraction of the Church is the result of the collective distraction of individuals within the Church, one mudcake at a time!

Lucifer knows his time is short as he sees the stage being set for the ad-vent of the Kingdom, but he also believes that he can still gain the victory by making the world so evil and undermining the Church so fatally that God will finally in His anger destroy all of creation. Like the stereotypical outlaw, if he is going to go down, he will go down in a blaze, taking as many with him as he can. Lucifer, since the very beginning, has believed that he could be like God and is so prideful that he still believes that he can cause God to break His Word and destroy creation, and then he would finally have the victory.

So in this final age, he is stepping up his activity against all the mudcakes, including the Church. He goes about his evil work with such a passion that in his jealous rage he fails to see that he is playing right into God's plan to eliminate him, and at the same time, eliminate the presence and potential of evil eternally.

Chapter 23

The World War to End All Wars

————— ·•· —————

In the time of transition between the *Church Age* and the *Kingdom Age,* the emerging *overcomers* will seek a greater intimacy with the Holy Spirit, and then they will begin to manifest the miraculous. As the miraculous increases within this group, they will be noticed by the world. More and more mudcakes will seek the face of Jesus, receiving the free gift of salvation. Some churches decline while others grow exponentially as more and more redeemed mudcakes within the Church seek to become *overcomers* in an increasingly difficult world. The rest are swept away in a powerless faith. This is the *"falling away"* prophesied for the last days! (See Second Thessalonians 2:3.) This is often where there is confusion. Some believe that the Church will have a revival in the last days while others believe we will have a falling away. *The truth is that we will have both!*

While all this is going on within the Church, what about the rest of the world? What about the biblical prophecies yet to be fulfilled that were for the *"time of the end,"* as the prophet Daniel told us? (See Daniel 12:4.)

Will the world end? Will it end in 2012 like Nostradamus, the Mayans, and others have predicted? You have probably heard about much of this in the media, and even a movie has been made about this date.

I will tell you this emphatically—*the world is not prepared for what is coming!*

Up until this time, two-thirds of all prophecy in the Bible has been fulfilled to the letter, but there is still another one-third that has yet to be fulfilled. Those prophecies have to do with the times we are in now and also a time yet to come. What about these prophecies? What can we expect to see happen in this world as God continues His pre-creation plan to develop the *seen* Kingdom upon the Earth from the *unseen* Kingdom of Heaven?

We are going to take a look at where we are now in the history of the world and in God's plan in the light of the teachings of Jesus Christ—the one who walked among us and knew God's plan best. We will be looking specifically at what He said in Matthew 24 and also in Luke 17, drawing from the prophet Daniel as well as other prophetic Scriptures.

My intent here is to give you a snapshot overview of what is prophesied for this age. In this book, I have not been able to stop and discuss every detail of every event in history along the way since creation; I cannot do that here either.

In looking at the prophecies of that which is to come, we must realize that the "timepiece" for God to carry out His plan *has been and always will be* the nation of Israel. Many have purported the idea that the Church replaced the nation of Israel in God's plan (replacement theology). This theory is hogwash to those who know and understand the Scriptures; this erroneous theory was developed during a dark period in the history of the Church to justify an anti-Semitic attitude that had entered the Church during a time of corruption.

By the term *timepiece*, we mean that by watching the nation of Israel we can approximate just about where we are in this plan of God. If you recall, the nation of Israel did not have a national home from the days that it was conquered by Babylon, but has been scattered throughout the whole world and under the authority of other nations. Jews have contributed much to the world, and while they have represented a fraction of a percent of the world's population, many of the greatest contributions have been made by them. No other race of people has more patents and Nobel prizes than the Jews. They have also endured incredible persecutions by nations, the most notorious of which was Nazi Germany, and they in centuries past have also been persecuted by the Church. The Holocaust perpetrated by the Nazis of Germany under Adolf Hitler killed six million Jews. Why would God allow such a thing? God did not cause it, but He allowed it for a season. Why?

Worldwide sentiment up until that time was not very favorable to the Jews. Anti-Semitic attitudes prevailed throughout the whole world. As hard as it is to believe, there was a silver lining in the Holocaust, for after Germany was defeated, there was much sympathy toward the Jews in the world at that time, especially in Europe and the United States. After the war, many Jews began to return to their national roots, and by the end of the 1940s, many Jews had resettled in what became known as Palestine, which was the ancient land of Canaan where the nation of Israel was located until conquered by the Babylonians. There was a desire on the part of the world to see the Jews have their own home again.

I recall one of my college professors bringing an old book to class that I believe he found in a garage sale or perhaps a used book store. The book was popular in its time and was written about the turn of the 20th century; it was critical of Christianity and the Bible. He read us a part of the book's comments concerning the nation of Israel and the return of the Jews in the last days to the original land of Israel. The book stated that this improbable prophecy was one of the strongest evidences against the veracity of the Bible. According to the author, it was ridiculous to think that such a scattered and demoralized people could, after thousands of years, organize and gather again within the land where they originated. How could they organize such an effort? And if they did, what would motivate the world to let them do such a thing? After all, the land of Israel had been captured and recaptured over and over again. How could they ever stake their claim to the land? It would take a world council to allow such a thing.

With that, my professor closed the book, dropped it to the desk, and proclaimed, "God approved of it; that's who!" He went on to tell us how that book containing the lies of lucifer was "reduced to trash" in 1948. Yes, the major argument of the book against the veracity of the prophetic Scriptures was silenced when a world council led by the United States recognized the nation of Israel once again located in the same land they were taken from close to 2500 years before!

Only the Spirit of the Living God could accomplish such a thing.

Since that time, the nation of Israel has grown and taken more land under miraculous circumstances during the Six Day War in 1967. Israel today is a thriving nation, the center of the attention of the world, with one of the most powerful armies in the world. If you study this process of the reestablishment of Israel, you become increasingly aware that all this only could have occurred through divine intervention.

In Ezekiel 37 we find one of the most significant prophecies regarding the establishment of the nation of Israel once again on their original land. Even people who are not familiar with the Bible know the lyrics of the famous old song, "Dem Bones Dem Bones, Dem Dry Bones." In this prophecy given over 2500 years before it occurred, Ezekiel sees a vision of a valley of dry bones where the flesh comes back on them, and they rise up once again.

I recall that we were watching the news one night when it was reported that the number of Jews who had returned to Israel had reached six million people. My wife Andi suddenly had a very interesting revelation, and she said to me, "There were six million Jews killed in the Holocaust, and now the population of Jews in Israel is six million. Would you say *dem dry bones* have come alive?" It was an exciting thought as we contemplated the intense effort by lucifer to destroy the Jews at the hands of Adolf Hitler and the Nazis. You would think that killing six million people of a specific race would devastate that race, yet it backfired in the face of lucifer, for it paved the way for the creation of the nation of Israel and the regathering of the same number as those who perished in the Holocaust. All of this has occurred much to the dismay of the surrounding Arab nations who, as you recall, are descendants of Ishmael. Historically, since the days of Ishmael and Isaac, these descendants have been the adversaries of the nation of Israel.

The land of Israel today can be driven north to south in just a few hours and east to west in even less time. However, this tiny nation, about the size of the state of New Jersey in the United States, has become the focal point of the whole world. All eyes are on Israel and specifically the city of Jerusalem in these last days. Israel has few friends in this world, and even its most obvious friends, the United States and Great Britain, are beginning to backpedal in the wake of their personal interests with the Arab nations.

These Arab nations and their leaders have sworn to work together against Israel, and some have been very outspoken about pursuing the total annihilation of Israel. Throughout history, those nations that have risen up against Israel have in the end seen their own demise because of the promise made to Abraham by God: *"I will bless those who bless you, and whoever curses you I will curse"* (Gen. 12:3). One of the reasons the United States has been so blessed over the years is due to their support of Israel. I fear for the United States; the current administration has taken a more sympathetic role to the Muslim nations (ironically, nations also sworn to the defeat of the "great satan," the USA). Certainly, these leaders lack something vastly important—an understanding of and a respect for the Word of God. According to prophecy, this support for Israel will diminish to the point that when the nations do in fact rise up against Israel, no one will support her. However, little Israel will again survive, and the nations will be defeated, *this time by God Himself!* (See Ezekiel 38:18-23.)

Lucifer has moved upon the Muslim world and given them a hatred for the two most significant groups of people in our world today through whom God is carrying out His plan to establish the Kingdom of Heaven upon the Earth. Those two groups of people are:

1. The nation of Israel

2. The Church

The Muslim religion and its holy book, the Koran, teach that Israel and the Church are *infidels* and must be destroyed. In fact, murdering an infidel provides an immediate ticket to their idea of heaven. The number of Muslims in Great Britain and the United States is growing and having an adverse effect on the friendship of these two influential countries with Israel. The leadership of these nations, under the guise of tolerance, is playing into their hands because of a lack of understanding, not only of the Bible, but also of the teachings of the Koran and Mohammed. If one believes the teachings of the Koran, then one accepts or approves that all Jews and Christians, as well as the "great satan," the United States, are infidels and must be killed in the name of Allah. That is what it teaches!

We stand around singing "We Are the World," while lucifer is rallying his forces in an attempt to destroy Israel, the United States, and the Church. The good news is that the King of Glory, Jesus Christ, is also preparing for battle at this very moment.

Christians are viewed as intolerant and are condemned by the media as the cause of the problems in these societies that were originally founded on Christian principles. The Muslim religion is very intolerant of those outside its religion, and even more so of women, yet so much is done by our society to protect and cover for them. The radical Muslim is the one who is practicing the teachings of that religion; others just bear the label, much in the same way that many bear the name of Christian without any commitment to Christ. All one needs to do to reach this conclusion is to read the Koran. Islam is a religion of deception, even to the point of befriending the *infidels* in order to lull them to complacency and defeat.

The Muslim influence will grow so much within these nations that they too will not support the nation of Israel in the future. The good news is that the ungodly decisions currently being made by our elected officials are playing right into God's plan to destroy lucifer and those who follow him in preparation for the coming Kingdom.

Please do not lose sight of the magnitude of this prophecy that was fulfilled in 1948 when the nation of Israel was reestablished. The prophecy that Israel would be a nation scattered throughout the world with no home of their own and then would be gathered together again in the last days was uttered by multiple prophets and goes all the way back to Moses himself. We find Moses's prophecy in Deuteronomy 4; it was uttered around 1450 B.C.—about 3400 years before it was completely fulfilled in 1948! It is a miracle that in all that time the Jews never lost their national identity or traditional culture, even though they did not have a country or government to unify them.

This single, fulfilled prophecy sets the stage for the appearance of Jesus Christ to establish the Kingdom of Heaven on Earth. This dramatic event will also set the stage for one, last, mighty battle known as *Armageddon* between the forces of lucifer and the forces of the Kingdom led by Jesus.

The rumblings of this coming battle are heard every day in the news. However, the complacency in the Church and in the world makes it so they are not aware that they are following a script word for word. A copy of this script is also most likely laying on their coffee tables or on their shelves or is somewhere in most homes in the United States.

The bestselling book of all time, the Bible, lays there quietly while the scenes of its prophetic script are played out on the television!

So, is the world going to end in 2012 like these ancient civilizations and non-biblical prophets like the Mayans seem to believe?

First of all, let me clear something up. The world will never end! What will end is life on the Earth as we know it, with all its attendant evil and grief. Jesus, working through His agents on Earth, will once again establish dominion, then defeat the forces of lucifer, and establish His eternal Kingdom.

In the process of this battle for the Kingdom, the Earth will be re-created into the perfect world it once was in Eden. It will be created again with just a Word, the Word of the Lord. In it, there will never again be any evil.

No, class, we have no biblical reason to believe the world will end in 2012. The world will never end, but I believe 2012 will be a part of some very significant events currently unfolding from the pages of that dusty black book on many shelves. Why do I believe that? Because I know the Word of God! There is so much going on in the world today that as I watch the news reports with a knowledge of the Scriptures as we have discussed, I become aware, as others educated in the Scriptures are, that events are lining up daily with the prophetic word of the Bible. I know what is in those pages, and you can too. Yes, it's as simple as that!

While He was on the Earth, Jesus gave us much information to add to the Old Testament prophecies so that we could know when it was near, *"even at the doors!"* (See Matthew 24:33.) He also told us in Mark 13:32 that *"no one knows about that day or hour,"* but that the fulfillment of the *"signs"* of His coming would reveal its nearness. However, Jesus also warns that when it occurs, the world will not be expecting it!

Those who know the prophetic words and the words of Jesus cannot give you a date, but can see the scriptural signs and know that at any moment Jesus's knock could be at the door. The exact moment is not known, but the expectation of a soon arrival is there. Let me give you a simple illustration so you can understand this concept better.

This kind of expectation is like when my daughter Mindy was a student at Messiah College, about a five-hour drive away from home. This was before the days when everyone had a cell phone to keep in constant contact. When she would come home for a visit at the holidays and such, we would know what day she would be free to leave. We would know the approximate time she guessed she would leave, but we could not tell you the exact moment she would arrive at the door. There were many variables that could affect her departure and travel time—especially how long it would take her to get her goldfish ready for the trip! Yes, she had a goldfish that she loved, and it was her traveling companion on these trips. If Mindy arrived home before we expected, Andi, Ben, and I were happily surprised, but if it was later than expected, we would be concerned.

Such it is with the coming of Christ. We who know Jesus as Lord of our lives look expectantly for His return, but do not know exactly when that will be. All we have are guidelines for an approximate arrival time.

Using the illustration of my daughter Mindy coming home from college, I would say that at the present time Jesus is preparing for His trip, getting the car packed, gassing it up, getting some snacks for along the route, and preparing the travel tank for His goldfish. Though I don't expect Him at this moment, we won't have to wait for much longer before He is here. The process of His return has started, but we still have time to prepare for His arrival.

So what are these signs to which Jesus was referring, and where are we now in the whole scheme of things? We need to look at the recorded words in Matthew 24, and I want you to read them here since no one can teach this like He can. Let me set the stage for you.

In Matthew 23 we find that Jesus had just given His final statements in public before His crucifixion. He warns about seven woes that would come upon the people because of their rejection of Him. Again His message was not received by the leadership, and He cries out to Jerusalem in grief for what lies in their future:

> *O Jerusalem, Jerusalem, you who kill the prophets and stone those sent to you, how often I have longed to gather your children together, as a hen gathers her chicks under her wings, but you were not willing. Look, your house is left to you desolate. For I tell you, you will not see Me again until you say, "Blessed is he who comes in the name of the Lord"* (Matthew 23:37-39).

They had just welcomed Him triumphantly as He came into the city. The people were thinking He would deliver them from the Romans, and then they lost their enthusiasm when He did not mount a military coup. Then, in verse 39, He refers to the fact that they will not see Him again until the day He appears in the Temple at His second coming. It would be then that they would say the words, *"Blessed is He who comes in the name of the Lord."* After Jesus speaks these final words, He leaves the Temple never to return until the time of His second coming to Earth.

Signs of the End of the Age

Now let's pick up the action again in Matthew 24 as Jesus tells it. Let's read it, and then I will make some comments afterward:

> *Jesus left the temple and was walking away when His disciples came up to Him to call His attention to its buildings. "Do you see all these things?" He asked. "I tell you the truth, not one stone here will be left on another; every one will be thrown down."*

> *As Jesus was sitting on the Mount of Olives, the disciples came to Him privately. "Tell us," they said, "when will this happen, and what will be the sign of Your coming and of the end of the age?"*

> *Jesus answered: "Watch out that no one deceives you. For many will come in My name, claiming, 'I am the Christ,' and will deceive many. You will hear of wars and rumors of wars, but see to it that you are not alarmed. Such things must happen, but the end is still to come. Nation will rise against nation, and kingdom against kingdom. There will be famines and earthquakes in various places. All these are the beginning of birth pains.*

> *"Then you will be handed over to be persecuted and put to death, and you will be hated by all nations because of Me. At that time*

many will turn away from the faith and will betray and hate each other, and many false prophets will appear and deceive many people. Because of the increase of wickedness, the love of most will grow cold, but he who stands firm to the end will be saved. And this gospel of the kingdom will be preached in the whole world as a testimony to all nations, and then the end will come.

"So when you see standing in the holy place 'the abomination that causes desolation,' spoken of through the prophet Daniel— let the reader understand—then let those who are in Judea flee to the mountains. Let no one on the roof of his house go down to take anything out of the house. Let no one in the field go back to get his cloak. How dreadful it will be in those days for pregnant women and nursing mothers! Pray that your flight will not take place in winter or on the Sabbath. For then there will be great distress, unequaled from the beginning of the world until now—and never to be equaled again. If those days had not been cut short, no one would survive, but for the sake of the elect those days will be shortened. At that time if anyone says to you, 'Look, here is the Christ!' or, 'There He is!' do not believe it. For false Christs and false prophets will appear and perform great signs and miracles to deceive even the elect—if that were possible. See, I have told you ahead of time.

"So if anyone tells you, 'There He is, out in the desert,' do not go out; or, 'Here He is, in the inner rooms,' do not believe it. For as lightning that comes from the east is visible even in the west, so will be the coming of the Son of Man. Wherever there is a carcass, there the vultures will gather.

"Immediately after the distress of those days 'the sun will be darkened, and the moon will not give its light; the stars

will fall from the sky, and the heavenly bodies will be shaken.'

"At that time the sign of the Son of Man will appear in the sky, and all the nations of the earth will mourn. They will see the Son of Man coming on the clouds of the sky, with power and great glory. And He will send His angels with a loud trumpet call, and they will gather His elect from the four winds, from one end of the heavens to the other.

"Now learn this lesson from the fig tree: As soon as its twigs get tender and its leaves come out, you know that summer is near. Even so, when you see all these things, you know that it is near, right at the door. I tell you the truth, this generation will certainly not pass away until all these things have happened. Heaven and earth will pass away, but My words will never pass away" (Matthew 24:1-35).

Jesus, after describing the times leading up to the end of the age, then turns His focus on that specific day itself. He goes on to speak to His disciples about the mystery of the day and hour of His second coming and to exhort them to be alert, wise, and faithful.

The Day and Hour Unknown

No one knows about that day or hour, not even the angels in heaven, nor the Son, but only the Father. As it was in the days of Noah, so it will be at the coming of the Son of Man. For in the days before the flood, people were eating and drinking, marrying and giving in marriage, up to the day Noah entered the ark; and they knew nothing about what would happen until the flood came and took them all away. That is how it will be at the coming of the Son of Man. Two men will be in the field;

one will be taken and the other left. Two women will be grinding with a hand mill; one will be taken and the other left.

Therefore keep watch, because you do not know on what day your Lord will come. But understand this: If the owner of the house had known at what time of night the thief was coming, he would have kept watch and would not have let his house be broken into. So you also must be ready, because the Son of Man will come at an hour when you do not expect Him.

Who then is the faithful and wise servant, whom the master has put in charge of the servants in his household to give them their food at the proper time? It will be good for that servant whose master finds him doing so when he returns. I tell you the truth, he will put him in charge of all his possessions. But suppose that servant is wicked and says to himself, "My master is staying away a long time," and he then begins to beat his fellow servants and to eat and drink with drunkards. The master of that servant will come on a day when he does not expect him and at an hour he is not aware of. He will cut him to pieces and assign him a place with the hypocrites, where there will be weeping and gnashing of teeth (Matthew 24:36-51).

Let us break down Jesus's teaching here into categories to give us a good overview of these last days about which He spoke.

We read in this passage that, as Jesus was leaving the Temple Mount, the disciples were admiring the buildings and were calling His attention to them. Jesus responds with a prophecy telling them that these buildings would be destroyed, one stone at a time. This prophecy was fulfilled 37 years later when Rome became upset with the Jews and destroyed Jerusalem, burning the buildings of the Temple Mount and then tearing them down stone by stone to recover melted gold. The Temple would never be rebuilt again until a time just before Jesus's return. Presently work is under way, plans are being drawn, and Temple furnishings and implements for Temple worship are being created. Many of the Temple implements can be seen at the *Temple Institute* in Jerusalem today. Andi and I have been there and seen them. Take a look at their Website; you can see them there yourself.[1] There are also plans under way to resume animal sacrifice once the Temple is rebuilt.

The biggest impediment to the building of the Temple right now is that the Temple Mount is under the control of the Muslims, and the Dome of the Rock sits where the Temple is to be built. For many years scholars believed that the Dome of the Rock would need to be removed first, but evidence is increasing that the Temple itself was at another location on the mount, where currently no building is erected. I suppose you can see the potentially volatile situation that exists at the present time since the Temple Mount is still under Muslim control. The point is this: whether the Dome is removed, or the Temple is to be built at another spot, it's going to happen soon!

Jesus's prophecy of the destruction of the Temple by Titus in A.D. 70 prompted the disciples to inquire as to when this would occur and what would be the signs of His coming. We will break down His response into sections with some commentary for ease of understanding.

Beginning of Birth Pains

Just as birth pains signal the beginning of labor, Jesus said there would be signs that the time of the end was beginning. The King James Version refers to this as the *"Beginning of Sorrows."* The Greek word *odin* translated "sorrows" is the same word used in that language for the pains of labor.[2] In the King James English, one would describe a woman in labor as being "in sorrow" or "feeling sorrows."

I feel I must stop here for a moment and discuss why there are different versions of the Bible, for some have misunderstood. The different versions or translations are just varied efforts to translate from the early biblical texts. Different versions are not a result of contradictions in the Bible, as some uninformed people believe. Languages change, and the versions have been created to keep up with changing languages. I have often heard critics say that with the contradictions and so many versions, how do you know which Bible to believe? This is a question from lack of knowledge because the versions say the same thing in different ways, drawing on the original Hebrew and Greek words, which have more specific meanings and usages than do English words.

Work on a new translation is also under way now, spearheaded by the Messianic Jewish Community (Jews who accept Jesus as their Messiah), a project with which I am involved in the leadership. This Bible is published by Destiny Image, the publisher of this book, and we are translating the original Scriptures from the oldest documents illuminated by the culture and traditions of the Jewish people who originally wrote almost the entire Bible. I believe this translation will bring the Bible full circle as we approach the Kingdom Age. Understanding Jewish culture and traditions illuminates the words of the Bible; I believe this translation due out starting in 2011 will be an incredibly popular version throughout the Christian community.

Now back to the *"birth pains"* Jesus was talking about. Jesus said that there were some things that would occur to signal the beginning of the end of the corrupted earthly Kingdom. Let's take a look at these birth pains. It is safe to say, and theologians overwhelmingly agree, that we are currently in the time to which Jesus is referring.

1. Many Versions of Jesus

Jesus warned that there would be many different versions of Him who would arise to deceive many away from the truth. Since the time of Jesus, we have seen the growing influence of the religions of Hinduism, Buddhism, and Islam, as well as many cults and New Age religions. Books are written that will lead astray those who do not know or accept the Word of God. Christians are portrayed as intolerant purveyors of hate; it seems that it is "open season" on criticizing the Jews and the Christians, but not on other religions, even in nations founded on Christian principles like the United States.

President Barak Obama, soon after becoming president of the United States, in an effort to please the Muslim world, announced that the United States, which was founded on Christian principles was, in his words, "not a Christian nation."[3] Ironically Christians played a large part in his election due in part to their desire to pursue a worldly agenda over the agenda of the Kingdom of our Lord. I do believe, however, that those leaders who have an openly non-Christian agenda potentially have what I call a "Cyrus Anointing." Cyrus was a king of Persia, an ungodly man who was used by God to accomplish His purpose upon the Earth. These endtimes will be marked by leaders who will speak out of both sides of their mouths trying to please everyone. As it has been said, *"When you try to please everyone, you end up pleasing no one."* The leaders in these endtimes will be in hot pursuit of what they believe will lead to a utopian society with a one-world government distributing equally the wealth around the Earth. Of course, in the minds of most of these leaders, this government would be led by them.

The global financial crisis of 2008 advanced the cause of the establishment of people's idea of the new world order and a one-world economic system. At the G20 summit held in Pittsburgh in September 2009, the groundwork was laid for this new world order. The Financial Stability Board (FSB) made up of representatives from each of the 20 nations was established to form international regulations and bylaws. President Obama agreed that the United States, who has the largest GDP (Gross Domestic Product), three times the size of number two Japan, will have only one vote, the same as nations whose GDP is a fraction of that of the United States, effectively subjecting the future of the U.S. economy to a world council. A group of the nations led by China called for the creation of a new currency to replace the U.S. dollar as the standard, and U.S. Secretary of the Treasury Timothy Geithner then let slip that the Obama administration is open to the idea. The Prime Minister of England, Gordon Brown, called this meeting, "a defining moment: an unprecedented period of global change." He went on to say at this event that "I think a *new world order* is emerging with the foundation of a new progressive era of international cooperation."[4]

I heard President Obama speaking in Prague following the summit, recapitulating the direction of the current administration's attitude toward a global one-world financial system and currency: "All nations must come together to build a stronger global regime."[5] The word *regime* according to Webster means "rule or governmental system."[6] This is exactly the type of system where you cannot buy or sell without a "mark" that is employed by the antichrist or the beast in the prophecy found in the Book of Revelation.

What we see going on here, my friends, is "counterfeiting." Remember, I referred to satan as the great counterfeiter. Not only does he raise up counterfeit faiths and supernatural powers, but he is also playing off an inward desire that is in the hearts of most mudcakes. That inward desire is for peace on Earth and a utopian society that is governed by a single "good" leader. Satan is trying to create a *counterfeit* new world order, and he has done so using governments, organizations, and societies like the Illuminati and the Masons. His plan mimics God's plan to create the *seen* Kingdom of Heaven on Earth with Jesus as King. Satan has caused mudcakes to pursue a counterfeit kingdom that is based on the humanistic philosophy that "people are basically good," which is in direct opposition to what God says about people in His Word. It has been proven over and over again since the dawn of time that power corrupts people! Satan is orchestrating those who would use human wisdom without the influence of the Word of God to pursue this end, and as we shall see, he nearly destroys the world when it is accomplished. That fits right into his plan to destroy creation himself if he cannot get God to do it. Remember what Jesus told me, "Evil always oversteps itself!" Jesus said that satan's mission was to seek, kill, and destroy (see John 10:10). Let me ask you again, who are you following? Whose mission are you supporting?

2. Increase in Global Conflict

The 20th century was unprecedented in history with regard to the number of people killed in wars. Those who believe people are "evolving" into an enlightened creature must beware. Mudcakes have just become more sophisticated and efficient in their abilities to kill and destroy. The beginning of the 21st century indicates that it will be no different; it will, in fact, be worse as the stage is being set for a battle of unprecedented proportions. For the first time in history, nuclear weapons are now in the hands of all sides of the conflict.

Jesus said in Matthew 24 that *"nation would rise up against nation."* When we look at the original Greek word translated "nation," we find that it is the word *ethnos.*[7] Do you see the English word *ethnic* in that word? In actuality, the word means "ethnic group," so what Jesus was saying was that *"ethnic group will rise up against ethnic group."* We have seen this all over the world in China, India, and Africa. We even see it in the gang warfare on the streets of the United States where people are killed just because they belong to another gang. In Africa in recent years, over 100,000 people have been shot and hacked to death just because they were from a different tribe than their killers. In the "War on Terror," terrorist groups attack people because of their belief that they are superior and must destroy all who do not believe as they do. In this war known as a holy war or *jihad*, it is not a particular country that seeks to destroy the Jews and the Christians, but a group with a particular philosophy and belief.

Why do the Muslim world and their god Allah seek the destruction of the Jews and Christians? Do you remember who the current remnants are that God is working out His plan through to create the Kingdom of Heaven on Earth? (The Jews and Christians!) Perhaps now you see who Allah really is. Allah is an intolerant, demanding demon-god who never tells his people he loves them. The God of the Bible is a patient Father, a long-suffering, giving, and loving God, who was willing to die for our redemption. It frustrates me when I hear people say, "Well, we are just worshiping the same god in our own ways." This is not true!

3. Increase in Famine and Pestilences

Much of the world is daily becoming non-tillable, and world hunger has become a problem of epic proportions. The organizations who are attempting to feed those in areas where people are dying daily due to the lack of food are frustrated because the need is so much greater than their means. In the United States we throw food away while people are starving to death (ask a restaurant some time how much food gets thrown out there in a day, and you will be amazed). We have been a blessed nation because we honor God, and we have blessed Israel, but the leadership and the people of this country are putting that blessing in jeopardy. If the hand of God ever comes off of the United States, we will experience the grief and the hardship that much of the world experiences now while we go about our day unaware of how our behavior and the actions of our government can affect us.

Every American should spend a week in Africa or India, and we would look at our "waste" much differently. I was so changed after being in Africa that I cannot stand to see food wasted or thrown out. I recall being in a restaurant where they got my order mixed up and brought me the wrong food. They were going to take this perfectly good food and throw it out when I refused to let them. Confused as to why I would not let them, I offered the simple explanation, "I've traveled in Africa. I consider food a precious blessing, not to be wasted." They understood, and a discussion ensued with the waitress about how much food is thrown out in one day in that restaurant. Jesus tells us in Matthew 24 that famine will increase as a sign of the end of this age. Disease will also increase, and as experts tell us, the HIV virus is only getting started; the strains seen in Africa and in other parts of the world are stronger and more deadly than the earlier ones, and they are spreading.[8] Experts tell us that we have only seen the tip of the iceberg. During this time, the prophecies of the Bible indicate that food will become a very valuable commodity.

4. Increase in Earthquakes

Geologists tell us that there have been more recorded earthquakes since 1950 than in all time prior to that date (Israel became a nation again in 1948). Geologic and volcanic activity is also increasing. The apostle Paul tells us in Romans 8:22 that all creation groans and travails in pain in anticipation of the coming Kingdom. Geologists warn of the continued increase of this type of activity in the years to come; in 2009 and 2010, many of these earthquakes were not only of great magnitude, but took place in places where there is a greater population. In a recent prophetic word, the Lord revealed to me that a large quake is coming to the midsection of the United States in the near future, which will shake this nation in many ways besides physically.

The Church Age started with the sending of the Holy Spirit to baptize believers on the Day of Pentecost and has continued until this day. These birth pains that we discussed are for the purpose of signaling a transition into a new age, the Kingdom Age. The birth pains are just a sampling, a mere taste of what is to come, because as we shall see, it will intensify; this period known as the Church Age will have a very violent end.

During the days of birth pains, it is very important that the Church is prepared and steps up its mission of advancing the Gospel and advancing the Word and will of the Creator God.

Jesus referred to these days as the *"days of Noah,"* and He also said they were like the days of Lot (see Luke 17:26-30). Jesus said that the days preceding this violent end of the Church Age will resemble the world during the pre-Flood days of Noah as well as the days preceding the destruction of Sodom and Gomorrah with fire and brimstone. Prior to both of these events, there was much evil in the world, immorality, homosexuality, murder, and the like. Just as the condition of the world in those days signaled a coming judgment, the condition of this world at this present time signals the end of the age. The Church Age will come to a sudden end with violence unprecedented in history.

The Nephilim were also present in those days, driving the growth of evil, and that brings me to the conclusion that in order for Jesus's words to be true, the Nephilim would also need to return; in fact, I believe and discern that they are here at this present time. The prophecy of Enoch, which we talked about in Chapter 11, tells us that the spirits released upon the deaths of the Nephilim of Noah's days became evil spirits that have oppressed men and women and have risen up against them because *"they have proceeded from them"* (see Enoch 15:8-10). Viruses (stray DNA) and diseases from their corrupted DNA have proceeded from them as well and are one of the ways they continue to oppress the mudcakes.

I have stated before that the Nephilim of the last days are probably not giant warriors, but evil beings, some of whom are and will become incredibly evil leaders carrying out the will of satan. These leaders will inspire many to carry out satan's mission to steal, kill, and destroy (see John 10:10). I believe that the Nephilim through the continued reproduction of their offspring have corrupted the spirits of groups of people until evil reigns supreme in the hearts of these people. These are individuals and groups whom we observe with disbelief because of the level of evil with which they oppress others. I believe that many of the terrorist societies may be made up of people whose spirits are corrupted by the Nephilim and the continued reproduction of their offspring.

This may sound too hard for you to believe, but if you believe that Jesus does not lie and that He said that these last days would be like the days of Noah, then the conclusion must be drawn that the Nephilim are still here, and they will keep on working until they bring this age to a violent end. They will do so in an effort to fulfill lucifer's will to destroy creation! In destroying all creation, they will have, in their evil minds, rendered the Cross of Calvary null and void and destroyed God's plan to establish His Kingdom upon the Earth.

Once again we need to peel the onion of the Word here in Luke 17 and look deeper at what was going on during the times of Noah and Lot. Jesus was not only referring to everyday activity, but there was also much evil going on that brought the judgment. The evil was increasing due to an evil influence growing in the world at that time. What was that evil influence? The world was increasingly being corrupted by the influence of the Nephilim, just as the influence of these Nephilim spirits is at work today.

Lucifer's plan would appear to be successful as we move toward the end of the age. The situation also becomes increasingly violent and destructive as we get to the end of the age. With this understanding in mind, let us move forward with Jesus's teaching illuminated by some of the other words of biblical prophecy regarding the end of the age.

In Matthew 24:9, Jesus warns His followers that there will be persecution of those who believe in Him. Here we see Him reference two groups of people within the Church. We see His first reference to the end-time *remnant* known as the *overcomers* who come out of the seven types of churches of the Book of Revelation that we discussed in the last chapter.

This passage also underscores my belief that there will be both a revival and a falling away in the last days. Many *"will turn away from the faith,"* while others will *"stand firm to the end"* and overcome (Matt. 24:9-13). These *overcomers* will not only be "saved," but they will finalize the Great Commission given by Jesus to His disciples at His ascension. The fulfillment of His command to preach the Gospel to all nations is the key, the defining moment! Once Jesus's followers have preached the Gospel to all the nations, *"then the end will come"* (Matt. 24:14).

We then immediately ask the question, has the Gospel been preached to all nations? The answer is a resounding *"yes!"* In fact, in recent years, where the Gospel has been oppressed, doors have been opened again to evangelism, and *overcomers* can be found in every nation of the world, regardless of their hostility or openness to the Gospel. I recently compiled some figures that I found very interesting from the World Christian Encyclopedia and David Barrett Research.[9]

In 1900, the number of Christians in China and in South America was not measurable. However, today it is estimated that there are 100 million Christians in China, which is expected to grow to 200 million in the next 30 years; there are 50 million Christians in South America. In Africa in 1900, there were 10 million Christians while today there are 360 million. In addition, Christians and Gospel-preaching churches are found in each and every country in this world. Perhaps we are already in the last days' revival as prophesied. Christianity is growing fast and is still the largest world religion.

However, in the last days, this fast-growing Church is also a persecuted Church, causing some to move away from the faith while others become more stalwart and begin to tap into the *dunamis* power of the Holy Spirit, engineering a great move of the Holy Spirit before the event referred to as the "calling away." This end-time Church of *overcomers* will resemble the early Church of the Book of Acts and move in the miraculous power of the Holy Spirit. The *"calling away"* of the Church is the next major event on the prophetic calendar after the establishment of the nation of Israel and the gathering of the Jews back to their homeland which, as we have seen, has already occurred. Six million Jews have been gathered back to their original land, and the nation was officially established in 1948.

The "calling away" of the Church has been a much-debated doctrine over the years as to when and if it will occur. Some say it will occur before the Tribulation, some say during it, and some say it occurs at the end at the second coming of Jesus. I must confess that over the years I have wavered a bit between the views as I studied the Bible. However, today I can say that after many years of "peeling the onion" of the Word of God, and as a result of my near-death experience, I have no doubt that it occurs somewhere from the beginning of the Tribulation to somewhere just before the Great Tribulation (the second half of the Tribulation). Even during the writing of this book, I became even more impressed with this fact as I contemplated the information I wished to present here. Let me simply state that this "calling away" is a lightning-like moment when the Church is called away by Jesus into Heaven with Him in preparation for His second coming. Meanwhile, it is a time of great tribulation on the Earth as the wrath of God is poured out on the unrepentant mudcakes.

Now for those of you who have trouble accepting this "calling away" or "rapture" of the Church, I want you to know that the Lord gave me revelation in my encounter with Him regarding this as well. The reason there is so much confusion and disagreement about this is due to the way time-bound physical minds like ours view it. *We must overlay the physical with the spiritual so that we can understand.*

As we have discussed before, a day is as a 1000 years to the Lord and vice versa. I told you that I experienced an *ever-present* **now** when I was in His presence. The point is that time means nothing to God, and all the events of humankind are played out in what is a microcosm or *flash moment* of eternity to God. The Tribulation is seven years long, and the Great Tribulation is three and a half years—or the second half of the seven-year Tribulation. What is that time to God—nothing!

We must look at the events of this time as God sees them and not as separate events as we would tend to view them. We must look at it as He does, *as one event*, the second coming of Jesus!

Let me illustrate it to you this way.

Let's say that you and I decide to go together to a major sports event. I arrange to pick you up after work, and we plan to have dinner on the way to the stadium at a nice restaurant that we both like. The day comes, and I pick you up; we stop and have a wonderful meal, and then we go to the big event, which is the crowning activity of our evening. While we do this, the rest of the world goes about their business.

Months later when we are talking, I asked you to recall the time when we went to the restaurant. You would most likely respond by saying, "Oh yes, the time we went to the game together!" The fact is that we would view the different activities of the evening—me picking you up, driving to the restaurant, having dinner, driving to the game, and then watching the game—as different aspects of the same event.

Well, I learned from the Lord that this is exactly how He views the event of His second coming. He sees that seven-year period as a time when He comes and picks us up *(the calling away)*, takes us to eat *(the marriage feast of the Lamb)*, and then takes us with Him to the big event *(His return to defeat the forces of satan)*. While He is doing all this, the rest of the world is going about their business in the Tribulation. *We cannot return with Him as the Scriptures say unless we are with Him, so Jesus picks us up, takes us to dinner, and then we go with Him to the big event—the Second Coming!*

We find in Revelation that after Jesus addresses the seven churches, giving correction and also commending the *overcomers*, the next thing that He does is to say, *"Come up here"* (Rev. 4:1). The apostle John to whom Jesus gave this vision has been on the Earth viewing the events up until this point. At the beginning of Revelation 4, he sees the door of Heaven open and hears the words of Jesus *calling him away* and saying, *"Come up here."* From this point on in the Scriptures, we see that the Church is no longer situated on Earth, but with Jesus as the remaining prophesied events unfold. The Church is only on the Earth again when they return with Jesus at His second coming to do battle with Him against the forces of satan. The simple conclusion is that if the Church is with Jesus when He returns, then somehow, somewhere during this time, they must have left the Earth to join Him.

One of the other things we have learned from studying the Scriptures is that God often gives a pre-type event depicting a coming or future event. We have discussed these pre-types before with regard to the birth and death of Jesus Christ, which are recorded in the Old Testament. Just like the pre-types we have already discussed, we have some that depict this "calling away" as well.

In the days just before the destruction of Sodom and Gomorrah, Lot and his family were called out of the city to avoid the judgment of God. In the same way, Noah and his family were called out of the world to a safe place in the ark before God unleashed His judgment upon the Earth in the form of the great Flood.

We have seen that Enoch was called from the Earth in a sudden disappearance, a kind of "calling away," not experiencing death. The same thing happened to the prophet Elijah. These two men are the only two people in all of recorded history who have never tasted physical death. Why? Scriptures tell us that *"man is destined to die once, and after that to face judgment"* (Heb. 9:27). Many theologians consider that it is possible that Enoch and Elijah will be the *"two witnesses"* who will appear from Heaven upon the Earth during the Great Tribulation and will be killed for their witness (see Rev. 11:3-12). No matter who they are, these two witnesses will be left lying dead in the streets, and then they will rise before the eyes of the people and be once again taken to Heaven. It would be unjust in God's eyes, and not in accordance with His Holy Scriptures, for them to have died twice, so possibly God took them in anticipation of this future event. We shall see that a "second death" is reserved for those who die without ever receiving the redemption provided by Jesus. This "second death" is an eternal and spiritual death (see Rev. 20:14). *Perhaps you thought death could not get any worse, but it can, as you shall see!*

First Thessalonians 5:9 tells us that God *"did not appoint us to suffer wrath";* instead, He *"rescues us from the coming wrath"* (1 Thess. 1:10). The coming judgment upon the Earth known as the Great Tribulation is also known as the *Day of Wrath. Wrath* throughout Scriptures refers to judgment. When we become children of God through the acceptance of Jesus Christ as Lord of our lives, we pass from being *"children of wrath"* (Eph. 2:3 KJV) into God's family. God's family is those for whom the wrath was already poured out on Jesus at Calvary. God already judged Jesus for our sins, so we have no need to suffer the judgment yet to come. *Those who have not accepted Jesus as standing in their place as God poured out judgment on Him will have to face the judgment to come themselves. God will pour out wrath on them because they did not claim Jesus as their own, suffering the wrath of God for them.*

The calling away of the Church will unleash a fury of evil upon the Earth. The presence and influence of the Holy Spirit within these called-away children of God will also now be missing upon the Earth. The presence of the Holy Spirit within the Church is what restrains the evil forces of lucifer from being able to freely move among the mudcakes. In this calling away, the beginning of the event of the second coming, graves will be opened and the dead will be raised first to meet Jesus; then the living will be called up to meet Him in the air and be with Him forever. (See First Thessalonians 4:16-17.) Lucifer and his forces will now be allowed to move about upon the Earth unchecked by those possessing the *dunamis* power of the Creator.

It is interesting to note here again that the New Age teachings of this current day under the inspiration of lucifer have developed a teaching to explain this sudden, massive disappearance of people from the Earth. They refer to this as "the cleansing."[10] They will declare that this disappearance will be due to the reappearance of the "enlightened ones" (the watchers, the fallen ones), extraterrestrials who had visited the Earth thousands of years before. According to these present-day New Age teachings, the missing people, the Church, those who in their opinion are the unenlightened ones, the purveyors of hate who hold the world back and keep evolution from achieving the full purpose of humankind (I think that one is funny!) will be abducted by aliens!

According to them, a spaceship takes all the Christians away! Now the world can evolve into its full purpose!

Counterfeit! Counterfeit! Counterfeit! Guess whose handiwork that is? Lucifer, the devil, old satan himself. He does not give up, but he is running out of time here.

According to Jesus, the Jews and those others who have chosen to follow these "enlightened ones" and not Jesus will be left upon the Earth at the calling away and turned over to the Great Tribulation or to the *Day of Judgment* upon the Earth. Throughout the Scriptures, this Great Tribulation is referred to by numerous other names as well. These names really give us a picture that this time following the calling away is definitely not going to be a "Teddy Bear Picnic." This violent time to come is referred to in Scripture by such names as *"The Time of Jacob's Trouble," "Day of Israel's Calamity," "Day of the Lord," "Day of Indignation," "Overflowing Scourge," "Day of Wrath," "Wrath That Is to Come," "Hour of Trial That Comes Upon the Earth," "Year of Recompense,"* and *"Hour of Judgment."* Whew! Glad I got a ticket to ride that train! How about you? Got that ticket yet? The Kingdom of God is coming fast, *"forcefully advancing,"* and you don't want to get run over by that train. Let death or the calling away, whichever comes first, put you on board!

The fact is that prophetic Scriptures in the Bible record more about the Great Tribulation than any other event. It is mentioned 49 times by the prophets and is discussed 15 times in the New Testament. Every unfulfilled prophecy in the Bible will precede and occur during the Tribulation; the stage is being set for this event right now. The alliances are being developed. Ironically, as I was writing these words, I saw a picture of President Obama praying Muslim-style to Allah with a group of Muslims in the *White House* in this "Christian," Israel-supporting nation. The lines are being drawn because, as we discussed, Allah is not the Creator God, and according to Mohammed, the enemies of Islam are Jews and Christians— the *infidels* spoken about in the Koran who must be destroyed! Of course, I have already heard this president not only declare numerous times that he is a Muslim but also that "the United States is not a Christian nation." Yes, the stage is being set!

It is interesting to note that within the last year a 17th-century Islamic prophecy was so noteworthy that a pro-Iran Web site posted it; our press ignored it. Yes, satan reveals prophecy too. Satan is not all-knowing as God is, but he does know what his future plans are. While the prophecy has been trumpeted around the Muslim world, I have not once seen it mentioned on the television news in the United States. In the 17th century, a Muslim by the name of Ali Ibn Abi-Talib predicted that during this time the strongest army in the world would be commanded by a tall black man who will have assumed the reins of government in the West. It also prophesied that this man's name would be *Hussein* (Barack *Hussein* Obama). The prophecy says that this man in the endtimes will pave the way for the *Mahdi* (lucifer's counterfeit Messiah) to conquer the world.[11] This is the reason there was so much excitement in the Muslim world at the election of President Obama. Do we see any connection here? Is the stage not being set for a conflict, for an attack upon Israel as the signaling event of the beginning of the Tribulation prophesied in the Bible?

What event am I talking about?

In Ezekiel chapters 38 and 39 we read of an event that takes place in the Middle East. Under the leadership of Gog, Magog, Meshech, and Tubal, or what today is modern-day Russia, an alliance is formed with the Arab nations. They come against the nation of Israel to destroy it, or as the current reigning president of Iran says, that "with God's grace Israel will be annihilated" and the President Zahar of Hamas says that they will "drive them into the Mediterranean sea."[12]

However, God says He has a different plan: *"I will bring you* [Gog] *against My land, so that the nations may know Me when I show Myself holy through you before their eyes"* (Ezek. 38:16).

How is God going to show Himself holy before the nations? This alliance will be utterly defeated, for as Ezekiel 39:12 says, it will take seven months for Israel to bury their dead enemies and cleanse the land.

The interesting fact here as we study this passage is that *this mighty alliance led by Russia will not be defeated by Israel in a military conflict, but by God Himself*. The account tells us of earthquakes, fire and brimstone, and hail—an incredible natural calamity will come upon these forces surrounding Israel from the hand of God, totally destroying them. Ezekiel says that even the animal kingdom will look at it and tremble, knowing that this is the hand of God! (See Ezekiel 38:20.) Then God says something interesting: *"I will pour out My Spirit on the house of Israel"* (Ezek. 39:29).

The Bible teaches us that *"all Israel will be saved"* in the end (see Rom. 11:26-27; Isa. 59:20-21). What that means is that Israel will suddenly realize that their Messiah has already come and that His name is Yeshua (Jesus). I believe that this miraculous event showing the hand of God on Israel combined with the event of the calling away of the Church will be the catalyst for the saving of Israel. Israel puts two and two together, so to speak, and realizes the truth as their eyes are opened to it.

The forces of evil are released unhindered after the calling away because the world is devoid of Spirit-filled believers; lucifer's plan is for the unredeemed mudcakes left behind to destroy themselves and with them God's plan to redeem creation.

In Jesus's teaching in Matthew 24:15, He references the prophet Daniel. Daniel's prophecies were precise in foretelling the history of the Jews and the world up to the time of Jesus's death on the Cross. During the Babylonian captivity, he interpreted a dream for King Nebuchadnezzar that prophesied that they would be conquered by the Persians, who in turn would be conquered by Alexander the Great and the Greek Empire. This empire would in turn be conquered by the Romans who interestingly were never conquered; they just became so corrupt they defeated themselves. Daniel then tells of a revived Roman empire and a coalition of ten nations. There has been much written about who this coalition might be, but we do not have time to get into that information here. Some believe it could be the European Union, and some believe it is a coalition of Muslim nations. At the end of Daniel's prophecy, however, there is one Kingdom, an eternal Kingdom that comes and crushes them all!

Daniel foretold of 70 weeks in his prophecy—70 groups of years according to the Hebrew tradition. The beginning of these 70 weeks began when the word went out to rebuild the Temple under Zerubbabel and the Wall of Jerusalem under Nehemiah. This prophecy concerns the Jews and the city of Jerusalem. The 69th week ends when *"the Anointed One will be cut off"* (Dan. 9:26), and the city and the Temple are destroyed. Specifically, this word refers to the crucifixion of Jesus in A.D. 33 and the later destruction of Jerusalem and the Temple in A.D. 70 by Titus.

The last group of seven is reserved for the *"time of the end,"* at the end of the Church Age, and refers to the Tribulation, which lasts for seven years and is divided in half—with the second half being much more intense and evil. In fact, it is so bad that Jesus says that the days will be shortened for the sake of the *"elect"* (Israel) because if they were not, no one would survive. The "birth pains" give rise to the birth of the time of Tribulation, which ends with the second coming of Jesus. Again, Jesus views all these events as one event—the event of His second coming.

It is at this time that a significant individual leader arises. This individual is trusted by both the Arab nations as well as the Jews, and he makes a covenant with the nation of Israel. He further wins their trust by allowing them to resume the animal sacrifices and Temple worship in the newly rebuilt Temple on the Temple Mount in Jerusalem.

This appears to be what the world needs—except that this individual is none other than a Nephilim possessed by the spirit of lucifer. We see him referred to in Scripture as the *"beast," "the Man of Sin,"* or the *"antichrist."* By the way, the word translated "anti" actually means "against," or *counterfeit!*

The Jews begin to believe he is their long-promised Messiah until a moment comes that Jesus warned us about:

> *So when you see standing in the holy place "the abomination*
> *that causes desolation," spoken of through the prophet Daniel—*
> *let the reader understand—then let those who are in Judea flee*
> *to the mountains. Let no one on the roof of his house go down*

to take anything out of the house. Let no one in the field go back to get his cloak. How dreadful it will be in those days for pregnant women and nursing mothers! Pray that your flight will not take place in winter or on the Sabbath. For then there will be great distress, unequaled from the beginning of the world until now—and never to be equaled again. If those days had not been cut short, no one would survive, but for the sake of the elect those days will be shortened (Matthew 24:15-22).

Jesus warns of a big betrayal of the Jews three-and-a-half years into this Tribulation period by this leader. It results in persecution and violence against the people of God (Israel) as the *beast* makes his move to destroy Israel. What happened? Daniel told us over 2500 years before. (Note that the word *week* here refers to a period of seven, the seven years of the Tribulation.)

Then he shall confirm a covenant with many for one week; but in the middle of the week He shall bring an end to sacrifice and offering. And on the wing of abominations shall be one who makes desolate, even until the consummation, which is determined, is poured out on the desolate (Daniel 9:27 NKJV).

The Book of Revelation says that the *beast* deceives and betrays the Jews and then takes over the Temple, setting up his own image in the Temple to be worshiped, in what Jesus calls *"the abomination which causes desolation."* This signals the second half of the seven-year Tribulation, a period known as the Great Tribulation.

The Great Tribulation will be a time like none other upon the face of the Earth, so intense that all of creation is on the brink of destruction. This destruction is coming not only from wars and conflicts, but also from persecution, natural disasters, famines, disease, and the worst you can imagine multiplied.

Jesus says that the Earth will be so distressed that even the sun will be darkened, and the moon will not be seen at night. Stars, most likely meteorites and asteroids, will fall from the sky, and all the heavens will be shaken. Astronomers are currently predicting this inevitable shower of meteorites and asteroids, and geologists expect an increase in earthquakes and volcanic activity.

I am giving you here a brief snapshot of what is expected to happen. The Bible, and specifically the Book of Revelation, gives us many details that I have left out as space will not allow for them. Knowing the details of what will happen during the Tribulation is not as important as knowing Jesus. Why? If you know Jesus, you will not be here, but called away from the *"wrath to come."* You will be with the rest of the Church enjoying what is known as the *Marriage Feast of the Lamb*. We will be with Jesus as *"joint heirs"* of all that the Father God has given to Him. We will be celebrating our presence eternally with Him, and we will be preparing for yet another event upon the face of the Earth in which we will play a major role. Oh, I hope you will join us!

Meanwhile, *global warming* finally comes to Earth, not in the manner, however, that the world is working so hard to prevent. Their global warming is a politically motivated farce; they should really be concerned about another source of global warming—the condition of their souls! Those who are seeking things to be "green" should first be seeking the red blood of Jesus! There is no reference in the Bible to global warming ever being an issue; in fact, the Earth was warmer in early creation under the canopy of vapor that came down at the Flood. The apostle Peter talks about the real global warming the world should be concerned about:

> *But the day of the Lord will come as a thief in the night; in which the heavens shall pass away with a great noise, and **the elements shall melt with fervent heat,** the earth also and the works that are therein shall be burned up* (2 Peter 3:10 KJV).

Yes, all of creation is on the brink of destruction, and lucifer and his forces are rejoicing as the clock runs down. Victory is apparently at hand for his forces and for him. The sun and moon are now darkened from the violent activity, but that is but a sign, a sign of the end.

Lucifer dances in the Temple in Jerusalem—surely, finally, now he has won! He shouts with glee, *"I will be like the Most High God"* (see Isa. 14:14).

Chapter 24

In the End

———•———

"In the beginning God..." Those famous words open the Bible in Genesis 1:1 and were also the first words of Chapter 1 of this book—but what about "In the end God"?

In the end?

The end of what? The end of time? The end of the Earth? I thought God did not have an end?

No, class, God is like a circle; He has no beginning or end. He lives in an "ever-present now," as I experienced in that near-death experience. He is not bounded by time.

Did God know that lucifer would rebel if given the kind of power and authority God gave Him? Did God know Adam and Eve would rebel and sin—and that He Himself would have to become a mudcake in order to redeem them? If God is an all-knowing and perfect God, then why did He create all this grief for Himself? Did God make a mistake? Did God know that in the end lucifer could bring all of creation to the brink of destruction?

Did God know all of this *"in the beginning"*?

Of course He did!

Then why did He do it?

God is the Alpha and Omega, the beginning and the end; God saw the beginning and the end at the same moment, and the end result was good!

In the end, He would have a family whom He could love and who could love Him back. *In the circle of God's existence, in that ever-present now, there was a momentary flash in eternity; in that **flash moment,** God created a family and destroyed evil and its potential to exist in the universe. The 6000 years it took to accomplish this, for those of us bound by time, is but a momentary, miniscule flash in eternal time.*

God might have said, "I will allow evil to exist, and I will then destroy it eternally. It won't take me long; it will be done in a flash! Then I can create a safe place for My family for eternity."

This whole process that we call world history is part of the creative process. Eden was not intended to be the final product of creation, but a stepping stone in the process of the creation of a *seen* Kingdom full of His family upon whom He could lavish His love. The process of creation is not finished yet!

Your life is an even briefer moment during this **flash** (a flash within a flash). If you so choose, you can be freed from evil and become part of Creation's final product—the Kingdom!

I have repeated often throughout this book—*your life is just a brief moment in eternity for the purpose of your redemption.* Those not choosing this redemption will be forever sealed as evil with all that is evil *"in the end."* The only end a redeemed mudcake will see is the end of evil and the end of this world *as we know it.*

So what happens at the end of this flash moment in eternity?

As we concluded the last chapter, it appeared that satan was winning! The Earth is a smoking cinder, and the sun and the moon cannot be seen. Death and destruction, famine and disease are everywhere. It's a dark place on the brink of total destruction. Lucifer dances in the Temple proclaiming victory and saying, *"I will be like the Most High God!"* He is thinking, "Let Jesus have those believer mudcakes He has taken to the *unseen* Kingdom, for I am the prince of the *seen* Kingdom!"

That is what is happening in the *seen* world, but we must stop and ask ourselves, "What is happening in the *unseen* world?"

Let's pick it up at the "calling away" of the Church before the Tribulation, which we talked about in the last chapter.

When the Church arrives in the heavenly Kingdom, Jesus and those who have gone on before them will be there to meet them. The first thing Jesus does is to prepare a meal for His Bride, the Church. The Bride, as joint heir with Him, will celebrate what is known as the *Marriage Feast of the Lamb* (the Lamb being Jesus who was sacrificed for us). (See Revelation 19:6-9.) This is an incredible celebration that will last for years while the Earth is in great turmoil during the Tribulation. It's the better place to be, let me tell you!

Then something awesome happens!

At the end of this meal, Jesus organizes a "posse" of angels and of the *saints*. The saints are all those redeemed mudcakes who were at the *Marriage Feast of the Lamb*. The Bible refers to redeemed mudcakes as *saints* (see 1 Cor. 6:2; Eph. 3:17-19). The Catholic Church has declared certain significant people to be saints, but Jesus Christ declares all who have accepted His sacrifice of redemption as *saints*. Sainthood is conferred upon you by Jesus when you receive Him as Lord.

Jesus gives all these *saints* majestic, powerful, and heavenly horses, and for people like me, supernaturally quick riding lessons, and He empowers us with the ability to ride these horses. His horse, as the King, is the most majestic horse of all, and on His red robe and on His thigh is written *"King of kings and Lord of lords!"* (See Revelation 19:16.) This mighty King possesses a secret weapon that is the most powerful weapon in the entire universe. The weapon is like a sharp sword able *"to strike down the nations"* (Rev. 19:15). This sword comes out of His mouth. We know it as the Word of God. This weapon has been tested before, for it is the same power that flung the Earth, sun, moon, and stars into their places. John 1:1 says, *"In the beginning was the Word, and the Word was with God, and the Word was God!"*

The Rider on the White Horse

Let's pick up the biblical account of this event in the Book of Revelation and see what happens:

> *I saw heaven standing open and there before me was a white horse, whose rider is called Faithful and True. With justice He judges and makes war. His eyes are like blazing fire, and on His head are many crowns. He has a name written on Him that no one knows but He Himself. He is dressed in a robe dipped in blood, and **His name is the Word of God. The armies of heaven were following Him, riding on white horses and dressed in fine linen, white and clean. Out of His mouth comes a sharp sword** with which to strike down the nations. "He will rule them with an iron scepter." He treads the winepress of the fury of the wrath of God Almighty. **On His robe and on His thigh He has this name written:***
>
> *King of kings and Lord of lords.*
>
> *And I saw an angel standing in the sun, who cried in a loud voice to all the birds flying in midair, "Come, gather together for the great supper of God, so that you may eat the flesh of kings, generals, and mighty men, of horses and their riders, and the flesh of all people, free and slave, small and great."*

Then I saw the beast and the kings of the earth and their armies gathered together to make war against the rider on the horse and His army. But the beast was captured, and with him the false prophet who had performed the miraculous signs on his behalf. With these signs he had deluded those who had received the mark of the beast and worshiped his image. The two of them were thrown alive into the fiery lake of burning sulfur. *The rest of them were killed with the sword that came out of the mouth of the rider on the horse,* and all the birds gorged themselves on their flesh (Revelation 19:11-21).

Wow! Just at the moment lucifer begins to celebrate, with creation on the brink of total destruction, every eye is turned toward the heavens to behold the most unbelievable sight. Descending upon the armies of lucifer is the most majestic army equipped with the most powerful weapon, the Word of God, led by the King of kings and Lord of lords Himself: Jesus Christ, the Messiah, the Son of God, the Son of Man, the Lamb that was slain! Jesus's feet touch down upon the Mount of Olives in Jerusalem just as He promised the disciples, the very place from which He ascended. (See Zechariah 14:4.) Yes, this is the final event of His second coming, which has been anticipated for so long. This time He is coming with justice and judgment; this time He will judge those who rejected Him and the salvation bought with His blood. Evil is forever defeated under a wash of the very blood of the Creator's Son, Jesus. All that is left is the judgment of evil and of its purveyors!

The Lord Comes and Reigns

Let's look at another word of prophecy about this event, this time from the prophet Zechariah. This word of prophecy was given in the sixth century *before* the birth of Jesus.

A day of the Lord is coming when your plunder will be divided among you.

I will gather all the nations to Jerusalem to fight against it; the city will be captured, the houses ransacked, and the women raped. Half of the city will go into exile, but the rest of the people will not be taken from the city.

Then the Lord will go out and fight against those nations, as He fights in the day of battle. On that day His feet will stand on the Mount of Olives, east of Jerusalem, and the Mount of Olives will be split in two from east to west, forming a great valley, with half of the mountain moving north and half moving south. You will flee by My mountain valley, for it will extend to Azel. You will flee as you fled from the earthquake in the days of Uzziah king of Judah. Then the Lord my God will come, and all the holy ones with Him.

On that day there will be no light, no cold or frost. It will be a unique day, without daytime or nighttime—a day known to the Lord. When evening comes, there will be light.

On that day living water will flow out from Jerusalem, half to the eastern sea and half to the western sea, in summer and in winter.

The Lord will be king over the whole earth. On that day there will be one Lord, and His name the only name.

The whole land, from Geba to Rimmon, south of Jerusalem, will become like the Arabah. But Jerusalem will be raised up and remain in its place, from the Benjamin Gate to the site of the First Gate, to the Corner Gate, and from the Tower of Hananel to the royal winepresses. It will be inhabited; never again will it be destroyed. Jerusalem will be secure.

This is the plague with which the Lord will strike all the nations that fought against Jerusalem: Their flesh will rot while they are still standing on their feet, their eyes will rot in their sockets, and their tongues will rot in their mouths. On that day men will be stricken by the Lord with great panic. Each man will seize the hand of another, and they will attack each other. Judah too will fight at Jerusalem. The wealth of all the surrounding nations will be collected—great quantities of gold and silver and clothing. A similar plague will strike the horses and mules, the camels and donkeys, and all the animals in those camps.

Then the survivors from all the nations that have attacked Jerusalem will go up year after year to worship the King, the Lord Almighty, and to celebrate the Feast of Tabernacles. If any of the peoples of the earth do not go up to Jerusalem to worship the King, the Lord Almighty, they will have no rain. If the Egyptian people do not go up and take part, they will have no rain. The Lord will bring on them the plague He inflicts on the nations that do not go up to celebrate the Feast of Tabernacles. This will be the punishment of Egypt and the punishment of all the nations that do not go up to celebrate the Feast of Tabernacles.

On that day Holy to the Lord will be inscribed on the bells of the horses, and the cooking pots in the Lord's house will be like the sacred bowls in front of the altar. Every pot in Jerusalem and Judah will be holy to the Lord Almighty, and all who come to sacrifice will take some of the pots and cook in them. And on that day there will no longer be a Canaanite in the house of the Lord Almighty (Zechariah 14:1-21).

Who is this great military leader? Who is this one whom Israel at this time finally embraces as their Messiah?

Yes, Israel, this time it **is** *a military coup, just like you have always wanted!* And what is best of all is that all Israel will be saved! (See Romans 11:26-27; Isaiah 59:20-21.) It will be truly liberating, not just for Israel, but for all of creation.

Yes, class, this time the answer truly is *Jesus!* Go ahead; shout it out! I did! I am really smiling and nodding this time too! And you know who is behind it all? *God!* Yes, class, that other right answer!

Now, do you know who's really in trouble here? You're right! The third answer—*the devil!* No frowns and cautious looks this time here from the teacher, just a little church lady dance!

Without being able to fire a useless shot, lucifer stands face-to-face with the warring angel Michael, and he and his heavenly forces grab hold of "old slew foot" by the scruff of the neck, throw him to the ground along with his sidekick, the false prophet who deceived so many and made them wear the *"mark of the beast"* on their forehead or hand (see Rev. 19:20).

You see, the *beast* (satan) and the false prophet controlled the people by placing a computer chip in their foreheads or on their hands to identify those who had sworn allegiance to the beast. Those who did not have this informational chip could not buy or sell anything, including food.

By the way, this technology exists today and is currently in use, mostly for the identification of animals. Plans are under way to use it with people for "identification purposes" and to replace your credit or debit card. The company who produces it, *Veri Chip Inc.*, (www.verichipcorp.com) is a NASDAQ publicly traded company. In November of 2009, this corporation acquired another corporation known as *Steel Vault Corp* and changed its name to *PositiveID Corporation* with its ticker symbol *PSID*. All we need is one single authority to command this technology to be used worldwide! What *Veri Chip* (now *PositveID Corp.*) intended for good will be used by the beast for evil. *PositiveID Corporation*, the manufacturer, says that this chip "could be inserted under the skin on the hand or forehead for identification, tracking and information purposes."[1]

Ironically, on the very day, I wrote this chapter, Andi, not knowing what I had been writing, came to me with an article appearing in *The Jerusalem Post* with the headline, "Knesset Approves Controversial Biometric Database Law." Let me quote from the article:

> After months of heated debate, the Knesset approved the Biometric
> Database Law Monday night paving the way for the introduction
> of "smart" identification documents for all Israelis. Once the law
> goes into effect, there will be a trial period of two years, during
> which participation in the biometric database will be voluntary. If
> the trial period is deemed successful, Interior Ministry officials will
> be authorized to make fingerprints and facial contours of all Israeli
> residents before providing them with identifying documents. *The
> documents will include a micro-chip,* which will contain photos of two
> fingerprints and the person's facial contours.[2]

By the way, this information went unreported in the United States because the news services do not understand its significance, because they do not know the Word of God. The big news that day was a great sports figure's disclosed infidelity! So many of the mudcakes and their leaders of today are much like Nero who played the fiddle while pending destruction is all around.

This technology was revealed to the apostle John in a vision recorded in the Book of Revelation 2000 years ago! Still think the Bible is boring and outdated?

This is yet another sign that we are presently at the end of the Church Age preparing for the Tribulation transition into the Kingdom Age.

I am not just blowing smoke here! However, lucifer is about to do just that!

Yes, lucifer in the form of the beast is cast down to the ground once again and bound; then he and the false prophet are thrown into the lake of burning sulphur! Yes, sir, stink into the stink!

> *I beheld the earth, and indeed it was without form, and void;*
> *and the heavens, they had no light.*

I am not quoting Genesis here; no, I am quoting Jeremiah 4:23 where the prophet Jeremiah utters a word of prophecy about this coming day. The results of this day will be as the result of lucifer's first casting down to the ground. Just as in Genesis 1:2, *"The earth was without form and void, and darkness was upon the face of the deep"* (KJV), we will see the Earth become *"without form and void; and the heavens, they had no light"* (Jer. 4:23 NKJV).

Andi likes to point out that the best lucifer can come up with at the end of his rampage is to bring darkness upon the Earth, just like he did the first time he was cast down to the ground.

Do you remember this verse I have often quoted throughout this book? *"The thing that hath been, it is that which shall be; and that which is done is that which shall be done: and there is no new thing under the sun"* (Eccles. 1:9 KJV). Here we have another example of the truth of this passage as the events of the past are also a picture of the future.

Let's look at this account in the Book of Jeremiah before we go on:

> *And at that day the slain of the Lord shall be from one end of*
> *the earth even to the other end of the earth. They shall not be*
> *lamented, or gathered, or buried; they shall become refuse on the*
> *ground* (Jeremiah 25:33 NKJV).

> *I beheld the earth, and indeed it was without form, and void;*
> *and the heavens, they had no light. I beheld the mountains, and*
> *indeed they trembled, and all the hills moved back and forth.*
> *I beheld, and indeed* **there was no man,** *and all the birds*

of the heavens had fled. I beheld, and indeed the fruitful land
*was a wilderness, and all its cities were broken down **at the***
presence of the Lord, by His fierce anger (Jeremiah
4:23-26 NKJV).

The prophet Jeremiah reveals that as a result of this battle there will be
no one left on the battlefield after the Day of the Lord. Is this a bittersweet
victory for Jesus? All that is left are broken-down cities, and dead soldiers;
the enemies of the Lord are lying on the ground utterly defeated. The Earth
is extremely unstable and trembles. Survivors in the world are terrified in
their hiding places because even the hills are moving back and forth. This
is the result of God's fierce anger and the presence of the Lord as He spoke
the word of judgment against the Earth. The forces of lucifer are brought to
nothing in one day!

It is a total annihilation of God's enemies. And you know what? The forces
of Heaven do not suffer one casualty in this greatest battle of all time!

Yes, Earth, this is in your future!

Is it over?

Not yet!

The Thousand Years

Let's pick up the biblical account where we left off at the beginning of
Revelation chapter 20:

*And I saw an **angel coming down out of heaven**, having*
the key to the Abyss and holding in his hand a great chain.
He seized the dragon, that ancient serpent, who is the
devil, or Satan, and bound him for a thousand years.

He threw him into the Abyss, and locked and sealed it over him, to keep him from deceiving the nations anymore until the thousand years were ended. After that, he must be set free for a short time.

I saw thrones on which were seated those who had been given authority to judge. And I saw the souls of those who had been beheaded because of their testimony for Jesus and because of the word of God. They had not worshiped the beast or his image and had not received his mark on their foreheads or their hands. They came to life and reigned with Christ a thousand years. (The rest of the dead did not come to life until the thousand years were ended.) This is the first resurrection. Blessed and holy are those who have part in the first resurrection. The second death has no power over them, but they will be priests of God and of Christ and will reign with Him for a thousand years (Revelation 20:1-6).

We find that the Nephilim possessing the spirit of lucifer himself and known as the *beast* is bound and thrown into the lake of fire, also known as the abyss, but the text says that it was only for 1000 years.

What? You mean he is coming back?

Yes, he is! Rather like those movies where you think the monster is dead, then it starts moving again—the monster will move again! He was defeated, but he was not yet judged and eternally condemned.

Before he meets his final demise and evil and the potential for evil is completely defeated, we will see Jesus reigning from Jerusalem just as the prophets said He would in what is known as the *Millennium,* or the 1000-year reign of Christ upon the Earth. Lucifer is bound for 1000 years so that he cannot counterfeit anything and deceive the nations during that time. It is a wonderful life upon the Earth, this time ruled by a totally good and righteous

King just as Israel has always dreamed. People are born, and long life is restored as the Earth is repopulated. The saints of Heaven also are present upon the Earth. It is at this time that a resurrection, known as the *first resurrection* occurs.

Jesus reverses the injustice meted out by the beast, who killed those who refused to follow him. This first resurrection is for the *Tribulation saints*—those who refused to follow the beast and refused to take his mark in their foreheads or hands. These are the people who accepted Jesus as Lord during the *Tribulation* and were beheaded because of it. (It is interesting to note at this point that the method Islam has for dealing with *infidels* is to behead them.) Jesus rewards them by resurrecting them and giving them ruling positions upon the Earth as they repopulate the Earth during this 1000-year reign. The bodies of the faithful who died *before* the *Tribulation* were resurrected and glorified when Jesus called the Church away. They too are upon the Earth and will rule and reign with Jesus as He takes control of the Earth from satan. The Earth is ruled by the Church and the Tribulation saints with Jesus the Messiah as their King.

The 1000-year millennial reign of Jesus is a time of universal peace, prosperity, long life, and prevailing righteousness and goodness. Wrong and injustice disappear, and Jesus reigns for 1000 years as children are born and repopulate the Earth. Satan is nowhere to be seen.

Understand that this still is not the Kingdom of Heaven upon the Earth. This is a restored earthly Kingdom ruled by the Son of Man, the King of kings Himself. This fulfills all the prophetic words of both the Old and New Testaments as the Messiah rules in Jerusalem.

However, at this point, there is still one issue to be dealt with: The potential for evil still exists. Satan is only bound, and once and for all he must be dealt with, judged, and condemned eternally. How? How can a spiritual being be eliminated? The *seen* Kingdom of Heaven cannot exist on Earth with satan lurking outside its gates. If that were so, the potential for another mudcake rebellion such as was in Eden would always be a possibility. The Earth is corrupted with accumulated sorrow and grief, and the dirt and ashes to which the unredeemed mudcakes' bodies had returned had spiritually polluted it. What is more, the "heavens" (the Earth's atmosphere) had been polluted by the activities of satan, who is known also as the *"prince of the power of the air,"* and his forces (Eph. 2:2 KJV). Ephesians 6:12 tells us that there are *"spiritual forces of evil in the heavenly realms."* We discussed earlier that some of the unexplained phenomena we have dubbed UFOs are a result of this heavenly activity.

Evil must be finally judged and the Earth purged of the disease of evil; therefore, at the end of the 1000 years satan is released from his prison. Needless to say, this prison did not do much to rehab him, for immediately he returns to his old ways and begins to deceive the people. We see another mudcake rebellion reminiscent of the rebellion in Eden on the horizon.

He goes to the surrounding people, the Gog and Magog, so to speak, of that day, deceives them, and then brings them once again against Jesus's Kingdom just as He had done to Israel before the *Tribulation*. Lucifer surrounds this Kingdom led by Jesus Christ. He leads many astray and gets an army to march across the *"breadth of the earth"* to attack the Kingdom of Jesus Christ centered in Jerusalem. This insurrection and its leader are quickly and finally dealt with in the last battle for all eternity to come. This battle was over before it even got started. Let's read the account of this event:

> *When the thousand years are over, Satan will be released from his prison and will go out to deceive the nations in the four corners of the earth—Gog and Magog—to gather them for battle. In number they are like the sand on the seashore. They marched across the breadth of the earth and surrounded the camp of God's people, the city He loves. But fire came down from heaven and devoured them. And the devil, who deceived them, was thrown into the lake of burning sulfur, where the beast and*

*the false prophet had been thrown. They will be tormented day
and night forever and ever* (Revelation 20:7-10).

Then we read:

*Then I saw a great white throne and Him who was seated on it.
Earth and sky fled from His presence, and there was no place
for them. And I saw the dead, great and small, standing before
the throne, and books were opened. Another book was opened,
which is the book of life. The dead were judged according to what
they had done as recorded in the books. The sea gave up the dead
that were in it, and death and Hades gave up the dead that were
in them, and each person was judged according to what he had
done. Then death and Hades were thrown into the lake of fire.
The lake of fire is the second death. If anyone's name was not
found written in the book of life, he was thrown into the lake of
fire* (Revelation 20:11-15).

We find that fire once again descends from Heaven and cleanses the
Earth from this latest and *final* mudcake rebellion. All rebelling mudcakes
are destroyed; their leader, lucifer, is captured by the forces of Jesus Christ
and cast into the lake of burning sulfur—this time forever. Yes, class, the
monster stays dead this time! Then there is a final cleansing action by this
Great God King in Jerusalem, for there is now another resurrection. In this
enormous resurrection, all those who had rebelled against God and refused
to receive His salvation all the way back to the Garden of Eden are raised.
Their spirits, which have been in Hades, are now rejoined to the dirt and
ashes that made up their bodies, and they now stand before the Lord. Yes,
people like Cain, Nimrod, Herod, the Pharisees, Nero, Mohammed, Buddha,
Adolf Hitler, Saddam Hussein, and current-day leaders who oppose Israel
and Christianity will find themselves before the *Great White Throne* of judgment. Doctors, lawyers, businesspeople, social leaders, Nobel prize winners,
clergy, philanthropists, housewives, renowned scientists, talk show hosts,

movie and television stars, musicians, theologians, judges, prominent people, unknown people, white, black, Hispanic, Asian, and people of all creeds and colors from every walk of life will also be present. They now all stand before this throne.

One by one they are called forward. At that moment, they stand alone, and neither their status nor their accomplishments in life matter. An angel peers into a book known as *"the Lamb's book of life"* looking for their names (Rev. 21:27).

The only thing that matters is the answer to one question: "Do you know Jesus?"

Revelation 20:15 tells us what happens next; *"If anyone's name was not found written in the book of life, he was thrown into the lake of fire"* (KJV). They join lucifer and his demons, the Nephilim, and other rebelling mudcakes in the lake of burning sulfur to be tormented *"forever and ever,"* as the Scripture says. They are dealt the same fate as the one who deceived them, even if they made the decision to follow him by default.

Yes, this is hell. Hell has never been occupied until this time. It is a place from which no one returns, not even lucifer. It was created for lucifer and the angels who fell with him; there is no opportunity for redemption for these spiritual beings. It was not created for mudcakes. God provided a way for fallen mudcakes to escape following their leader lucifer into hell; all they must do is choose Jesus as their Savior and Lord, and their names will be written in the Lamb's book of life. *It is a benefit that is free, but one that you do not get unless you apply.* Those who do not find their names in this book are cast into eternity with lucifer and his demons, forever separated from others and, most importantly, from their Creator.

What about you? Do you know Jesus? Is your name written in the *Lamb's book of life*? If you haven't done so yet, perhaps now you should visit the part of this book called "The Secret of Eternal Life."

Most people hold back from making this decision because they do not want to change their lifestyle; they are afraid of what their friends, spouses, or others think. You must understand that it only matters what Jesus thinks. His is an eternal opinion; theirs are just temporary!

Don't live this temporary life without looking into and making a decision about your eternal future! The clock of your life is ticking down; you have no idea when it will stop and your opportunity will come to an end. There is no second chance, just this life, that's all! It does not matter where you have been, what you have done, or how unworthy or bad you think you are, for in this life there is a second chance! Jesus gives you a second chance. You were born into this world and, therefore, subject to lucifer, the *"prince of this world."* All you have to do is rebel against him and choose to follow the King; you will then become a citizen of the *new world order*, the Kingdom of Heaven.

"Jesus answered, 'I am the way and the truth and the life. No one comes to the Father except through Me'" (John 14:6). Jesus is the only road to Heaven; following anyone else just leads to hell.

Those who choose Jesus, who make Him Lord of their lives, have a glorious and an unbelievable future ahead of them. The Book of Revelation and the whole Bible ends with the promise of the eternal *unseen* Kingdom becoming the *seen* Kingdom of Heaven upon the Earth.

With the finality of the Great White Throne judgment, God's original plan for creation is restored and completed. Evil and the potential for evil are eradicated, not only from the Earth, but from the entire universe. No evil will befall God's beloved mudcakes, now in restored bodies as they were before their fall in Eden. No temptation will ever come before their eyes; there will be no *Tree of the Knowledge of Good and Evil* in the Earth, for they will already possess this knowledge. In their lives upon the Earth, they would have chosen *good* in their own personal mudcake rebellions. Evil can no longer tempt them.

It is at this moment that we see another re-creation of the world, as we saw between Genesis 1:1 and 1:2. Not much detail is given, but we find in this prophecy of Revelation chapter 21 that the Earth and its atmosphere has passed away and a new heaven (atmosphere) and new Earth have been re-created as it was fully and originally intended.

The New Jerusalem

Let's read the account in chapters 21 and 22:

> *Then I saw a new heaven and a new earth, for the first heaven and **the first earth had passed away, and there was no longer any sea.** I saw the Holy City, the new Jerusalem, **coming down out of heaven from God,** prepared as a bride beautifully dressed for her husband. And I heard a loud voice from the throne saying, "**Now the dwelling of God is with men, and He will live with them.** They will be His people, and God Himself will be with them and be their God. He will wipe every tear from their eyes. **There will be no more death or mourning or crying or pain, for the old order of things has passed away.**"*
>
> *He who was seated on the throne said, "**I am making everything new!**" Then he said, "Write this down, for these words are trustworthy and true."*
>
> *He said to me: "It is done. I am the Alpha and the Omega, the Beginning and the End. To him who is thirsty I will give to drink without cost from the spring of the water of life. **He who overcomes will inherit all this,** and I will be his God and he will be My son. But the cowardly, the unbelieving, the vile, the murderers, the sexually immoral, those who practice magic*

arts, the idolaters and all liars—their place will be in the fiery lake of burning sulfur. This is the second death."

One of the seven angels who had the seven bowls full of the seven last plagues came and said to me, "Come, I will show you the bride, the wife of the Lamb." And he carried me away in the Spirit to a mountain great and high, and showed me the Holy City, Jerusalem, coming down out of heaven from God. It shone with the glory of God, and its brilliance was like that of a very precious jewel, like a jasper, clear as crystal. It had a great, high wall with twelve gates, and with twelve angels at the gates. **On the gates were written the names of the twelve tribes of Israel.** *There were three gates on the east, three on the north, three on the south and three on the west.* **The wall of the city had twelve foundations, and on them were the names of the twelve apostles of the Lamb.**

The angel who talked with me had a measuring rod of gold to measure the city, its gates and its walls. The city was laid out like a square, as long as it was wide. He measured the city with the rod and found it to be 12,000 stadia in length, and as wide and high as it is long. He measured its wall and it was 144 cubits thick, by man's measurement, which the angel was using. The wall was made of jasper, and the city of pure gold, as pure as glass. The foundations of the city walls were decorated with every kind of precious stone. The first foundation was jasper, the second sapphire, the third chalcedony, the fourth emerald, the fifth sardonyx, the sixth carnelian, the seventh chrysolite, the eighth beryl, the ninth topaz, the tenth chrysoprase, the eleventh jacinth, and the twelfth amethyst. The twelve gates were twelve pearls, each gate made of a single pearl. The great street of the city was of pure gold, like transparent glass.

I did not see a temple in the city, because the Lord God Almighty and the Lamb are its temple. The city does not need the sun or the moon to shine on it, for the glory of God gives it light, and the Lamb is its lamp. The nations will walk by its light, and the kings of the earth will bring their splendor into it. On no day will its gates ever be shut, for **there will be no night there.** The glory and honor of the nations will be brought into it. **Nothing impure will ever enter it, nor will anyone who does what is shameful or deceitful, but only those whose names are written in the Lamb's book of life** (Revelation 21:1-27).

The River of Life

The angel takes the apostle John on a further tour of the holy city:

Then the angel showed me the river of the water of life, as clear as crystal, flowing from the throne of God and of the Lamb down the middle of the great street of the city. On each side of the river stood the tree of life, bearing twelve crops of fruit, yielding its fruit every month. And the leaves of the tree are for the healing of the nations. **No longer will there be any curse.** *The throne of God and of the Lamb will be in the city, and His servants will serve Him.* **They will see His face, and His name will be on their foreheads.** *There will be no more night. They will not need the light of a lamp or the light of the sun, for the Lord God will give them light.* **And they will reign forever and ever.** *The angel said to me, "These words are trustworthy and true. The Lord, the God of the spirits of the prophets, sent His angel to show His servants the things that must soon take place"* (Revelation 22:1-6).

Yes, class, we see that God re-creates again and that this new Heaven-on-Earth Kingdom comes down from Heaven. There are no longer any curses, sicknesses, or tears; all evil has been banished, and *"there will be no more death or mourning or crying or pain, for the old order of things has passed away"* (Rev. 21:4). Everything is new! Yes, it is the *new world order* the heart of humankind has sought throughout the ages.

The dimensions of this city are given, and it has been estimated to be comparable in size to the land mass now of the eastern United States north to south and from the east to the Mississippi River. It has 12 gates named after the 12 tribes of Israel and 12 foundations named after the 12 disciples or apostles. *This signifies the eternal uniting of the remnant earthly nation of Israel with the remnant spiritual nation of the Church, and it is also symbolic of the joining of the spiritual* **unseen** *Kingdom of Heaven (the Church) with the physical* **seen** *Kingdom (Israel) on Earth.* The foundations are named for the apostles because they were the foundations laid by Jesus for His eternal Kingdom when He was upon the Earth. The 24 elders around the throne, who worship the Lord in Revelation 4, represent the uniting of the physical and spiritual Kingdoms as well because these 24 elders are the founders of the 12 tribes of Israel and the 12 apostles.

This city also has a river flowing crystal clear and pure from the throne of God, flowing with the *"living water"* Jesus promised while on Earth because there is a *"Tree of Life"* on both sides of the river. These trees are like the tree that sustained life for the mudcakes in the Garden of Eden, the very tree they were forbidden to eat of when they rebelled and were banished from Eden (see Gen. 3:22-24). The fruit of this tree sustained their life in the mudcake body. Do not confuse this with the *Tree of the Knowledge of Good and Evil.* Adam and Eve in Eden knew they were not to eat of its fruit, but they did so, creating this mess we now live in. The *Tree of Life* is only mentioned three places in the Bible; in Genesis, in the beginning of the Bible; in Proverbs, in the middle of the Bible; and twice at the end of the Bible, here in Revelation (see Rev. 2:7; 22:2).

The account also says something else very interesting. It says that there are *"no more seas."* Why?

If you recall, we discussed earlier that the seas were created when the canopies that encircled the Earth fell to the Earth, the last one being the canopy of vapor that fell at the time of the Flood. This canopy created a "greenhouse effect" upon the Earth. What we see here, my dear mudcake friends, is that God in His re-creation after the judgment once again restores the original canopies to their places through the purging with fervent heat of the fire of judgment. Talk about going "green!" The New Jerusalem is the environment you environmentalists should be pursuing! You can find it by following Jesus!

We also see that the original light and presence of the Almighty God Himself is also what lights the world: *"Now the dwelling of God is with men, and He will live with them"* (Rev. 21:3).

It also says that there is no need of a Temple because God dwells with man. You see, the presence of God lights up all creation. Light is projected from creation. When I was in the presence of Jesus in Heaven, I noted that everything and every color was illuminated from within. On Earth we see colors only when light shines on things reflecting their color, but where God indwells everything, the light comes out of all things. Even the people I saw wore an "illuminated robe" shining from within, and there was an illuminated presence about them that covered them.

I remember sharing this concept at my mother's funeral and referring to the fact that while we were left with the "empty shell," Mom herself was in the presence of God because she made Jesus Lord of her life. I shared the fact that the light that went out in Eden had just come back on within Mom's new glorified body. That is the best way I can describe it although it is not accurate; I just do not have the words, and there are none that can depict truly what I experienced. Such it is for all who die having received Jesus's gift of salvation provided at Calvary. When God's presence left Adam and Eve, they noticed they were naked—why? They noticed they were naked because the light of God's presence no longer indwelt and illuminated them!

Yes, in the New Jerusalem, we will be naked!

Don't worry, though; we will wear the robe of Christ's righteousness, and the presence of the Holy Spirit within us will illuminate us once again as it did Adam and Eve before the fall. We will be once again perfect mudcakes, no sickness, no fat, no cellulite, no bad breath, just good through and through! According to this passage, we will not only see His face, but He will also illuminate us with His presence. We will truly then be the *"enlightened ones!"* The New Age believers will be the *"lit up ones"* in the *lake of fire* for having rejected *"so great a salvation."*

The process of creation of the new world order, the **seen** *Kingdom of Heaven upon the Earth started* **"in the beginning,"** *is now completed!*

Who will indwell this new Heaven and new Earth, this majestic and glorious eternal city, the *seen* Kingdom of Heaven upon the Earth?

The answer this time, class, is *"God,"* and it is *"Jesus";* it is also the *overcomers:* **"He who overcomes will inherit all this"** (Rev. 21:7).

Yes, the *overcomers* appear here again, everyone throughout the ages whose name was found in the *Lamb's book of life* will be part of this last-day remnant that transitions the world into the Kingdom Age. These *overcomers* are those who make up the Kingdom. All who overcame sin and death throughout all the ages by following the One who defeated sin and death are *overcomers*. They became *overcomers* not only by the blood of the Lamb, but also by confessing Jesus as Lord—the *"word of their testimony"* (Rev. 12:11 KJV).

An *overcomer* is one as described in the following passages from the Bible:

That if thou shalt confess with thy mouth, and shalt believe in thine heart that God hath raised Him from the dead, thou shalt be saved (Romans 10:9 KJV).

*Whosoever shall confess that Jesus is the Son of God, **God dwelleth in him,** and he in God* (1 John 4:15 KJV).

He that overcometh, the same shall be clothed in white raiment; and I will not blot out his name out of the book of life, but I will confess his name before My Father, and before His angels (Revelation 3:5 KJV).

Are you an *overcomer*? Your destiny and purpose in this life can be summed up in this phrase—to be an *overcomer* with Jesus, not only in this life, but in the life to come. Do you remember, as I said throughout this book, *that your life is a brief moment in eternity for the purpose of your redemption in order to share in the inheritance of Jesus Christ?*

Just as God did with the re-creation of world, God *"hovers"* or *"broods"* over you to re-create you. It does not matter where your life has been or what has happened; God always has a plan to redeem that which is ruined, in darkness, and in chaos. If that describes you, then He has a plan for you!

Just like the train in the dream I shared in a previous chapter, the Kingdom of God is forcefully advancing, running over everything in its way. It has a defined direction, and it is on track, and lucifer has no claim to those it picks up along its way. He has no claim on them or the world that they will inhabit because *God has bought and paid for it with His own blood!* He distributes that purchase price freely just as the conductor in the form of tickets did on that symbolic train to those it picked up along the way. *The Kingdom of God* forcefully advances through the fallen world until it reaches the *seen* Kingdom upon the Earth, and then it crushes all others like the stone the prophet Daniel saw (see Dan. 2:44-45).

Any other purpose you might be seeking is temporal and will burn in the *lake of fire* when the Kingdom of Heaven comes to Earth. Do not leave God's gift of love lying on the ground unopened—and be less than all that you were purposed to be.

Let me sum up this book with the words of the most famous verse in the Bible:

> *For God so loved the world that He gave His only begotten Son, that whosoever believeth in Him should not perish, but have everlasting life* (John 3:16 KJV).

Now, class, let me personally paraphrase it for you in the light of all that we have learned:

> *For God so loved **you** that He gave for **you** His only begotten son, **Jesus**, that if you believe in Him, you will not perish in the lake of fire with lucifer, but will have everlasting life in the New Jerusalem with Jesus* (see John 3:16).

The Gospel is simple: You + Jesus = Overcoming Eternal Life.

OK, class, here is what we have learned. You now know how and why the world was created and why so much evil has prevailed in the world over the ages.

You now know why Jesus had to come as a man and die and why you need a Savior. You now know how the world is going to end and what the options are for *you* and all humankind.

You now know that eternal life after death is for all people, and you now know that where they spend this eternity is a choice that each one must make individually during this life. You also know that the default choice is to spend eternity with lucifer and the fallen ones.

You now know why you were created and that your purpose is to glorify God and to live eternally with Him in His love as part of His family!

You now know the choice is yours and yours alone.

Oh, and who am I to tell you all this?

I am merely a mudcake who is a blood-bought child and servant of the Most High God, one of His called-out ones from death into eternal life.

I am a member of God's family who has been called to a specific purpose in this life through a unique experience.

I have become His "friend" with whom He has shared His secrets as He promises He will share with all His family.

I am called to share His Word and His love for the world in hopes that more mudcakes will choose to do the same and become His friends too before it is too late.

I do this task because I love you. I cannot help but love you because He first loved me, and the Bible says that He sheds His love abroad through the Holy Spirit who is given to us (see Rom. 5:5).

My ultimate purpose is to glorify God and live eternally with Him.

That is who I am!

He desires to do the same for you!

May God bless you as you seek Him and lay hold of the purpose, the promises, and the calling He has for you. It is a gift that you must but receive.

Final Words

I was considering what might be my closing word or paragraph in this book when I heard the Lord say to me, *"Let Me close the book with a word."* So

I bid you blessings, and we will close out this book with the words of Jesus Christ Himself to you. Listen as He, the King of kings and Lord of lords, the Messiah, the Mighty King, the One who loves you, speaks:

Behold, I am coming soon! My reward is with Me, and I will give to everyone according to what he has done. I am the Alpha and the Omega, the First and the Last, the Beginning and the End.

Blessed are those who wash their robes, that they may have the right to the tree of life and may go through the gates into the city. Outside are the dogs, those who practice magic arts, the sexually immoral, the murderers, the idolaters and everyone who loves and practices falsehood.

I, Jesus, have sent My angel to give you this testimony for the churches. I am the Root and the Offspring of David, and the bright Morning Star (Revelation 22:12-17,20).

"Yes, I Am Coming Soon!"

Appendix

The Secret of Eternal Life

———•———

If you are a reader who has never made a decision to make Jesus Christ Lord of your life, or if you are unsure you are part of God's family, would you make that decision now? You would be a welcome addition to the family of God, and we sure would love to have you with us forever in Christ's Kingdom. Being a member of God's family would entitle you to all that God has promised in this life and in the Kingdom life to come. Let me review these important points with you that will lead you to make a decision for Christ and qualify you as a child of God, as well as other things we talked about throughout the book. I have included ample Scripture references to substantiate these points.

The Bible tells us:

1. *All people are sinners.* (See Romans 3:10, 3:23; Isaiah 64:6; Jeremiah 17:9; James 2:10.)

2. *The penalty of sin is death.* (See Romans 6:23; Ezekiel 18:20.)

3. *You must be perfect and sinless to enter Heaven.* (See Revelation 21:27; Habakkuk 1:13; Psalms 5:4.)

4. *You cannot do anything on your own to obtain perfection.* (See Ephesians 2:8-9; Galatians 2:16; Romans 4:5.)

5. *God provided a perfect sin-bearer (Jesus) and imputes to us His righteousness.* (See Second Corinthians 5:21; Philippians 3:9; Isaiah 53:6; First Peter 3:18.)

6. *You need only to believe in the Lord Jesus Christ as your personal Savior and confess that there is salvation in no other.* (See John 3:16; Romans 10:9; John 1:12; Acts 16:31.)

7. *You can be certain of your salvation now and know that your salvation cannot be lost because eternal life is eternal.* (See John 6:37,39; First John 5:13; John 10:28; Hebrews 10:10,14; First Peter 1:5.)

It does not matter what your past has been or what you have done. God is a God of restoration, and His grace is sufficient to save you and turn your life around. Just as no one is good enough to get into Heaven on their own merit, no one is bad enough not to receive so great a salvation as Jesus provided.

I don't care (more importantly, God doesn't care) whether you are Catholic, Baptist, Methodist, Presbyterian, Lutheran, Charismatic, Pentecostal, or another faith or background, or what your Mama or Daddy was. God and I just want to know: Do you know Jesus?

I don't mean, do you know about Him or what He has done—but do you have a personal relationship with Him? Answering this question is the most important thing you can ever do in this *temporary* life because it determines where you will spend eternity. There is no second chance after this life. Eternity is a long time, so you better make your reservations with Christ in Heaven. The default decision is to spend eternity according to the plans God has for satan, which is eternal separation from God and from all others. Remember, your body dies, but your soul or spirit does not. All you must do is accept the free gift of eternal life provided by God through Jesus Christ. So let me ask you again: Do you know Jesus?

Answer this question now before you read further because the Bible tells us that the time of Jesus's coming again will come upon us as a *"thief in the night."* The world will be caught by surprise—will you?

> *But of the times and the seasons, brethren, ye have no need that I write unto you. For yourselves know perfectly that the day of the Lord so cometh as a thief in the night. For when they shall say, Peace and safety; then sudden destruction cometh upon them, as travail upon a woman with child; and they shall not escape* (1 Thessalonians 5:1-3 KJV).

What Is Your Answer?

If you would like to be part of God's family—or maybe you are not sure you have ever asked Jesus to be Lord of your life, leading you to abundant life—would you pray the following prayer with those of us in God's family who already have? If you can, read it out loud; if you are not able to do that where you are, then say it quietly to Him in your mind. *He can and will hear you!*

> *Lord Jesus, I acknowledge that I am a sinner and that I need a Savior to be seen as righteous in God's eyes. I believe You died on the Cross for me and that Your sacrifice has covered my sins. I ask You to come into my life and save me and to be Lord of my life. Change me, Lord, and lead me into the abundant life that You have promised. Thank You, Lord, for saving me. In Your precious name, I pray. Amen.*

If you have prayed that prayer, let me welcome you to the family of God and to eternal life in Jesus Christ!

Perhaps some of you have made a decision for Christ in the past but are not living for Him today. Why don't you now take this opportunity to recommit yourself to Him and begin to walk in obedience to His will? If you would like to recommit yourself, take a moment and ask His forgiveness and renew that commitment to Him. Begin to walk in obedience to the One who loves you with an everlasting love. Pray your own prayer—or pray the following prayer if you need help.

> *Lord Jesus, I am sorry that I have been disobedient and have strayed from You. Forgive me for my unfaithfulness. I thank You for Your faithfulness to love me in spite of my sins. Create in me a clean heart, Lord, and renew a right spirit in me. I recommit myself to You and ask that You help me to walk in obedience to Your will in my life. Thank You, Lord. In Your precious name, I pray. Amen.*

Now, this is important! Let me encourage you to find a Gospel-preaching and Bible-teaching church to become part of, a church where you can be encouraged and taught the Word of God so that you can grow further in your walk with Jesus Christ. Look for a church where the *overcomers* are going... one where they use the Bible often in the service and people actually bring their own. Look for a church that is growing and teaches and preaches salvation through Jesus Christ. Remember the seven churches Jesus spoke to in Revelation; only two out of seven was He pleased with. Those churches represent the churches that are operating in the world today, so not every church is teaching the Word as they should.

If you have accepted Jesus Christ while reading this book, or if you have recommitted your life to Christ, I urge you to let us know by completing the page at the end of this book and sending it to us at the address on the form. You can send us a letter as well by mail or by E-mail. We have something we would like to send you to help you in your new walk with Christ.

Endnotes

Chapter 2

1. *Merriam-Webster's Collegiate Dictionary*, 11th ed., s.v., "Ordain"; "Anoint."

2. F. Brown, S. Driver, C. Briggs, *Brown-Driver-Briggs Hebrew Definitions* (Peabody, MA: Hendrickson Publishers, 1996); Ludwig Koehler and Walter Baumgartner, *The Hebrew and Aramaic Lexicon of the Old Testament, 2 Vols.* (Boston, MA: Brill Academic Publishers, 2002).

Chapter 4

1. For more information see M. Alan Kaslev, "Palaeos Mesozoic: The Mesozoic Era," http://www.palaeos.com/Mesozoic/Mesozoic.htm (accessed November 26, 2010).

2. Ibid.

Chapter 5

1. "America's Volcanic Past: Big Bend National Park, Texas," *U.S. Geological Survey,* http://vulcan.wr.usgs.gov/LivingWith/VolcanicPast/Places/volcanic_past_big_bend.html (accessed November 26, 2010).

2. James Oberg, "ArabSat bites the dust, dashing hopes: Team's plans for daring space rescue go for naught," *NBC News* (March 24, 2006) http://www.msnbc.msn.com/id/11999597/ (accessed November 27, 2010).

3. Charles Q. Choi, "Violent Planet: The Forces that Shape Earth," *Live Science* (March 4, 2010) http://www.livescience.com/environment/violent-planet-earth-100304.html (accessed November 27, 2010).

Chapter 6

1. *Merriam-Webster's Collegiate Dictionary*, 11th ed., s.v., "Firmament."

2. *Scofield Study Bible* (Oxford University Press, 2002), Genesis 1:3 reference note.

Chapter 7

1. Matthew Henry, *Matthew Henry's Commentary on the Whole Bible* (Grand Rapids, MI: Zondervan, 1992), 6.

2. "The Old Testament Hebrew Lexicon" *Study Light.org*, s.v. "Adam"; http://www.studylight.org/lex/heb/view.cgi?number=0119 (accessed November 27, 2010).

3. James Strong, *Strong's Complete Dictionary of Bible Words*, Hebrew 5048.

4. "The Old Testament Hebrew Lexicon" *Study Light.org*, s.v. "Bara"; http://www.studylight.org/lex/heb/view.cgi?number=01254 (accessed November 27, 2010).

Chapter 8

1. Buck Stephens, *The Coming Financial Revolution* (Shippensburg, PA: Destiny Image Publishers, 2005), 172-174.

2. *The Hebrew and Aramaic Lexicon of the Old Testament* (Boston, MA: Brill Academic Publishers, 1994).

3. *Ibid.*

Chapter 9

1. James Montgomery Boice, *Genesis: an Expositional Commentary, Volume 1* (Grand Rapids, MI: Zondervan, 1982), 201.

Chapter 10

1. *International Standard Bible Encyclopedia, Volume 4,* Geoffrey W. Bromiley, ed. (Grand Rapids, MI: Eerdmans Publishing Company, 1956), 423.

2. F. Brown, S. Driver, C. Briggs, *Brown-Driver-Briggs Hebrew Definitions* (Peabody, MA: Hendrickson Publishers, 1996), Hebrew 2233.

3. James Montgomery Boice, *Genesis: an Expositional Commentary, Volume 1* (Grand Rapids, MI: Zondervan, 1982), 245.

Chapter 11

1. F. Brown, S. Driver, C. Briggs, *Brown-Driver-Briggs Hebrew Definitions* (Peabody, MA: Hendrickson Publishers, 1996), Hebrew 582.

2. James Montgomery Boice, *Genesis: an Expositional Commentary, Volume 1* (Grand Rapids, MI: Zondervan, 1982), 232.

3. *International Standard Bible Encyclopedia, Volume 4,* Geoffrey W. Bromiley, ed. (Grand Rapids, MI: Eerdmans Publishing Company, 1956), 63.

Chapter 12

1. F. Brown, S. Driver, C. Briggs, *Brown-Driver-Briggs Hebrew Definitions* (Peabody, MA: Hendrickson Publishers, 1996), Hebrew 2490.

Chapter 13

1. James Strong, *Strong's Complete Dictionary of Bible Words,* Hebrew 7650.

2. "Meaning of Numbers in the Bible," *Bible Study.org;* www.biblestudy.org/bibleref/meaning-of-numbers-in-bible/7.html (accessed November 29, 2010).

Chapter 16

1. For a complete discussion on this subject, see Rick Larson, *The Star of Bethlehem;* www.bethlehemstar.net (accessed November 30, 2010).

2. Monk Themistocles (Adamopoulos), "The Magi and the Infant Jesus," *Orthodox Research Institute;* http://www.orthodoxresearchinstitute.org/articles/bible/themistocles_magi.htm (accessed November 30, 2010).

Chapter 17

1. Contact our ministry for a CD or DVD of this teaching on *Breaking the Curse of Poverty,* or better yet, bring it to your place of worship.

2. Cahleen Shrier, "The Science of the Crucifixion," *Azusa Pacific University;* http://www.apu.edu/infocus/2002/03/crucifixion/ (accessed December 1, 2010).

Chapter 18

1. "The New Testament Greek Lexicon," *Study Light.org,* s.v. "Gehenna"; http://www.studylight.org/lex/grk/view.cgi?number=1067 (accessed December 1, 2010).

2. "The New Testament Greek Lexicon," *Study Light.org,* s.v. "Hades"; http://www.studylight.org/lex/grk/view.cgi?number=86 (accessed December 1, 2010).

3. "The Old Testament Hebrew Lexicon," *Study Light.org,* s.v. "Sheol"; http://www.studylight.org/lex/heb/view.cgi?number=07585 (accessed December 1, 2010).

4. "The New Testament Greek Lexicon," *Study Light.org,* s.v. "Tartaroo"; http://www.studylight.org/lex/grk/view.cgi?number=5020 (accessed December 1, 2010).

5. "Astronomers pinpoint time and date of crucifixion and resurrection," *Ananova* (2003); http://clippednews.wordpress.com/2003/05/09/ did-jesus-christ-die-at-3PM-on-3rd-april/ (accessed December 1, 2010); and Rick Larson, "The Day of the Cross," *The Star of Bethlehem;* www. bethlehemstar.net/day/day.htm (accessed December 1, 2010).

Chapter 19

1. Spiros Zodhiates, *The Complete Word Study Dictionary, New Testament* (Chattanooga, TN: AMG Publishers, 1992), 487 (#1411).

Chapter 20

1. *Fausset's Bible Dictionary,* Electronic Database Copyright ©1998 by Biblesoft.

2. Buck Stephens, *The Coming Financial Revolution* (Shippensburg, PA: Destiny Image Publishers, 2005), 182-185.

3. *Ibid.*, 185-191.

4. C.S. Lewis, *A Mind Awake: An Anthology of CS Lewis,* Clyde Kilby, Ed. (Mariner Books, 1980, 2003), 233.

5. *Strong's Greek Dictionary,* s.v. "Endunamoó"; http://strongsnumbers. com/greek/1743.htm (accessed December 1, 2010).

6. Buck Stephens, Prophetic Word (January 6, 2007).

Chapter 21

1. Buck Stephens, Prophetic Word (September 23, 2009).

2. Spiros Zodhiates, *The Complete Word Study Dictionary, New Testament,* (Chattanooga, TN: AMG Publishers, 1992), 1493 (#5586).

Chapter 22

1. For more information on Tunnelling, see "Quantum Tunneling," *Science Daily;* http://www.sciencedaily.com/articles/q/quantum_tunnelling.htm (accessed December 2, 2010), and Leonardo Motta, "Tunneling," *Eric Weisstein's World of Physics;* http://scienceworld.wolfram.com/physics/ Tunneling.html (accessed December 2, 2010).

Chapter 23

1. See www.templeinstitute.org (accessed December 2, 2010).

2. Spiros Zodhiates, *The Complete Word Study Dictionary, New Testament* (Chattanooga, TN: AMG Publishers,1992), 1027 (#3601).

3. Arthur Delany, "Obama: U.S. 'Not a Christian Nation or a Jewish Nation or a Muslim Nation," *Huffington Post* (April 6, 2009); http://www.huffing-tonpost.com/2009/04/06/obama-us-not-a-christian_n_183772.html (accessed December 2, 2010).

4. Andrew Porter, Robert Winnett, and Toby Harnden, "G20 summit: Gordon Brown announces 'new world order,'" *The Telegraph* (April 3, 2009); http://www.telegraph.co.uk/finance/financetopics/g20-summit/5097195/G-20-summit-Gordon Brown-announces-new-world-order.html (accessed December 2, 2010).

5. Ibid.

6. *Merriam-Webster's Collegiate Dictionary*, 11th ed., s.v., "Regime."

7. *The Complete Word Study Dictionary, New Testament*, 503 (#1484).

8. "The Global HIV/AIDS Epidemic," (PDF) *U.S. Global Health Policy* (November 2009); http://www.kff.org/hivaids/upload/3030-14.pdf (accessed December 2, 2010).

9. "Religions of the World," *Religious Tolerence.org;* www.religioustolerance. org/worldrel.htm (accessed December 2, 2010).

10. "The Cleansing for the Kingdom," *Let Us Reason Ministries;* http:// www.letusreason.org/latrain14.htm (accessed December 2, 2010).

11. Amir Taheri, "Obama and Ahmadinejad," *Forbes.com* (October 26, 2008); http://www.forbes.com/2008/10/26/obama-iran-ahmadinejad-oped-cx_at_1026taheri_print.html (accessed December 2, 2010).

12. "Ahmadinejad: 'With God's grace,' Israel 'will be annihilated,'" *Jihad Watch;* http://www.jihadwatch.org/2010/03/ahmadinejad-with-gods-grace-israel-will-be-annihilated.html (accessed December 2, 2010).

Chapter 24

1. See www.positiveidcorp.com (accessed December 3, 2010).

2. "Knesset Approves Controversial Biometric Database Law," *Jerusalem Post,* December 7, 2009; the article goes on to say that the bill has been dubbed "the Big Brother Bill."

For More Information

Contact Buck Stephens at:

Buck Stephens

Advancing the Kingdom Ministries

PO Box 274

Syracuse, New York 13214

315-424-6180

or

E-mail: atkm@atkministries.org

www.atkministries.org